TOWARD DEFINING THE PRAIRIES
REGION, CULTURE, AND HISTORY

TOWARD DEFINING THE PRAIRIES
REGION, CULTURE, AND HISTORY

Edited by
Robert Wardhaugh

THE UNIVERSITY OF MANITOBA PRESS

The University of Manitoba Press
Winnipeg, Manitoba R3T 2N2
www.umanitoba.ca/uofmpress

Printed in Canada.

Cover Design: Kirk Warren

Canadian Cataloguing in Publication Data
Main entry under title:
>   Toward defining the prairies

>   Includes bibliographical references
>   ISBN 0-88755-672-8

1. Prairie Provinces—Social conditions. 2. Prairie Provinces—In literature. I. Wardhaugh, Robert Alexander, 1967-

FC3237.T69 2001   971.2   C2001-910331-X
F1060.T69 2001

The University of Manitoba Press gratefully acknowledges the financial support for its publication program provided by the Government of Canada through the Book Publishing Industry Development Program (BPIDP); the Manitoba Arts Council; and the Manitoba Department of Culture, Heritage and Tourism.

This book has been published with assistance from St. John's College, the University of Manitoba, and from the Social Sciences and Humanities Research Council of Canada.

CONTENTS

Robert Wardhaugh
Introduction: Tandem and Tangent • 3

Gerald Friesen
Defining the Prairies: or, why the prairies don't exist • 13

Alvin Finkel
Alberta Social Credit and the Second National Policy • 29

Royden Loewen
From the Inside Out: The World of Mennonite Diaries • 51

R. Rory Henry
Making Modern Citizens:
The Construction of Masculine Middle-Class Identity
on the Canadian Prairies, 1890-1920 • 79

Alison Calder
Who's from the Prairie?
Some Prairie Self-Representations in Popular Culture • 91

Gerald T. Davidson
An Interdisciplinary Approach to the Role of Climate in
the History of the Prairies • 101

Molly P. Rozum
Indelible Grasslands:
Place, Memory, and the "Life Review" • 119

Birk Sproxton
Novels that Named a City: Fictional Pretexts of Flin Flon • 137

Jason Wiens
The Prairies as Cosmopolitan Space: Recent 'Prairie' Poetry • 151

J'nan Morse Sellery
Western Frontiers and Evolving Gender Identity
in Aritha van Herk's *The Tent Peg* • 165

Claire Omhovère
The Female Body as Garrison in Three Prairie Biotexts • 179

Karen Clavelle
Life Sentence, *passwords*, and local pride:
prairie in the poetic journals of Eli Mandel and Dennis Cooley • 195

Robert Kroetsch
Don't Give Me No More of Your Lip;
or, the Prairie Horizon as Allowed Mouth • 209

SELECTED BIBLIOGRAPHY • 217

CONTRIBUTORS • 231

Acknowledgements

This book grew out of the "Defining the Prairies" conference held at St. John's College at the University of Manitoba in September 1998. The essays gathered here reflect only a sampling of a fine group of presentations. I would like to thank all those who participated in the conference, as both presenters and observers. I would also like to thank the committee of readers who helped to select the essays in this collection.

The conference would never have been possible without the creativity, dedication, and tireless efforts of the organization committee—Dennis Cooley, Kathryn Young, Karen Clavelle, and Doug Reimer. The staff at St. John's College also deserve a special note of thanks for all their work in hosting the very successful event.

I owe a special thanks to the staff at the University of Manitoba Press. To David Carr and to editors Pat Sanders and Sharon Caseburg, I offer my heartfelt thanks. You have made this a better book.

TOWARD DEFINING THE PRAIRIES
REGION, CULTURE, AND HISTORY

Introduction: Tandem and Tangent

Robert Wardhaugh

HOW DOES ONE DEFINE A PLACE? How does one define a region? An area's physical features, particularly those that make it distinctive, are probably the most obvious defining elements. Geography plays a major role in determining a society's economic development, as well as its resulting social and cultural structures. Landscape usually establishes political boundaries. Societies emerge with particular cultural patterns, based upon the geography, economics, and politics of a place. But peoples moving into an area also arrive with an established cultural framework. Gradually, societies come to identify and be identified with particular locales, and likewise, a region becomes identified with particular societies.

But identity is also perception. It is not determined exclusively by external forces. A region, in the words of Richard Allen, is very much a mental construct, "a state of mind."[1] According to Patricia Limerick, "regions are much more the creation of human thought and behavior than they are products of nature."[2] A place can mean different things to different people. Societies record perceptions of a place in oral imagery, such as stories, songs, and myths, in visual imagery and structures, such as paintings and photography, architecture, sculptures, and monuments, or in written imagery, such as poetry, novels, travel accounts, diaries, and histories. These images become active agents, further shaping perceptions of place.

Over time, dominant images emerge (from inside and outside the region) that define a place and time, and people use them (whether through acceptance or rejection) to express their identity. Shared experience, and the manipulation of that experience through memory, forges a sense of community reinforced (or divided) by the forces of class, ethnicity, gender, politics, religion, and language. Thus, a regional consciousness emerges. But region is a relative term; its definition is based on its relation to other regions. Regional consciousness, therefore, is usually framed in terms of these relationships and can, to an extent, transcend these other, singular, forces that shape identity.

While there may be a dominant sense of region, it rarely stands uncontested. There are usually multiple competing identities, all vying for position within (or from outside) that regional consciousness. According to John Thompson, it is the myths of the people that shape regional identity, but there are different peoples and different myths. Similarly, Richard White points out that there is not a single myth, a single imagined region, but rather myths "constantly in competition," just as peoples have always been in competition.[3]

The process of defining a region is further complicated by the fact that identity is not static. "All identities," Philip Buckner notes, "are socially constructed and all are fluid and unstable and frequently in a state of re-negotiation."[4] Societies and cultures are continually redefining themselves over time. If a region is a state of mind, inextricably attached to identity, and that identity is changing, then it is logical to assume that regions also are changing and indeed being redefined.

Producing a definition of a region, therefore, is extremely complex. The very concept of "defining" has come into question by new theoretical approaches such as postmodernism, poststructuralism, and postcolonialism. It may now seem a hopeless endeavour. But the process of defining is just as important, if not more important, than the actual production of a definition.

This book provides an attempt to highlight recent approaches "toward defining the Prairies." The essays included offer ways of thinking about place that are as diverse as the region itself. Robert Kroetsch refers to "tandem and tangent," a phrase coined by literary critic Mark Libin, and these approaches to defining a region are marked by tangential investigations, operating in tandem, towards that objective.

Regionalism has long played a prominent role in debates on Canadian identity. "Contemporary Canadians," Thompson points out, "routinely think about their country as a segmented sequence of regions."[5] For generations, however, Canadians have been urged to think in terms of nation and this nationalism usually runs counter to regionalism. Regional divisions are acceptable as long as a vision of nation remains paramount; nationalism must transcend regionalism. Scholars have made the regional flavour of the Canadian nation more palatable by offering it up in terms of "limited identities."[6] Canada is divided into regions but it is exactly this division, we are told, that provides the nation with its distinct identity.

Interest in regionalism among Canadian scholars, however, has waxed and waned. There was a time, from the 1970s through the first half of the 1980s, when the West was the subject of considerable academic debate. The annual Western Canadian Studies conferences organized by the University of Calgary from 1969 to 1987, for example, demonstrated this interest. They were highly successful, multidisciplinary meetings, focussing on the region. Most of the proceedings were published and came to form an important corpus for studying the area. The volumes of papers offered a literal "who's who" in Prairie scholarship, with names such as G.F.G. Stanley, W.L. Morton, L.H. and L.G. Thomas, John Warkentin, Gerry Friesen, Eli Mandel and Robert Kroetsch, to name only a few.[7]

Alas, by the late 1980s, interest in the Prairies, and in regionalism, for that matter, had waned. Threats to the country's unity, posed by the spectre of Quebec separation and augmented by western grievances, led to a new wave of nationalist sentiment among Canadian historians. Ramsay Cook, for example, announced in 1983 that "as a tool of analysis, 'regionalism' is a concept whose time is gone."[8] The Western Canadian Studies Conference series ended. Regionalism as an analytical tool lost favour; the idea of the Prairies as a distinct unit worthy of study had, at the very least, diminished. The importance of place as a "defining" element had been so overshadowed by such transcending giants as gender, class, and ethnicity, and so deconstructed by poststructural, postmodern, and postcolonial critics, that "place" as a defining construct seemed to have disappeared. Work being done by historians in the United States pointed to a "New West," one which was still distinct but which questioned the traditional notion of that distinctiveness by emphasizing hegemony, inequality, and plurality.[9] If the traditional definition of the Canadian Prairies was no longer acceptable, why was an alternative not being constructed, or at least discussed?[10] Canadian historians offered little in the way of a constructive response. They were more interested in criticizing and dismissing regional history because it threatened their desire for a national history.[11]

Only recently has the Prairie region again begun to receive attention from scholars. The ensuing discussion, however, lacks its prior interdisciplinary tone. Unfortunately, the ending of the Western Canadian Studies conferences also seemed to signal an end to interdisciplinary discussion on the Prairie region. Cultural, political, and economic forces ensured that regionalism has remained an important force in Canada, but differences in perception and conception are obstructing constructive communication across the disciplines.

Canadian historians have now come to question the structure of power in the Canadian West by emphasizing the influence of hegemony. Like their counterparts in the US, they criticize traditional interpretations that privilege particular ethnic, gender, or class groups. The myths of the dominant culture, such as the North West Mounted Police and the Pioneer, are now placed alongside the myths of the Métis, the First Nations, and the ethnic communities formed through immigration. In addition, the history of the region has been forced open to include previously excluded groups such as women and the working class. Historians have successfully dismantled the dominant view of Prairie history, and in place of one distinct region, we have been taught instead to think of many Wests. If we wish to focus on one "region," we are told to question the boundaries employed and possibly even to think in terms of a new region, one that is based not on political or economic lines, but one that is cultural in definition, and one that is constantly changing.

In this the historians concur with their literary colleagues, but language, ironically, has become a barrier to interdisciplinary communication. Despite their emphasis on new notions of region, historians still maintain an approach to constructing identity that privileges "representational" language. According to some literary critics, historians accept representational forms of definition, yet fail to question their processes and modes of reconstruction. Janine Brodie observes that "references to region are so familiar and pervasive that we have accepted these divisions as natural and self-evident without ever questioning why we have come to think of the country in these terms or what meanings these spatial abstractions actually convey."[12]

Literary scholars, on the other hand, have taken a different approach and to their credit have produced considerably more new work on the Prairie West.[13] In their view, the rise of such theoretical constructs as postmodernism requires a response. Many postmodern writers and poststructural critics have moved attention away from an emphasis on traditional notions of place and "context" by instead focussing on language and "text." They are critical of the modernists' "introspective gaze" that "only perpetuates attempts to disengage critical enquiry from the flux of historical change," urging "a rejection of any such claims to temporal disengagement." As David Jordan points out, "to the postmodernist regionalist, regional identity is neither a transcendent symbol, nor a fixed identity, nor an abstract structure defined by subjective patterns of coherence; it is 'in the midst' of this temporal difference."[14] In the meantime, some writers "inside" the Prairie region have used postmodernism to focus on the meaning of their place.[15] While questioning and deconstructing traditional definitions of

Prairie that rely on landscape and environment, nostalgia and idealism, they maintain and present a powerful reconstructed notion of place.[16]

Some historians, however, argue that "contextual" historical forces, such as provincialism, communication technology, cultural change, and globalization, have so transformed regional constructs in the Canadian West that a completely new definition is necessary. That new definition shatters old notions of region and, as a result, "Prairie" is no longer an applicable or useful concept with which to discuss the area.

Those in literature are not content with this new definition and view it as little more than a reassembling of old parts held together by traditional notions of representation. These notions continue to privilege geographic, economic, and political boundaries. They argue that it merely offers a replacement of one singular definition for another and, as a result, is necessarily exclusionary or reductive. Instead, the literary critics argue for a more multiple, more mobile, and perhaps even more uncertain definition. The Prairies still exist, they assert, as much as any cultural formation "exists." It is the process of definition that is changing. The historians' re-definition of the Prairie West clearly threatens the "place" of Prairie writers, including the regional basis and consequence of their work.

Historians and literary critics no longer seem to speak the same language when discussing the Prairie West. Their conceptions of this place, as a result, appear very different. There is at least one conclusion, however, upon which both disciplines can agree: the traditional definitions that long dominated discussions of Prairie, "where place has overwhelmingly been defined in narrow, deterministic terms, as 'the land' or the natural physical environment," are no longer adequate.[17] The meaning of the Prairie West has been transformed to such an extent in the last thirty years that new definitions, or at least a new discussion, is necessary.

This book is a product of the "Defining the Prairies" conference held at St. John's College at the University of Manitoba in September 1998. The conference was designed to encourage a return to the multidisciplinary discussion that marked the previous Western Canadian Studies conferences. The thirteen essays included in this book deal with various aspects of Prairie history, literature, climate, society, culture, and identity. They offer a sampling of the diverse myriad of perspectives and approaches employed to study the Prairie West today, and they attempt to demonstrate the necessary multiplicity in "defining" or even discussing this one region. Above all, the work seeks to make clear that definitions of the Prairie West are constructs with constantly shifting boundaries.

The collection is "bounded" by insightful essays from two of the most prolific writers on the Prairie West: historian Gerald Friesen and literary writer Robert Kroetsch. Both authors played significant roles in the Western Canadian Studies conferences, but both now articulate very different approaches to the region. Their essays, to a large extent, reflect the gulf that separates their two disciplines.

The book opens with Friesen's controversial essay, which argues that the Prairie West has been transformed by such forces as provincialism, modernization, and globalization. The Prairies, according to Friesen, were a construct built by historical forces mainly in the first half of the twentieth century. As a result, we should now "re-imagine" the West (including British Columbia) and view the region instead as four distinct provinces with a few important elements in common. "Our perceptions of the past," he claims, "may stand in the way of our seeing its present reality clearly."[18] Nostalgic and romantic notions of a Prairie identity are not enough to define a region. "It is time," Friesen argues, "to take stock of a new West. It is time to leave behind the imagined Prairie region. The new ways of thinking about this part of the country are the result of changes in the western economy, in the structure of government, and especially in the cultural and communication contexts of contemporary life." The Prairies, quite simply, no longer exist.

The diversity of the Prairie region becomes evident in the essays that follow by Alvin Finkel and Royden Loewen. Finkel's essay on the Social Credit party alludes to the dangerous assumptions of "Prairie homogeneity." He discusses Alberta's distinctive reaction to the "social and economic interventions of the federal government" in the 1950s and 1960s, a response certainly not shared by the other two Prairie provinces. Loewen demonstrates the remarkable diversity of ethnic groups that peopled the Canadian Prairies by examining the "rural worlds of Mennonite diarists." He argues that the daily written record offers a fascinating glimpse into the everyday lives of ordinary people, while at the same time exposing the "often hidden contours of household and community." His essay emphasizes how perceptions of a particular society and culture establish identity.

R. Rory Henry argues that historians have not fully investigated the hegemonic power of the middle class, focussing instead on the interactions of "marginalized groups" as an expression of a Prairie identity. The influence of the middle class, Henry claims, has been ignored, "despite the fact it proved the dominant identity," and he calls for attention to be redirected to this pervasive force. Alison Calder looks at the processes of "self-definition" employed by Prairie dwellers, "working out of complicated mythologies of their own, developing narratives of identity to fill various individual or cultural needs." She calls for a critical examination of "the stories we tell about ourselves," in order to construct "images of the Prairie in popular culture that are as complicated, messy, and vibrant as the Prairie culture itself."

Despite recent emphasis on place as cultural construct, Gerald Davidson provides a convincing argument as to the very real importance of climate in "determining" the political and social structures of the Prairies. Molly Rozum argues that landscape was a powerful shaper of identity on the Northern Grasslands, not only as a physical force, but also in the relationship of "remembered landscapes" and their impact on "the creation of personal and regional 'sense of place'."

Definitions of Prairie are certainly grist for the mill among literary critics. By looking at the "fictional pretexts" for the naming of Flin Flon, Manitoba, Birk Sproxton examines "Prairie" as a literary construct. He also makes some important observations about the diverse geography encompassed by the Prairie region: "In the story of this city, which I will argue is at once both Prairie and not Prairie, we have a neat variation on Robert Kroetsch's notion that we don't exist until someone tells our story." Jason Wiens also looks at the Prairie construct, and provides an analysis of Prairie poetry, "re-reading the region as an internally differentiated cosmopolitan site."

J'nan Morse Sellery counters old representation, offering a gendered analysis of Prairie fiction through the work of Aritha van Herk. Sellery argues that "by colonizing gender, sexuality, and male language," van Herk has responded to "gender-defining and sexual Westerns, written mostly by men," and as a result offered new definitions of western Canadian frontiers. Claire Omhovère argues that representations of gender in Prairie literature are indeed distinct in that "the female body is constructed as a version of garrison where the collective, the individual and exterior space articulate." Karen Clavelle "takes the reader on a journey" by looking at the complex representations of Prairie in the works (and travels) of Eli Mandel and Dennis Cooley.

Finally, Robert Kroetsch concludes the collection by offering an entertaining and personalized discussion of the possibilities and impossibilities of defining Prairie:

> That's when I chanced to notice the slough-pumper. You see, the slough-pumper is so well disguised that it's almost impossible to recognize, standing as it sometimes does, in a rather unbirdlike way, rigidly still, its beak pointed

upward in what seems a slightly demented manner, its striped body all the while perfectly matching the reeds and grasses at the edge of a slough.

What if the slough-pumper, in trying to look like its surroundings, actually looked like its surroundings? Or—what if the slough-pumper, in trying to look like its surroundings, didn't succeed in looking like its surroundings? Hmmm.

Toward Defining the Prairies demonstrates the continued interest in this region, the possibilities offered by cross-disciplinary approaches and discussion, and the need for further scholarly interrogation. It is hoped that the essays in this collection can play a role in that process.

Endnotes

1. Richard Allen, ed., *A Region of the Mind, Interpreting the Canadian Plains*, Canadian Plains Studies No. 1 (Regina: Canadian Plains Studies Centre, 1973), ix.

2. Patricia Nelson Limerick, *The Legacy of Conquest: The Unbroken Past of the American West* (New York: W.W. Norton, 1987).

3. John Herd Thompson, *Forging the Prairie West* (Don Mills: Oxford University Press, 1998), ix-x; Richard White, *It's Your Misfortune and None of My Own: A History of the American West* (Norman: University of Oklahoma Press, 1991), 617.

4. Philip Buckner, "'Limited Identities' Revisited: Regionalism and Nationalism in Canadian History, *Acadiensis* XXX (Autumn 2000): 4-15.

5. Thompson, *Forging the Prairie West*, ix.

6. The term "limited identity" in this context was first used by Ramsay Cook to describe challenges to a national identity posed by such forces as ethnicity, class, gender, and region. J.M.S. Careless popularized the term. Ramsay Cook, "Canadian Centennial Celebrations," *International Journal* XXII (Autumn 1967): 659-63; J.M.S. Careless, "'Limited Identities' in Canada," *Canadian Historical Review* L, no. 1 (March 1969): 1-10.

7. David. P. Gagan, ed., *Prairie Perspectives* (Toronto: Holt, Rinehart and Winston of Canada, Ltd., 1969); A.W. Rasporich and H.C. Klassen, eds., *Prairie Perspectives 2* (Toronto: Holt, Rinehart and Winston of Canada Ltd., 1973); Susan Trofimenkoff, ed., *The Twenties in Western Canada* (Ottawa: National Museum of Man, 1972); David Jay Bercuson, ed., *Western Perspectives 1* (Toronto: Holt, Rinehart and Winston of Canada Ltd., 1974); A.W. Rasporich, ed., *Western Canada: Past and Present* (Calgary: McClelland and Stewart West Ltd., 1975); Henry C. Klassen, *The Canadian West: Social Change and Economic Development* (Calgary: Comprint Publishing Company, 1977); Howard Palmer, ed., *The Settlement of the West* (Calgary: Comprint Publishing Company, 1977); David Jay Bercuson and Philip A. Buckner, eds., *Eastern and Western Perspectives*

(Toronto: University of Toronto Press, 1981); R.D. Francis and H. Ganzevoort, eds., *The Dirty Thirties in Prairie Canada* (Vancouver: Tantalus Research Limited, 1980); Howard Palmer and Donald Smith, eds., *The New Provinces: Alberta and Saskatchewan, 1905-1980* (Vancouver: Tantalus Research Limited, 1980); A.W. Rasporich, ed., *The Making of the Modern West: Western Canada Since 1945* (Calgary: The University of Calgary Press, 1984); R.C. McLeod, ed., *Swords and Ploughshares: War and Agriculture in Western Canada* (Edmonton: The University of Alberta Press, 1993).

8. Ramsay Cook, "The Burden of Regionalism," *Acadiensis* VII, no. 1 (Autumn 1974); Cook, "The Golden Age of Canadian Historical Writing," *Historical Reflections* V, no. 1 (Summer 1977); Cook, "Regionalism Unmasked," *Acadiensis* XIII, no. 1 (Autumn 1983).

9. A good example is Jon Gjerde, *The Minds of the West: Ethnocultural Evolution in the Rural Middle West, 1830-1917* (Chapel Hill: The University of North Carolina Press, 1977).

10. Encouraging works such as that of Jeremy Mouat and Catherine Cavanaugh, eds., *Making Western Canada: Essays on European Colonization and Settlement* (Toronto: Garamond Press, 1996), demonstrate that some interest in "the West" among Canadian historians continues.

11. J.L. Granatstein, *Who Killed Canadian History?* (Toronto: HarperCollins Publishers, 1998); J.M.S. Careless, "'Limited Identities': Ten Years Later," *Manitoba History* 1, no. 1 (1980); Michael Bliss, "Privatizing the Mind: The Sundering of Canadian History," *Journal of Canadian Studies* 26 (Winter 1991-92); Doug Owram, "Narrow Circles": The Historiography of Recent Canadian Historiography," *National History* 1, no. 1 (Winter 1997).

12. Janine Brodie, *The Political Economy of Canadian Regionalism* (Toronto: Harcourt, Brace, Jovanovitch, 1990), 6.

13. David M. Jordan, *New World Regionalism: Literature in the Americas* (Toronto: University of Toronto Press, 1994); Christian Riegel and Herb Wyile, eds., *A Sense of Place: Re-Evaluating Regionalism in Canadian and American Writing, Textual Studies in Canada* (Edmonton: University of Alberta Press, 1997).

14. Jordan is quoting William Spanos, 105.

15. Eli Mandel, Robert Kroetsch, David Arnason, Dennis Cooley, and, most recently, Deborah Keahey are examples.

16. Deborah Keahey, *Making It Home: Place in Canadian Prairie Literature* (Winnipeg: University of Manitoba Press, 1998).

17. Keahey, *Making It Home*, 4.

18. Gerald Friesen, "Introduction," in *The West: Regional Ambitions, National Debates, Global Age* (Toronto: Viking/Penguin, 1999).

Defining the Prairies: or, why the prairies don't exist[1]

Gerald Friesen

IN A WONDERFUL LECTURE on Canadian regionalism delivered in 1980, British Columbia geographer Cole Harris employed the image of a nighttime flight from Atlantic to Pacific to suggest that, seen from above, the country "dissolves into an oceanic darkness spotted by occasional islands of light." And therein lay the metaphor that carried the rest of his talk: "Canada is a composition of islands," an archipelago situated "between an implacable north and the United States."[2] Because the geography of settlement is discontinuous, Canadians have been accustomed to thinking about their country in broad "regional" generalizations—regions being the names they apply "to blocks of country where they do not live." Over the decades, such broad terms as the West, Central Canada, the East, the North, labels that have "only fuzzy locational meaning," crystallized into something more: they became "part of our vocabulary of spatial ambition and resentment."

Harris suggested that the regional labels also conveyed interpretations of community identities. They established, he said, notions about the rhythms and realities of some Canadian community experiences against others. Thus, "in the older settlements of the Maritimes, the rhythms of the land, the traditional ways that earned a living, and the people who lived nearby comprised the context of most experience. Even today, genealogical conversation is a Maritime staple, a reflection of communities whose people have known each other through the generations." The West, by contrast, Harris argued, is not so rooted in history and in the chronicles of identifiable families. He wrote: "In the West such conversation is rarer for the local texture has been different, having less of custom and the generations and more of movement, technology, markets, and memories of other places."

These observations merit closer analysis. Yes, western family stories remain within the family and do not become community or regional conversations except in carefully edited, community historical volumes. But history has borne heavily upon westerners and *has* shaped community self-perception. Moreover, certain historical images are now a source of confusion because westerners utilize inherited concepts in circumstances where such notions no longer apply. And, as Harris emphasizes, region does play an important role in western Canadians' perceptions of the communities in which they live.

My purpose is, first, to outline the ways in which observers have defined the prairies. Second, it is to argue that our inherited regional folk tales have grown stale. And, third, it is to defend the relevance of region as a means of understanding western Canadians' social identities. Westerners define their community or citizenship identities in terms of their provinces, their cities, and their location as residents of the "West" in national conversation. The prairies, as a folk memory, inform their perception of these alternative identities but nothing more. The prairies have ceased to be a dominant citizenship image.

The notion of "region" bedevils analysis of the prairies. There are three main ways of thinking about it: the formal, the functional, and the imagined.[3] The formal region is built upon land forms and climate. It assumes that there are distinctive portions of the earth's surface that are more or less eternal. The prairies, in this approach, simply look different from the surrounding territories—the environment is distinctive—and life here must be different. The fur trader David Thompson, who first labelled "the great Plains," was proposing a formal region with these words.

The functional region is defined by the purpose of one's analysis. One could speak in terms of buffalo regions, or wheat-raising regions, or a region favourable to the Reform (now Canadian Alliance) Party. It discovers coherent patterns in the spatial distribution of certain defined elements and a larger system in which they are located. The two best-known academic discussions of prairie Canada, the frontier thesis and the staples or Laurentian thesis, posited the existence of functional regions. Each frontier zone was complemented by a settled civilization and each staple-producing territory by a metropolis. The frontier and Laurentian schools also sustained the notion of a formal prairie region because they were built upon several implicit economic assumptions: that the new societies would rely on the raising and export of primary products, especially farm goods; and that the distribution of natural resources was a crucial defining element in human history.

The imagined region is an approach much favoured by students of prairie literature. It asserts that a place must be imagined before it can exist. Though originally associated with environmentalism (and thus with the notion of a formal region), it was elevated to a new level of sophistication by the poet and critic Eli Mandel in the 1970s. In a number of papers, Mandel described the prairie region as a "mental construct ... a myth." He found a "certain coherence or unity or identity" in prairie literature, which was rooted in a few specific characteristics. These included a local landscape, a child's view of *first* things, a grotesque storyteller, a regional dialect, and stories of the past. Thus, prairie storytellers projected onto the land their chosen images and, in doing so, created a regional pattern within the broader corpus of world literatures.[4]

These three approaches have been employed to define the prairies during the past two centuries. Each has a part to play in the following discussion.

In pre-Contact Aboriginal societies, a definition of physical space would have been a matter of distinguishing resource zones, the homelands of particular cultural groups, and the band's perception of the trails to heaven. As the ice sheets retreated toward the Arctic, and as glacial Lake Agassiz shrank, Aboriginal peoples moved into the prairies. They established patterns of resource harvesting that reflected the distribution of food according to the season. Scholars have reconstructed these seasonal movements and proposed the existence of several different annual cycles of movement, including plains-parkland and parkland-forest patterns, that probably evolved over a period of several thousand years. By the time Europeans arrived in this territory in the seventeenth and eighteenth centuries, Aboriginal rhythms of movement and patterns of alliance and war were long established.

Did these Aboriginal lands in the northwestern interior of North America—the prairies—constitute a formal, functional, or imagined region? The answer lies in a combination of economy (notably food resources), diplomacy (including trade and defence arrangements but also effective sovereignty), and cultural inheritance (including language but also a collective memory). The presence of several different language groups, diplomatic alliances, and food-harvesting patterns in these lands suggests that the Aboriginal communities did not see the world in terms of a formal prairie region. However, one could describe the territory occupied by bands sharing a culture and language as a functional region—*their* homeland. Several such functional regions existed in the Aboriginal universe. Moreover, one could think of this cultural universe—including the stories of creation and of the natural world—as an imagined region, one in which such depictions were repeated by a number of bands or groups, and were handed down over time. Thus, one could speak of imagined and functional regions in this era but, because of the economic and political complexity of this land and because the cultural universe did not conform to geographic landforms, the prairies did not represent a formal region.

Between the mid-seventeenth and mid-nineteenth centuries, Aboriginal movements and the European fur trade reconstituted society in the northwestern interior. For purposes of company administration, this territory did become a unit. Both Nor'West and Hudson's Bay Company officers would have recognized a map that integrated the forests of the north and the plains of the southern interior. Such a zone encompassed the North and South Saskatchewan river basins and extended as far as Hudson Bay. Its boundaries rested in the west at the Rocky Mountains, in the east at the Petit Nord above Lake Superior, in the north at the Divide between Saskatchewan and Churchill River country, and in the south at the Missouri basin.

During this fur trade era, the Cree-Ojibwa-Assiniboine alliance also served to unite the interior. The chief enemies of the alliance included the Siouan-speaking peoples such as the Dakota southwest of Lake Superior, the Dene-speaking peoples north of the Churchill River, and the shifting group of western enemies of their ally, the Blackfoot, such as the Kootenay. On the east, the boundary was more difficult to define, largely because of the decimation of Aboriginal populations.

More important for a regional perception than Company administration or Aboriginal diplomacy alone was a new and distinctive pattern of European-Aboriginal relations. This pattern was facilitated by an extended period of peace, a great deal of trade, and large numbers of interracial marriages. Eventually, the signing of treaties during the 1870s ensured that the entire territory would recognize, and respond to, a single type of relation between Aboriginal people and the government of Canada. Though one could argue about the scope and location of what historians now describe as a distinctive "fur trade society," I suggest that it found a clear territorial expression in the northwestern interior.

At the heart of this community was the emergence of the Métis as a new people. As working families, as political actors, as founders of several distinct community ways of life, and as creators of a powerful historical tradition, the Métis reinforced the notion of a prairie region. Not that their sphere was limited to the prairies. There were mixed-race people from the

Atlantic to the Pacific and from the American states to Russian Alaska. Yet, because of the sinews of fur trade administration, the functional and imagined region found resonance in Métis activities associated with Fort Garry, Fort Ellice, and Fort Edmonton, as well as the Touchwood Hills, Cypress Hills, and Batoche. The songs of Pierre Falcon, the stories told about Paulet Paul, and the writings of Louis Riel established the bounds of this imagined region.

To summarize this era of prairie definition: there were functional and imagined regions in pre-Contact Aboriginal society but they did not coincide with a 49th parallel, Great Lakes-Rockies formal region *or* some narrower Great Plains formal region. During the fur trade era, however, formal and functional regions *did* coincide. One could talk about defining the prairies within their boundaries.

After several hundred years, in which European and Aboriginal communities lived together in the northwestern interior, the "technological arsenal" of the mid-nineteenth century enabled far-sighted politicians to create a new nation. The achievement of Confederation and Canada's subsequent annexation of the vast western and northern reaches of the continent reconstructed regional perceptions and realities.[5] One component of the new nation could be labelled "the prairies."

Why did this region take shape?[6] The staples theorists had a ready answer—wheat. A decade after leading the Confederation movement, Sir John A. Macdonald chose to build a national economy. Having just left the shelter of the Second British Empire (with its navigation, sugar, timber, and corn laws, 1784-1849), and having been rejected by the United States after a brief trial of North American free trade (the Reciprocity Treaty of 1854-1866), Canada would now be shaped by protective tariffs, railway subsidies, and land policy.[7] The centre would carry on the manufacturing while the prairies would produce grain for world markets. For a century thereafter, Canadians would think of nation-building as being synonymous with economy-building.

Political and cultural experience reinforced the economic. The election of third-party members in the federal election of 1921 must be part of the explanation for this sharpened image. But so, too, was the emergence of Winnipeg as a genuine regional metropolis. Similarly, the popularity of prairie novelists such as Ralph Connor, Nellie McClung, Robert Stead, F.P. Grove, Douglas Durkin, and Laura Goodman Salverson, and the presence of important institutions that seemed at the time to have a particular connection with prairie society, such as the North-West Mounted Police, the

One Big Union, and the United Church, also established aspects of a regional image. The lines on the map, the circulation of civil servants, and the slow and painful collective decision to accept English as the dominant language of public discourse all played a part in creating this imagined prairie community.

Proof that formal, functional, and imagined perceptions had coalesced can be found in the writing of prairie history. In 1946, W.L. Morton described the prairie experience as one of the "decisive fields of Canadian historical interpretation." Juxtaposed with French survival and Ontario domination, this third decisive sphere was built upon "the subordination of the West."[8] Morton argued that the then-dominant interpretation of Canadian history, the Laurentian school, would mislead generations of western schoolchildren: "Teaching inspired by the historical experience of metropolitan Canada cannot but deceive, and deceive cruelly, children of the outlying sections. Their experience after school will contradict the instruction of the history class, and develop in them that dichotomy which characterizes all hinterland Canadians, a nationalism cut athwart by a sense of regional injustice."[9] Morton believed that, in the prairie case, this sense of injustice had combined with economic and political and cultural factors to create a distinctive way of life. In his view, an identifiable prairie place was home to distinctive prairie people. Moreover, Morton suggested that western experience provoked a sectional political response: "For Confederation was brought about to increase the wealth of central Canada, and until that original purpose is altered, and the concentration of wealth and population by national policy in central Canada ceases, Confederation must remain an instrument of injustice."[10] Therein lay a community identity, Morton implied, as profound as Quebec's French nationalism and Ontario's British nationalism.

Morton argued that the West would have to "work out its own identity in terms of its own historical experience. It must realize its latent nationalism, a nationalism neither racial like the French nor dominant—a 'garrison' nationality—like that of Ontario, but environmental and, because of the diversity of its people, composite."[11] By understanding regional history, the prairie West could "free itself, and find itself."[12]

The seventy-five years between 1867 and the 1930s were sufficient to define a new prairie region. This was a space and society in which formal, functional and imagined territories coincided, thus imprinting upon Canadian consciousness the sense that not just group interests but even individual qualities might be different in this distinctive land.

It is so easy to assume that this prairie region still exists. It is even comforting to think that such continuity distinguishes our community life. The historic resentments of a peripheral community still spring immediately to mind when a slight occurs, as in the case of the federal government's allocation of an aircraft overhaul contract in 1986 or of Prime Minister Chrétien's appointment of an Alberta senator in 1998. But such reflex responses are only that—reflexes conditioned by past experience. Canada has moved on. The prairies, as a defined community, are far less relevant than they were in earlier days.

What has changed? Consider, first, some obvious economic differences. Among these, one of the most striking is the decline in rural population. An entire farm society constructed between the 1880s and the 1920s, which embraced several thousand places anchored by as little as a store or elevator or school, each place carrying a name and a meaning, has disappeared. In its stead, there is a new rural network, one that is changing so rapidly, year after year, that the eight percent of prairie Canadians actually engaged in farm production cannot be certain that their economic role will even exist a decade from now.

This small farm population creates far more wealth, measured by volumes of field crops, and dairy, poultry, and animal production, than its predecessor did. Paradoxically, the story of rural decline and decay must be accompanied by a narrative of export growth and individual wealth. This new agricultural economy is based on larger farm units and a much wider range of products. The fact that the Outstanding Young Farmer award for Manitoba now goes to a couple, not a man, and that the winning family must earn one-third of its household income off the farm, suggests the temper of the times.

The rural story is just one of the economic differences in the modern West. More important in terms of dollars earned and societies reconstructed is the resource sector. Oil and natural gas brought prosperity to Alberta after 1947. Potash, uranium and other mines, hydroelectric dams, and forest enterprises have brought jobs and investment to parts of every western province, not to the same degree as in Alberta, but still with sufficient effect that the passage of fifty years has made the Norths of each province unrecognizable to a pre-1940 resident. This is especially noteworthy for the change it has brought to Aboriginal communities.

Another profound economic difference lies in the cities. Much of the work in a service and knowledge economy occurs in urban areas, so cities have grown in relation to—indeed, at the expense of—the countryside. Anyone could cite the new industries, from Global Television and Palliser

Furniture in Manitoba to Ballard Power Systems and MacDonald Dettwiler computer applications in British Columbia.

A picture of the contemporary prairies as functional region is thus fragmented and confusing. It features, simultaneously, rural decline and rural prosperity; it adds to this the uneven development of resource industries; it also adds the rapid expansion of city-based enterprises, each provincial pattern being different from the other. The emergence of rural-urban, north-south, Aboriginal-non-Aboriginal tensions in each province mirrors this economic change. This is not enough to account for the end of old regional habits, perhaps, but it is sufficient to sustain a broader challenge to the prairie notion.

After economic factors, the biggest change in the post-1945 West is due to government. Confederation created provinces and the industrial age created cities. The combination of the two, the province with its governmental apparatus and the metropolitan centre with its social power, established two new territorial or spatial identities for Canadians. As bureaucracies and communications technologies grew in influence, these provincial and urban identities became ever more important in daily life.

Following the decade of depression during the 1930s and a world war in which the federal government took the lead in Canadian life, the province has come into its own.[13] The delivery of health care, the establishment of resource policies, and the management of industrial relations, to name just three immense jurisdictions, illustrate the significance of decisions within the provincial sphere.

The provinces are also responsible for much more activity in social and cultural realms, areas formerly reserved for personal and family supervision. It is obvious that Canadians spend more time in classrooms today than they did in the 1930s. Many of these educational moments, from daycare to college and trades training, are now administered and sponsored by the province. Research and development institutes, whether in medicine or farm machinery or social issues, also rely on provincial support. Peter Lougheed's $300 million fund for health research in Alberta may stand out, but there are sufficient other examples of university-related research to make the case convincing. The provinces are also more powerful forces in the conduct of national politics than they were fifty years ago. And they sponsor cultural and heritage programs, and networks of parks, sites, museums, and galleries that were undreamt of in the interwar decades.

The case that is made for provinces can also be made for cities. City-building strategies in Calgary, Vancouver, and Winnipeg differ one from the other, but each has shaped a cultural and political community. And cities have become powerful magnets, attracting newcomers from rural areas and overseas. Cities have become an aspect of citizens' identities. One need only observe the adaptation of a newcomer, the process by which new loyalties are forged and new patterns of life, including political and cultural views, are tested and adopted.

The alterations in economy and government have been the consequence of local initiatives. A third sphere of change, in culture and communications, has been driven entirely by developments in the wider world that have submerged local societies under a wave that could easily be mistaken for a global cultural consensus. Radio served as the dominant public medium on the prairies, the location of community conversation, between the 1930s and the 1950s. Television has been dominant since then. Both have increased the influence of the great entertainment production capitals of the world and diminished local centres. But within peripheral communities such as western Canada, both have also reinforced the power of the provincial metropolises. Both have elevated the role of the provincial government and established community conversations that adhere to provincial boundaries and yet seem excessively concerned about the experience of the metropolis. This is why Manitobans outside the capital region speak bitterly about Winnipeg's perimeter vision.

I am arguing that economic, governmental, and cultural forces have combined to elevate the provinces and the largest cities in the identities of individual Canadians. To define the prairies in this new circumstance is to say that the old notion of prairie unity has been eclipsed by three provincial societies and at least five—and probably many more—urban societies. These are both functional and imagined regions. The old formal region, and the vision of a common Winnipeg-to-Rockies identity, has outlived its usefulness.

Alberta can serve as a brief illustration. What is the most profound defining moment of Albertans' relations with the rest of Canada in the last three generations? I suggest it is their response to the National Energy Policy during the 1980s. What would Albertans pick out as the most important public policy decision to affect their lives in the last thirty years? I suggest the so-called Klein Revolution of 1993 to 1997. What do Albertans see as a collective birthright? Lower taxes than other Canadians pay? What is the archetypal story encountered by visitors from other parts? How about the "amazing true inspirational testimonial," told by someone who heard it from someone who knew the person, wherein a former gasfield worker or restaurant employee begins knitting toques or moulding fudge in a basement or garage and, before you can turn around, is worth a million, maybe two?

Alberta is the noisiest province in English-speaking Canada. It is the tempestuous—and slightly smaller—brother or sister who is not going to be hushed, thank you very much. It has money in its pockets and it's going to make its opinions heard. If it loses the money, it's probably your fault. And it will get it back, and more, and you'll probably want some when that happens. Significantly, it will share its good fortune. It is headstrong but generous, and it does care about others in the family. And remember, it will pipe up, uninvited and unrepresentative though its message may be, so take with a grain of salt its claim to represent the entire West.[14] That sounds like a cultural identity, an imagined community distinct from its neighbours, and a functional region, too.

What has happened to the prairies? I am arguing that, in the half-century since 1945, it has broken into three component provinces and at least five major cities, and that these units are far more important than any single prairie entity in contemporary Canadian life.

The final step in my argument is that a different Western region has coalesced during the past few decades. The view that there are two regions between Ontario and the Pacific, the Prairies and British Columbia, should be replaced by a new political reality and cultural perception—a single Lake of the Woods-to-Vancouver Island region. The case for a single West rests upon recent studies in psychology, reading, and opinion formation. It also relies upon popular culture and the media. The purpose of such an analysis is to establish the outlines of a new and distinct functional region, a "political West."

Cole Harris's observation quoted earlier suggested that regions were the names applied to blocks of land where one did not live—the Atlantic, the North, central Canada. It is noteworthy how often "western Canada" figures in public discussion today. One illustration: Diane Ablonczy, a Reform Member of Parliament, explained to a reporter that "in the West there is a can-do attitude. Instead of seeking help from government, it's 'get the government out of my face, I'll look after things.'"[15] David Bercuson and Barry Cooper, like Tom Flanagan, members of the University of Calgary faculty, refer regularly to "the West" in their columns for the *Globe and Mail*.[16] A featured session at a national Social Science and Humanities conference was entitled "Accommodating the New West" and all the panellists adopted the term without qualification.[17] These illustrations could be multiplied many times.

The image has spread from journalism to youth culture. This is not the old square-dance-and-string-tie image of the Stampede and the farm, but a new version featuring baseball caps and snowboards. One hears now of distinctions between a "west style" and an "Ont style" (for Ontario)—meaning that in the West one encounters greater informality in dress and pastime but, also, a superior, outdoors-and-exercise youth culture. The West has come to be defined by Calgary and Vancouver, by the Mountain Equipment Co-op and Kananaskis and Whistler, by Starbucks and Second Cups.

When these stereotypes of the West arise, is a new community taking shape? There is much overlap and confusion when this question arises, some of it intentional. An opinion always seems stronger if it can plausibly be shown to be shared by thirty percent of Canadians (the West's proportion of Canada's population for most of the twentieth century). But I believe the strength of such images lies less in some imagined social unity than in an imagined political force. Behind these generalizations about "the West" lies a functional region—a Canadian political region—that is much more important than the community labelled "prairies."

Why should a different region, a new West, have coalesced? Recent research on reading and political communications has relevance. An American study of news and the construction of political meaning argues that citizens employ just a few frames to capture and process information. At the broadest level, some of these frames offer capsule narratives that enable a concerned public to follow the drift of ongoing news stories such as a global economic crisis, a community's descent into war, a complex trial, or the like. Such narratives provide frames that involve economic assessment (as in profit-loss, prosperity-poverty), conflict (as in win-lose), the powerful and the powerless, individual emotion (as in concern for self and others), and morality (doing the right thing). Citizens utilize these frames actively as they filter, sort, and reorganize information.[18]

These frames have been likened to static pictures, on the one hand, and to narrative patterns, on the other, each serving to store knowledge in retrievable form and to organize it efficiently. Add to this research the study of short-term memory and background knowledge (labelled schema, or schemata) that scholars have employed to consider the development of cultural systems.[19] Whatever one thinks about E.D. Hirsch's use of these ideas to promote lists of essential names and dates in grade school education, one can be struck by the convergence of his analysis of reading with discussion in the disciplines of political science and communications about opinion formation.

I take from this research the following rough hypothesis. Canadian citizens cannot be expected to balance the interests and outlooks of thirty million compatriots, a hundred ethnic groups, and political districts, the provinces and territories, in all of their thinking about the evolution of the community. I suggest that they develop schemata or frames to deal with this circumstance. They learn a specialized "national language," a series of constructs that represent the whole. This language evolves slowly but it does evolve. It varies in content from one dominant communication system to another: in England's language, class will matter more, and in the United States, race; in Canada, region matters a great deal.

You might protest that the frames or schemata exist because the social phenomena preceded them. And you might also object that, by concentrating on the words rather than on the economic and social conditions, my approach permits rhetoric to supersede reality. I disagree. I prefer to see merit in recent scholarly work in language and communications that places the cultural (interpreted to mean words, ideas, and performance) on a par with the economic and the technological.

In adapting the recent scholarly discussions of frames and schemata, I am proposing that a cultural and political approach to the contemporary West reveals a significant component of Canadian thought, the functional political region. This is not a formal region based on physical geography. Nor is it, as yet, a fully realized, imagined region. It is certainly not united or homogeneous as a social system. The differences in provincial economies demonstrate that there is not a western economic region, though one might contend that the economic patterns, inevitably associated with the export of primary products, are similar in most of the West. Rather, popular perceptions have established the West as one of the "functional" regions in Canadian political life.

In recent years, the functional region, "the West," is said to be Reform/Canadian Alliance in sympathy. There is a rough justice in this label. Reform Members of Parliament held sixty of the West's eighty-eight seats in the House of Commons after the 1995 election, and sixty-six after the 1999 election. Similarly, we describe the Bloc Quebeçois faction as representative of Quebec. Our country requires greater subtlety in political thought, but it does indeed operate on these rough simplifications. As a consequence, this part of the country is made to stand for all the right-wing or conservative responses to the great issues of the modern world. Affirmative action? The West is made to answer, in unison with the Reform/Alliance Party, as an opponent. Alternative sexualities and the family? The West is said to represent opposition to the new and defence of the traditional. The role of the government in dealing with the market's excesses? The West stands for free enterprise. We may approve of or reject these crude labels, but they do serve a purpose in national politics and they do conform to the majoritarian character of the Canadian political system.

Cole Harris concluded his essay on Canadian regions by emphasizing that the scattered islands of settlement belonged to an archipelago. He insisted that Canadianness had, indeed, crystallized, that the nation had congealed around the political state itself: "But there could be, and was, an accumulating national experience.... A political space has been institutionalized across the archipelago, creating a web of experiences that are part of Canadian life...."[20] One of the entities in that political space, I am suggesting, is the contemporary West.

The shibboleths of prairie loyalties are with us still. But they are disappearing quickly. In September 1998, the Prime Minister appointed a senator to a vacant seat for Alberta during a provincially established campaign to elect senators-in-waiting for just such vacancies. Albertans described his action as a slap in the face for two imagined communities, Alberta and the West. Their responses did not mention the prairies.

There was once, in the days of Aboriginal dominance, a number of imagined and functional regions in the northwestern interior of North America. During the fur trade, all three types of region could have been discerned in the patterns of human action and reflection. After Confederation, another prairie region took shape, this one so firm and influential that W.L. Morton could see it as a complete social order. In recent decades, this prairie region has been replaced by two different levels of community, an Ontario-to-the-Pacific West, and one constructed upon four distinct provinces and numerous metropolitan centres.

This is not an attack on the old prairie stories. All Canadians can enjoy *Jake and the Kid*. But it is important to remember that nostalgia is just that, nostalgia—a sentimental evocation of some period of the past.

Robert Fulford, Toronto journalist, recently wrote a column on his first encounter with a spiky Vancouver magazine, *Geist*. Fulford noted a number of articles that had caught his eye, among them one on prairie hockey. This particular story, "a fantasy by Stephen Smith," concerned "a hockey player who chews on a puck to quiet pre-game nerves while reflecting on the suicide ritual an old player in the West performs when his time is over": "He skates out onto the ice of the big bay until he can skate no more, to wait for the final thaw."[21]

When I first read the account, I was delighted. The story smacked of American tall tales, of an Aboriginal folk memory conveyed in school classrooms, and of the current interest in hockey as an expression of Canadian nationhood. Unfortunately, it also rang a note that I eventually recognized as "soft news from the hinterlands," the sensation aroused when the national television news leaves the important, fast-breaking, and globe-shattering issues to feature a human-interest piece about a Saskatchewan town or a Newfoundland storm. What's wrong with that?

There is one great shortcoming in such genuflection to the "outlying regions." If this is all the nation is being told about the realities of today's Manitoba, Saskatchewan, or Atlantic community, the story falls short of the ideal. Neither the news story nor Stephen Smith's picture of the dying hockey player are reaching the important long-term matters of contemporary life in this part of the country. Thus, by smiling fondly on the image of an aging man in hockey pads sliding through the ice and into oblivion, I was letting Fulford and Smith get away with another piece of nostalgia. What is more, the larger structure of feeling, of which it forms a part, evaded the more difficult public issues that confront citizens in peripheral economies. One can't build countries on stories that miss the cuts and bruises of the everyday.

It is time to take stock of a new West. It is time to leave behind the imagined prairie region. The new ways of thinking about this part of the country are the result of changes in the western economy, in the structure of government, and especially in the cultural and communication contexts of contemporary life.

Endnotes

1. This essay is based on my book, *The West: Regional Debate, National Ambitions, Global Age* (Toronto: Viking/Penguin, 1999).

2. Cole Harris, "The Emotional Structure of Canadian Regionalism," lecture delivered at McGill University, printed in *The Walter L. Gordon Lecture Series 1980-81*, vol. 5, *The Challenges of Canada's Regional Diversity* (Toronto: Canada Studies Foundation, 1981).

3. This section summarizes an argument that appears in "The Prairies as Region: The Contemporary Meaning of an Old Idea," in *River Road: Essays on Manitoba and Prairie History* (Winnipeg: University of Manitoba Press, 1996).

4. Eli Mandel, "Images of Prairie Man," in *A Region of the Mind: Interpreting the Western Canadian Plains,* ed. Richard Allen (Regina: Canadian Plains Research Centre/University of Regina, 1973), 203; and Mandel, "Romance and Idealism in Western Canadian Fiction," in *Prairie Perspectives 2: Selected Papers of the Western Canadian Studies Conference, 1970, 1971*, eds. Anthony W. Rasporich and Henry C. Klassen (Toronto: Holt, Reinhart and Winston, Canada, 1973).

5. It also separated European from Aboriginal, thereby introducing the segregation in historical interpretation that is only in recent decades being transcended.

6. I agree wholeheartedly with Cole Harris's view (outlined in the article on regionalism cited above) of the creation of Canada. His approach asserts that the Industrial Revolution, read broadly to include such globe-changing innovations as steam transport, telegraphy, and commodities futures markets, made Canada possible. Harris wrote: "To say that Canadian Confederation requires this technological arsenal is to understate the case. Confederation became conceivable within an industrial technology and, in good part, is one of its by-products." This is, I suggest, why V.C. Fowke included the Confederation pact itself as one of the original "national policies." This view asserts too that changes in the technology of communication underlie the evolution of regional perceptions. (V.C. Fowke, "The National Policy—Old and New," *Canadian Journal of Economics and Political Science* 18, no. 3 [August 1952]: 271-86.)

7. These included some matters of great importance to the prairies, notably railway freight rates, immigration and homestead policy, western surveys, and western policing arrangements. This national framework was extended in later decades to include grain handling, grain marketing, industrial relations, and other important economic institutions.

8. W.L. Morton, "Clio in Canada: The Interpretation of Canadian History," in *Contexts of Canada's Past: Selected Essays of W.L. Morton*, ed. A.B. McKillop (Toronto: Macmillan, 1980), 105. The essay was first published in 1946. Morton explained that the Atlantic and Pacific provinces had their own importance but were not central to the story that concerned him because they had "destinies alternative to that of incorporation in Canada," whereas, without the other three, "there could have been, in the larger sense of the name, no Canada." All that was on offer in historical interpretations at the time, Morton implied, was the economic determinism of Laurentian scholars who placed metropolitan centres in positions of control and the West in a position of inferiority. This flawed interpretation, as he saw it, drew upon imperial political assumptions: "the historical interpretation follows the pattern of commercial imperialism it undertakes to trace." What was even worse, however, was that the Laurentian interpretation assumed not just metropolitan economic power and political imperialism but "uniformity of the metropolitan culture throughout the hinterlands."

9. Ibid., 108.

10. Ibid., 108.

11. Ibid., 110.

12. Morton held out the hope that Ontario's control might be ended, that Canada's subordinate regions might win equality, and that Lord Acton's prescription for a great nation might become the principle for Canada: "No power can so efficiently resist the tendencies of centralization, of corruption, and of absolutism, as that community which is the vastest that can be included in a State, which imposes on its members a consistent similarity of character, interest, and opinion, and which arrests the action of the sovereign by the influence of a divided patriotism." (Acton, *The History of Freedom and other Essays* [London 1907], cited in "Clio," 111.) Significantly, the prairie region was one of the sources of a "divided patriotism" in Canada.

   Prairie Canada did not find a comfortable home within the mythology of the newly constructed nation. Though the dominant peoples tried alternative definitions of the country, foremost among which was northernness, none was sufficiently inclusive to be convincing. As Cole Harris concluded: "The fact was that a satisfying national definition would not be found. If some islands could be defined easily

enough, the archipelago could not. Definitions that satisfied here, grated there...."
(Harris, "Emotional Structure")

13. Legally equal to Ottawa after the Judicial Committee rulings of the late nineteenth century, the provinces have actually become moulders of economic activity and even of cultural expression. This came about in part because of their resource income, but also because their constitutional responsibilities and even their political systems made them increasingly central in public life.

14. For an illustration of the interpretation that the economic downturn of the 1980s was the fault of outsiders, see "Albertans blame NEP for their economic woes," in *Globe and Mail*, 2 June 1987, B6.

15. Peter O'Neil, "Reform MP rejects traditional stereotype," in *Vancouver Sun*, 18 July 1998, B4.

16. David Bercuson and Barry Cooper, "Envoi: how the West was awakened," in *Globe and Mail*, 19 September 1998, D2.

17. The panellists at the University of Ottawa meeting in June 1998 were Doug Owram (University of Alberta), Tom Flanagan (University of Calgary), Gordon Gibson (Vancouver journalist), and Nick Taylor (Alberta senator).

18. W. Russell Newman, Marion R. Just, and Ann N. Crigler, *Common Knowledge: News and the Construction of Political Meaning* (Chicago: University of Chicago Press, 1992); a different approach is described in William L. Miller, Annis May Timpson, and Michael Lessnoff, *Political Culture in Contemporary Britain: People and Politicians, Principles and Practice* (Oxford: Clarendon Press, 1997).

19. "A schema functions as a unified system of background relationships whose visible parts stand for the rest of the schema. Because our narrow windows of attention confine us to just a few elements at a time, the technique of using surface elements to stand for larger wholes is an essential feature of our mental life. Schemata are our necessary instruments for making the surfaces of what we read connect significantly with the background knowledge that is withheld from immediate consciousness by the limits of short-term memory." (From E.D. Hirsch Jr., *Cultural Literacy: What Every American Needs to Know* [New York: Random House, 1988], 54-55.)

20. Harris, "Emotional Structure."

21. Robert Fulford, "*Geist* defies convention in its renderings of mundane culture," in *Globe and Mail*, 29 July 1998, A1.

Alberta Social Credit and the Second National Policy

Alvin Finkel

ALBERTA STANDS OUT from the other two Prairie provinces in its attitude in the 1950s and 1960s to the social and economic interventions of
the federal government that scholars now refer to as the "Second National
Policy."[1] The long-running Social Credit government (1935 to 1971), led
for most of the post-war years by Ernest Manning (1944 to 1968), was
largely hostile to federal programs throughout this period. This essay explores the attitude of Manning and his associates to federal policies from
1945 to 1971, when the Social Credit dynasty gave way to a Conservative
dynasty. A key concern here is the extent to which Social Credit resistance
to the federal agenda was ideological and the extent to which it was simply
the reaction of a newly wealthy province to programs that would redistrib-
ute wealth from richer to poorer provinces. In terms of ideology, an important consideration is the degree to which Socred attitudes were motivated
by social credit ideology and the degree to which they were motivated by
social conservatism.

Another explanation could lie in "western alienation." Certainly, the
western provinces had historical complaints about the tenor of the original
national policies of John A. Macdonald. But Social Credit was not consciously a party of western protest, even though it is possible to explain
some of its appeal in Alberta with reference to a general dislike of federal
parties whose power base was in central Canada. As this essay suggests,
Alberta did not present its complaints in the period before 1970 in the
discourse of "Prairie complaints" or "western alienation." It could hardly
do so, since most of its positions were not shared by the other two Prairie
provinces.

Both Saskatchewan and Manitoba largely welcomed the programs that
were introduced in the two and a half decades that followed World War II.[2]

In Saskatchewan, federal spending was welcome as a relief to the provincial treasury of a province that pursued an activist social agenda under its Co-operative Commonwealth Federation (CCF) government from 1944 to 1964, an agenda that Ross Thatcher's Liberals only partially undermined from 1964 to 1971. In Manitoba, federal spending was largely seen as an alternative to provincial spending in the days of the penny-pinching Liberal-Progressive administration that ended in 1958, and as a helpful add-on in the more activist years of Duff Roblin's Conservatives. Roblin sided with the private insurance industry against proponents of a national medicare scheme,[3] but rarely appeared to be a defender of provincial rights per se or an ideological opponent of government involvement in the economy, at least if it was limited to social services and to aid to the private sector.

By contrast, the positions taken by the Alberta government in the area of federal-provincial relations were generally hostile. It has been argued that the bad blood between Ottawa and Edmonton owed its beginnings to the federal government's disallowance of Social Credit's efforts in the 1930s to introduce social credit in the province. The province's efforts to control banks and currency clearly violated federal jurisdictions under the British North America Act, but that had not stopped William Aberhart from running his 1935 electoral campaign on a promise to introduce social credit provincially. Nor did it stop the Aberhart Social Credit government from excoriating the federal government when it asserted its authority in the area of finance and received the total support of the courts. The Alberta government's brief to the Royal Commission on Dominion-Provincial Relations in 1938 appeared to view Canadian federalism as an elaborate plot to plunder Alberta in the interests of central Canadian and foreign bankers. Prepared largely by L.D. Byrne and G.F. Powell, the minions of Social Credit founder Major C.H. Douglas, "The Case for Alberta" was not even presented directly to the commission. Instead, the Alberta government presented its brief to "the Sovereign People of Canada." It asked them to make their national government sovereign over not much more than foreign affairs, giving the provinces control over most jurisdictions, particularly the area of finance.[4]

In 1940, when the federal government proposed a national unemployment insurance program, both the Alberta government and the Social Credit members in Ottawa were early opponents of the legislation. The federal program involved contributions from individuals and from employers as well as a small contribution from the federal government. Social Credit argued that such a program subtracted from, rather than added to, national income. They supported a non-contributory program. So had the

Communists and the CCF in the 1930s. But while these parties believed that wealthier Canadians should be taxed to provide the funds necessary to sponsor unemployment insurance from general government revenues, Social Credit called for the government simply to print money necessary to fund the program. This would allow the unemployed to have spending money without taking it from anyone else. The Alberta government, however, wanted to cooperate with Ottawa during wartime and faced pressures from labour groups who were anxious to have unemployment insurance in any form. So the Aberhart government decided in the end to go along with the other eight Canadian provinces to give the federal government the all-province support required to pass a constitutional amendment allowing the federal government to introduce unemployment insurance.[5]

The circumstances of Aberhart's granting of consent to national unemployment insurance suggest that Alberta Social Credit was far from being reconciled to notions that Ottawa should play a larger role in social programs in Canada. The hostilities that had arisen by the mid-1950s in Edmonton–Ottawa relations may seem simply a continuation of the battles of the 1930s. But any argument that suggests a straight line in Alberta Social Credit relations with the federal government from the 1930s onwards is misleading. In fact, in the early post-war period, before it became clear that Alberta was not destined to remain another Prairie have-not province, overly dependent on the precarious markets for farm products, Alberta cultivated good relations with the federal government. Its attitudes bore some similarities to the other two Prairie provinces on the subjects of social welfare and the relative responsibilities of the two senior levels of government. There were, however, differences that resulted from Social Credit philosophy.

Ernest Manning's willingness in 1945 and 1946 to embrace, even if half-heartedly, Ottawa's blueprint for a welfare state was evident in the round of federal-provincial meetings that stretched from August 1945 to May 1946. The federal government presented in book form an elaborate set of proposals that would have established an advanced welfare state for Canada in one fell swoop. *Proposals of the Government of Canada*, usually referred to as the Green Book, was imbued with a centralizing philosophy. The federal government would take the primary responsibility for funding a national program of pensions for everyone over age sixty-five and a national health insurance program to cover all aspects of health care. It would run the former program and set the standards for the latter, which would be provincially administered. The federal government would also extend its role in caring for unemployed Canadians by assuming sole responsibility for the social welfare of unemployed employables who were not eligible to receive unemployment insurance. Finally, it would also provide the lion's share of funds for provincial public works programs to be timed with declines in the business cycle, and, in turn, would have to approve the programs to be carried out. So great an assumption of federal powers would not come without a price tag for the provinces. They were expected to agree to let the federal government remain, as it had been in wartime, the sole recipient of personal and business income taxes, as well as estate taxes. While the provinces would receive a small percentage of what the federal government raised, as a grant based on provincial population, their ability to raise taxes on their own would be limited to indirect taxes.[6]

None of the provinces particularly liked the tax arrangements that Ottawa proposed as the price of the 1945 version of the Second National Policy. Privately, Mackenzie King recognized that his government was, in fact, offering the provinces too little independence and too little money if they were to carry out their functions. Eventually, he decided that the programs he was promising to fund would be too costly for the federal treasury. It was best that agreement not be reached with the provinces, provided that the provinces rather than the federal government appeared as the villains.[7] The literature on the Green Book debate sometimes lays the blame for the failure of federal-provincial discussions on certain provinces and sometimes on Ottawa. Those who blame the provinces focus on Ontario and Quebec. But if they wanted to cast the net more widely to blame all the provinces that pushed Ontario's and Quebec's concerns at the conference, they might also blame Nova Scotia, British Columbia, and even Prince Edward Island.[8] Alberta, by contrast, sided with Saskatchewan, Manitoba, and New Brunswick in accepting the tax arrangements as an unpleasant, but acceptable, price to pay in order to get the programs that the Green Book promised, even though Manning had reservations about financing and control of some programs.

As Mackenzie King reflected upon his government's hard line on tax agreements at the plenary session of the Dominion-Provincial Conference on April 29, 1946, he noted with displeasure that he was "more sympathetic with his [Ontario Premier George Drew's] point of view than I was with our own." That day and the next he surveyed province-by-province the current stances on the Green Book package of proposals, particularly the tax proposals. Ontario, because it shared King's private views about the fairness and feasibility of the tax arrangements, was beyond the pale. Quebec was worse, with Duplessis having made a "fool speech" that accused the government of Nazism and gangsterism, while Angus Macdonald of

Nova Scotia was "seeking to side with Drew against the government," and Premier J. Walter Jones of Prince Edward Island was "just impossible." King listed as his four supporters Garson of Manitoba, McNair of New Brunswick, Douglas of Saskatchewan, and Manning of Alberta.[9]

Manning's support, whatever King thought, was lukewarm at best. At the opening of the Dominion-Provincial Conference on August 6, 1945, Manning's preliminary speech was a primer on Social Credit economic and political theory. Social Credit theory was opposed to centralization and maintained that each level of government could carry out its functions only if it had sufficient control over revenues. Manning complained to the conference that exclusive federal control over banking and currency left provinces in a poor position to fulfill their duties to provide for the welfare of citizens. "It is plainly the responsibility of the Dominion Government to ensure that Provincial revenues are adequate to enable the Provinces to discharge fully their constitutional responsibilities," argued Manning. This was a position in keeping with the concept of a Second National Policy based on federal underwriting of a substantial proportion of social program costs. But Manning, the Social Crediter, believed Ottawa should acquire the revenues required by both federal and provincial governments to run social programs from monetization of the nation's wealth.[10] Although he was insistent that each level of government should carry out the functions it was assigned, Manning indicated in his preliminary address, as he did several times throughout the conference sessions, his government's willingness to entertain constitutional changes. While he was vague about what responsibilities might be reassigned, subsequent statements by Manning and other ministers indicated they believed old-age pensions, care of unemployed employables, and housing should be solely federal responsibilities.

Communications between the Alberta government and the federal government regarding Green Book proposals were friendly. W. W. Cross, Alberta's long-time Minister of Health, made plain that his government wanted a national scheme of old-age pensions to be available at age sixty-five, free of a means test, with "the entire cost provided for out of the consolidated revenue of the Dominion."[11] Provincial Secretary A.J. Hooke, an ardent Social Credit ideologue, received a favourable response when he asked the federal Minister of Health and Welfare whether the proposed national medicare scheme would allow a province to charge a small deterrent fee for hospital stays and medical visits.[12]

Yet Manning, as a Social Crediter, could hardly be happy with Ottawa's approach to financing of social programs. When the Green Book had been tabled at the conference, Manning's first response was that there was too much emphasis on "redistributing purchasing power" as opposed to creation of new purchasing power through monetary means. He chided the government for its emphasis on full employment, suggesting that in a mechanized age of mass production, the concept of full employment "is as antiquated as an old maid's dream and as improbable of realization."[13] No doubt, such pessimism on the employment issue encouraged the province's decision to let the federal government take full responsibility for the unemployed. It also encouraged Social Credit to continue its traditional support for non-contributory social insurance programs, financed through monetary expansion, as a key to maintaining consumer purchasing power.

Manning summed up his scepticism regarding the Green Book approach to social programs in an address to the Saskatoon Canadian Club in August 1946: "Let us not delude ourselves into thinking that the mere redistribution of the national income increases the aggregate by one five cents piece. That, I submit, is the great weakness and inadequacy of the multiplicity of post-war social security insurance schemes and proposals being propagated today. The majority of them are based on the false premise that post-war economic security can be assured by a simple process of redistributing an inadequate over-all consumer income."[14]

Like many of Manning's post-war pronouncements, this speech was meant to please simultaneously conservative business representatives, who opposed programs that were either redistributive or inflationary, and Social Credit ideologues, who only supported programs that were financed by printing new money. Manning simply avoided the question of how consumer income should be increased, allowing business people to assume it would be via economic growth and low taxes, while Social Crediters assumed it would be via an increase in the money supply.

Such views on Manning's part, however, raise the question of why he would support the Green Book proposals, federal programs that were to be financed through taxation rather than expansion of the money supply. The answer seems to be simply that Manning was a pragmatic politician. His principal political opponents in the 1944 provincial election had been the socialist CCF, who claimed that the state profits from nationalized industries would provide much of the funding required to operate social programs. Manning had argued that socialism would mean a state dictatorship over people's lives and that squeezing the monies required for social programs out of productive enterprises was counterproductive. He espoused Social Credit's ideas for getting the monies needed for social insurance from monetary inflation. But, of course, as the evidence of the 1930s made clear, a province could play no role in setting monetary policy. The Green

Book would let the premier of a poorer province off the hook to some degree. The federal government, whose resources were greater than those available to the Alberta government, would provide the social programs most Albertans appeared to want. This would reduce the CCF's chances of ever ousting Social Credit from power.

As the premiers and the federal Cabinet met, Manning was also faced with a concerted campaign by the municipalities in his province to have the province assume the bulk of the costs involved in relief of the unemployed. In 1940, the Aberhart government had taken advantage of the relatively low unemployment rate during the war to pull out of its shared-cost program for unemployed employables ineligible for unemployment insurance. When the war was over and job-seekers once again exceeded jobs, the municipalities began to chafe at the provincial government for leaving them holding the bag. British Columbia was reimbursing municipalities for eighty percent of the costs of relief as well as fifty percent of the cost of medical services to recipients of old-age pensions, mothers' allowances, and relief allowances.[15] Alberta municipalities, large and small, pressured the province to follow suit. Calgary led the fray in early January 1946 with a resolution calling on the provincial government to follow the British Columbia example. For a month, Manning received a flurry of resolutions from municipalities endorsing Calgary's position.[16]

Still, Manning's explanation at the last session of the Dominion-Provincial Conference, of why Alberta was willing to be one of only four provinces prepared to accept the tax arrangements demanded by the federal government, largely ignored the Green Book proposals. Premier T.C. Douglas of Saskatchewan stressed his hesitation in supporting a set of tax arrangements that left unclear where the provinces would find sufficient revenues to carry out their obligations. His adherence to the federal proposals was largely predicated on his government's desire to have Ottawa establish or help provinces establish the social programs itemized in the Green Book.[17] By contrast, Premier Stuart Garson of Manitoba simply emphasized that a poor province could raise little revenue on its own from personal, corporate, and succession taxes, and Manitoba was happier to have the federal government collect these taxes and give the provinces a per capita share.[18]

Manning's reasoning was similar to Garson's, though he was careful not to appear to be grovelling in the manner of the Manitoba premier. He indicated that prospects for Canada's economic growth would be hampered by bickering among governments, since this would create uncertainty among investors. But "the most important reason" for concluding an interim taxation agreement along the lines suggested by Mackenzie King was that the alternative for some provinces was "complete bankruptcy." Provinces "would be faced with the responsibility of collecting, by means of dual taxation, sufficient revenues to maintain their present public services, to say nothing about providing for post-war development." In poorer provinces, it would mean "they would shortly be forced into the position of beggars at the door of the dominion treasury."[19]

Manning's support of the federal government package was by no means unconditional. While his government had publicly supported federal old-age pensions and federal authority in the area of housing, he was adamant that in areas that remained under provincial responsibility, the federal government should provide "unconditional supplementary grants for social services," rather than directing the provinces as to how they should spend the money. This demand, which reflected Social Credit's concern about centralization, separated Manning from both Douglas and Garson, who were too anxious to get federal funds for social programs to worry about federal efforts to control how these funds were spent.[20] On the whole, though, the positions taken by the government of Alberta on federal-provincial relations in 1945-46 seemed to reflect a realistic assessment that a poor province needed Ottawa's help if it was to establish a level of social programming acceptable to its citizens.

Hard-line Social Crediters, who denounced federal social insurance proposals, could not have been happy with Manning's acquiescence at the dominion-provincial meetings. But there was no outcry from them because Manning had thrown a large bone their way. In March 1946, his government introduced "An Act Respecting the Rights of Alberta Citizens," which largely echoed the Aberhart legislation that the courts had declared ultra vires in the late 1930s. All financial institutions would require a provincial licence permitting them to grant credit in Alberta.[21] As Manning indicated in a radio speech, a Board of Credit Commissioners would ensure that "for every dollar's worth of goods produced there must be made available to the consuming public a corresponding amount of Purchasing Power."[22] The premier suggested that this legislation was not ultra vires; he was proposing to control credit transactions, not currency per se. Nonetheless, Manning presumably knew that the courts would disallow his bill and may have viewed the Green Book arrangements, which would certainly add to the consuming power of Albertans as well as provide tax relief to the provincial treasury, as a desirable alternative. Or perhaps he hoped to soften up the federal government towards his provincial Social Credit bill by cooperating with federal proposals.

In early 1948, as expected, the Judicial Committee of the Privy Council of the United Kingdom agreed with lower courts that Alberta's legislation invaded federal jurisdiction. The reaction of the Alberta government in March 1948, only one month after the Leduc oil strike and therefore before this province could think of itself as wealthy, was a combination of Social Credit and poor-province thought. A resolution passed by the legislature suggested that the court decision meant that provinces could not fulfill their responsibilities under the British North America Act to provide for the welfare of citizens. So it was clear that the federal government would have to do so. But it should not do so on the basis that the Green Book had attempted, one that simply redistributed sources of revenues available to various levels of government. The Alberta legislature called on Ottawa to convene a new federal-provincial conference "for the purpose of considering and adopting a permanent solution based on the full utilization and monetization of the nation's production to replace the existing tax transfer agreement when it expires." In the interim, the federal government should give the provinces enough money for them to pay decent old-age pensions, to provide adequate medical services, and to build highways and other public works. Though the resolution was informed by Social Credit monetary theory, its emphasis on federal responsibility and on universal programs won it the support of the two CCF members of the legislature.[23] On the whole, then, in early 1948 the Alberta Social Credit government, while miffed that the courts had once again interfered with its monetary experimentation, was a supporter of the Second National Policy. It proposed a Social Credit version of the policy, of course, but, in general, it was after federal money to help a poorer province fulfill its social responsibilities as well as to pursue economic growth through the building of transportation infrastructure.

Indeed, it seemed to take several years after Leduc before the Social Credit government developed the notion that Alberta was a rich province that could, in fact, look after the social welfare of its citizens without federal help and indeed without control over monetary policy. After the federal government withdrew the Green Book proposals in June 1946, claiming that Ontario's and Quebec's recalcitrance made it impossible to find agreement on the issues raised by the federal proposals, the Alberta government remained open to federal initiatives for some time to come. There was no opposition from Alberta to the federal proposals for a national universal pension scheme in 1951, for example. But by the mid-1950s, there had been a change in the Alberta attitude that seemed to coincide with the change in Alberta's economic fortunes. The attitude shift was manifest in the positions it took at dominion-provincial conferences and in public statements regarding the allocation of taxing and spending powers between the provinces and the federal government. It was also manifest in a more conservative position on the question of social welfare. In fairness, however, there was continuity in the Alberta government's positions to the extent that, even in 1945-46, it had demanded a strict separation of powers between Ottawa and the provinces, and no conditions on monies given by Ottawa to provinces.

At the 1955 federal-provincial conference, Premier Manning protested that federal taxation practices left too little money to the provincial government to carry out its responsibilities. Federal revenue collections from the province were 252 percent higher in 1955 than they were in 1948. But the province had received only a marginal increase in funds from the "tax rental" agreements that the provinces continued to sign with Ottawa, despite the breakdown of the Green Book negotiations. Manning was concerned because in 1954 the debt-averse provincial government had to take $13 million from accumulated surpluses to fund its expenditures, despite a healthy increase in provincial oil royalties.

Manning's proposed solution, which eventually was put into practice, was for each province to set a tax rate as a proportion of the federal tax. Both sets of taxes could be collected by the federal government, which would then send the province its share. Obviously, this method favoured wealthier provinces over poorer ones. Before Ottawa had acceded to such a demand, it adopted a proposal favoured by Quebec and the Atlantic provinces, along with Manitoba and Saskatchewan: equalization grants. These were meant to be a redistribution of taxes collected from wealthy provinces in favour of the poorer provinces. While they were relatively small and meant mainly to allow the disadvantaged provinces to provide education and social services to their citizens that paralleled those available in wealthy provinces, Alberta begrudged these grants, claiming, as noted below, that it should share in any grants given to provinces.

From the Social Credit point of view, of course, programs that simply redistributed existing wealth added nothing to the overall economy and gave power to state bureaucrats, if not to the Money Conspiracy itself. But the government, and with it the Social Credit party, was moving away from the idea of large-scale social spending programs, whether financed by redistribution of wealth or by printing new money. A committee convened by the Department of Public Welfare in 1956 to review welfare legislation and policy assumed, in its recommendations, that public policy should favour means-tested programs over universal social programs.

The committee complained that the federal government had "seen fit to issue assistance to those not necessarily in need, by way of old age security and family allowances." So it wanted the Alberta government to approach Ottawa to "relinquish their present supervisory authority in connection with old age assistance, blindness allowances, disabled persons' allowances." The committee proposed that Ottawa simply give the provinces a grant to help them discharge their responsibilities in these areas.[24]

In an article in December 1956, in the Social Credit League's house organ, *The Busy Bee*, Ernest Manning outlined the government's position on both the purpose of social welfare programs and the desirable relative involvement of the federal and provincial governments in their elaboration and delivery. Manning emphasized that social welfare programs should be residual rather than universal. He wrote: "A major objective of organized society should be to assist each citizen to attain through his own enterprise sufficient financial resources to enable him to obtain for himself and his dependents an acceptable standard of social welfare without dependence on state welfare services. To the extent that this is impossible, society collectively must assume the cost of an acceptable standard of social services to bring such services within the financial reach of each individual citizen."[25]

Such a shift from Social Credit's one-time emphasis on handing money to all consumers regardless of their need made sense to many Albertans in the midst of an oil boom. In the 1930s it would have been dismissed as high Toryism in a province where the Tories would await the 1970s to form a government. Indeed, it reflected a right-wing philosophy rather than the Social Credit philosophy with its blend of right-wing and left-wing ideas, held together uneasily by a focus on the monetary panacea.

Manning's new views on federal-provincial relations still reflected in part the views he had expressed at the time of the discussions on the Green Book. He opposed all conditional grant programs "with the exception of limited national equalization grants" from which Alberta should not be excluded.[26] There should be a clear definition of responsibilities of all three levels of government, and clear sources of revenue for each. There should be no meddling by one level of government with the activities of another. But there was no longer a notion that the goal of full employment was an illusion, nor the view that the province of Alberta needed federal grants to avoid bankruptcy. Alberta's wealth had caused the Social Credit government to put some teeth into its doctrine of opposing centralization. It had less need of the federal government's money and its citizens had, at least from the provincial government's point of view, less need for any government's money. Why, then, should their money and the money that the

Alberta government might require as taxation be diverted to Ottawa and, via Ottawa, to other provinces?

This philosophy of minimalist government and opposition to centralization governed most dealings between the Alberta government and the federal government after 1956. Its opposition to a national medicare program, to regional development programs, and to grant-in-aid programs has been documented elsewhere.[27] But to what extent was this opposition based on Social Credit philosophy and to what extent was it based on the social conservative philosophy that was implicit in the Manning government's management of public affairs from the 1940s and explicit after 1963?

Throughout the 1950s, Manning continued to advocate expansion of the money supply to boost consumer purchasing power as an alternative to a tax-and-spend approach to dealing with problems of the business cycle and of poverty. But, as noted above, he also increasingly emphasized that respect for the individual's right to choose, always a key consideration in Social Credit philosophy, was incompatible with universal social programs. His speeches defending private enterprise demonstrated a conversion to the view that the marketplace, rather than government intervention, was the key to economic growth and greater wealth for individuals. Just as Depression-era socialism was watered down in the prosperous 1950s, Depression-era Social Credit lost its messianic fervour. While the conviction remained that reform of the monetary system was the key to forever solving the problems inherent in the business cycle, competing currents in the movement about how the government should ensure that each individual shared some of the benefits of prosperity had been resolved in favour of the right wing of the movement.

Manning let the penny drop in an interview with Southam reporter Charles Lynch in 1963. He argued that Canada was facing a "transition period," a period of political realignment. "Out of this a two-party system will emerge," he said. On the one side would be a party that supported the existing "monetary policies" that were turning Canada socialist: high taxation and increased public debt. On the other side would be a party of "social conservatism" that supported individualism and resisted spending programs that required increased taxation. What would happen to the Social Credit party and its philosophy when this new party was formed? "I do not see this new party of free enterprise as being primarily a Social Credit party. Social Credit is a philosophy first and a party second—it started as an educational approach and there is nothing in the monetary policies or philosophy of Social Credit that ties it to an individual party."[28]

The following year, the provincial Social Credit convention in Red Deer followed their leader's call to take the party into oblivion by agreeing to instruct both the provincial and federal Social Credit organizations "to encourage the realignment of all those who believe in the Free Enterprise Way of Life to band together in a program with as many points on which there can be general agreement."[29] In part, Manning's implicit rejection of the national Social Credit party was simply a recognition of the party's inability to sink roots outside the West. The breakthrough in Quebec in the federal elections of 1962 had simply caused fissures between the western and Quebec wings of the party, with many of the Quebec MPs leaving to form their own party, the Créditistes, under the leadership of Réal Caouette. But the party's failure to win support in most regions was only half the story. Manning's focus on higher taxes and increased debts, as the "monetary policies" he opposed, demonstrated the extent to which he was refashioning Social Credit ideas to make them indistinguishable from the ideas supported by chambers of commerce and by conservative ideologues. The Social Credit party, while being his power base, was worth sacrificing if it could help to fashion a genuine, national conservative party with a chance to form a federal government.

In the interim, however, the national Social Credit party might be a useful forum to express the provincial government's criticisms of federal policy towards the province. Manning campaigned for the federal Social Credit party during the 1965 federal election, in which his young son, Preston, was one of the Socred candidates in Edmonton. The premier's criticism of the federal Tories, and particularly the Tory members from Alberta, was not founded on Social Credit ideology. It seemed to be based in equal parts on social conservatism and on the complaints of a rich province. With regard to the former, Manning criticized the Tories for opposing his government's "co-insurance payments" for hospital patients (a daily fee for staying in the hospital) while allowing other provinces to levy premiums on their citizens for hospital insurance. That Alberta's system meant a tax on the sick while the premium system meant simply an insurance payment was of little concern to Manning since, from his social conservative point of view, a daily hospital fee was a deterrent to abuse of the system.[30]

The complaints of a rich province were evident in Manning's lashing out at both Tories and Liberals for having "penalized" Alberta in the awarding of equalization grants. The grants were determined by comparing the taxes that provinces were able to collect and comparing them to the taxes collected by the richest two provinces, Ontario and British Columbia. A formula then determined a grant that provinces with lesser incomes than those of the "big two" would receive. Alberta was the only province to receive nothing because of, as Manning put it, "Ottawa's insistence that revenue from our natural resources be treated the same as revenue from taxes."[31] The Alberta premier complained that the Conservative members from Alberta, who had held the overwhelming majority of the province's federal seats since 1957, had refused to support his call for Ottawa to exclude petroleum royalties from the federal government's calculations of Alberta's provincial revenues.

Both social conservatism and rich-province thinking informed Manning's reaction to the designated-area concept that the Tories had developed under Diefenbaker to help Atlantic Canada diversify its economy, and that the Liberals had extended to all areas of the country marked by poverty and lack of industry. While Manitoba and Saskatchewan welcomed a program that promised subsidies to most areas of their respective provinces, Alberta, which had far fewer designated areas proportionate to its population, was actively opposed to the concept of designated areas, and particularly to the idea of encouraging firms to establish themselves in these areas by giving them start-up subsidies as a reward. "This is not in keeping with the free enterprise concept and could well be in direct conflict with economic feasibility so important if Canada is to develop a solid competitive position in world export markets," Manning wrote Lester Pearson.[32]

While Manning's words to Pearson suggested simply social conservatism, his province's efforts to promote industrial development suggest he saw no violation of free-enterprise principles when a wealthy province built infrastructure with its own monies, which a poor province could not hope to duplicate without federal help. In northern Alberta, as he told the legislature in February 1965, the province planned to provide the capital to the Canadian National Railway to build rail lines to connect undeveloped mineral resource areas in the western portion of the province north of the CN main line, with CN outlets to the ocean. Manning saw subsidization of this sort as simply creating a better climate for investment, and expressed concerns about the policies of other provinces as well as of the federal government that involved "giving special concessions to a certain industry to locate in a particular area."[33] But Manning had once followed similar policies. In the 1950s his government had used the treasury branches to make interest-free loans to entrepreneurs with plans to diversify the provincial economy. They only abandoned this practice after some of these loans were not repaid and the government faced the main scandal of its years in office over the issue of political interference with the treasury branches.[34]

Manning and his ministers felt somewhat alone among the provinces in what they regarded as their principled opposition to federal intrusion in areas of provincial jurisdiction, an intrusion that is key to the concept of a second National Policy. So, for example, when Alberta Health Minister Dr. J. Donovan Ross blasted federal Minister of Health and Welfare Judy LaMarsh for recommending a federal-provincial conference on mental retardation, he could not resist taking a swipe at other provincial governments. After affirming that the federal government had no business at all in getting involved in the area of caring for individuals with disabilities, Ross lamented: "No doubt my sentiments may not be shared by other provinces, who too often are concerned with the possibilities of getting additional financial assistance from the federal treasury, rather than following out the principles contained in our major Dominion statute."[35] This was a rather self-righteous observation coming from a Social Credit minister, considering that less than two decades earlier his government had been happy to have the federal government take complete control over provision for the unemployed, the aged, and the inadequately housed. But the sweet smell of gasoline money over those two decades had allowed Alberta to become much tougher in its stance in favour of provincial control over jurisdictions that the British North America Act explicitly or implicitly gave to the provinces.

Manning was so convinced that other premiers wanted mainly to suck Ottawa dry, forcing the federal government to collect more taxes in Alberta, that he refused to consider working closely with the other provinces in the area of economic development strategy. At the third provincial premiers' conference, held in 1962 in Victoria, Premier Roblin suggested the creation of a body to study the provinces' difficulties in the areas of economic growth and to advise them on the best directions to take to improve economic performance. While most premiers liked the idea, Manning poured cold water on it. There was too great an ideological divergence among Canada's provincial governments for this to work, he argued. While some supported belt-tightening, others favoured "pump-priming the economy," usually with the federal government's help. He saw no point in trying to find advisors who could speak at once to the ideologically diverse provincial governments of Canada.[36]

Certainly Ernest Manning was, at times, given reason to believe that he alone among provincial premiers defended both private enterprise and a clear division of federal and provincial responsibilities. While Manning was hardly alone among the premiers to oppose a national medicare scheme at the federal-provincial conference of 1965, he was completely alone in his opposition to designated-area programs.[37] His long-term efforts to have the federal government rebate federal tax collected from investor-owned firms generating electricity were rebuffed by Finance Minister Walter Gordon, with no argument from the other provinces if only because Alberta was, at the time, the only province where private companies generated most of the electricity. [38]

Manning phrased his opposition to the tenor of federal policies and the policies of most of the other provincial governments not in the language of Social Credit, but in the language of social conservatism. The discriminatory treatment of private electrical utilities, he argued, encouraged provinces to nationalize these firms, which was not "in the interests of our national economy or the preservation of our free enterprise form of society."[39]

As for the designated areas programs, Manning's point of view coincided with the views of Alberta's major magnates. W. O. Twaits, president of Imperial Oil, wrote Manning in September 1968, to send him a copy of a letter he had sent to the federal Minister of Mines, Energy, and Resources, protesting federal financial aid to a refinery planned for Come-by-Chance, Newfoundland. Manning responded by indicating his agreement with Twaits, claiming that it was "a glaring example of the inequities which stem from various forms of government subsidies to induce industries to locate in specific locations."

> As you know we have always opposed this policy on the part of the Federal and various Provincial governments, and, frankly, we are much concerned that it is becoming such a widespread practice throughout the country. In addition to being inequitable to Canadian taxpayers, it is grossly unfair to require legitimate private industry to compete in the marketplace with plants which are exempt from carrying a fair and equitable share of the tax load and, in addition in many cases, are receiving substantial bonuses by way of capital funds from the federal treasury. [40]

By the 1960s, then—indeed, by the mid-1950s—the Social Credit government of Alberta can be seen to have become an opponent of the so-called Second National Policy. It did not accept the view that the federal government had an obligation either to raise the living standards of individuals regardless of the province in which they lived or that it should be attempting to favour disadvantaged areas in their efforts to achieve economic development. Rather, the federal government and the provinces should each stick to their own constitutional obligations and should have their own separate funds for their separate programs.

In this essay, as in my earlier work on Social Credit, I largely reject the conclusions of a recent volume on Social Credit in Alberta by Bob Hesketh, which concludes: "What is remarkable about Social Credit, then, is the very thing most often denied—the overriding continuity of its ideas. Though strongly influenced by Aberhart's and Manning's shared fundamentalism, Douglas social credit was the constant reference point of Alberta Social Credit ideology and government policy. The methods to achieve social credit were revised over the years, but the government remained the same. Only the people could free themselves. The government's job was to ensure they had the opportunity."[41]

Hesketh, in fact, deals only skimpily with the Manning period[42] and so does not have occasion to defend his view that the Social Credit government changed little over time. It is true, of course, that adherence to Douglasite social credit theory was at no time formally abandoned. But it might be noted that the Soviet Communist party at no time abandoned its adherence to Marxism–Leninism as its official philosophy. This supposed philosophical continuity, however, belies the radical differences in attitudes and policies on the part of different Soviet regimes, particularly the Stalin government as contrasted with the Gorbachev administration. Hesketh correctly emphasizes that the "Bible Bill" Aberhart vision of Social Credit, like Douglas's, "included an apocalyptic vision of world history and called for a radical revision of capitalism, a wholesale redistribution of the ownership of the means of production, and widespread social reform."[43] As the evidence presented in this essay suggests, none of these features could be found in the attitudes expressed by Ernest Manning in the latter stages of his Social Credit administration in Alberta.

There were, as we have seen, continuities and discontinuities in the Alberta government's attitude to federal proposals for intervention in areas of provincial jurisdiction in the quarter century after World War II. Throughout this period, Ernest Manning argued that a clear division of responsibilities and revenues between the federal and provincial governments was required. But, in the early years after the war, when Alberta could not go it alone, he foresaw a fairly large scope for the federal government, including full responsibility for care of the unemployed and full responsibility for housing. If only because the province was not to be allowed to have any control over currency, he also accepted the idea that the federal government would collect the lion's share of taxes and then distribute a portion of them to provinces on a per capita basis. This would ensure that the poorer provinces received more revenue than if they attempted to collect income and succession taxes on their own. Social Credit thinking argued for a clear division of powers; poor-province thinking argued for compromise with the federal government, and support, however grudging, for the Second National Policy. If the province could not have social credit, it could, at least, have federal funds.

By the mid-1050s, however, the Social Credit government recognized that it did not need federal funds. It soon realized that it also did not need social credit. It had oil; who could ask for anything more? Its earlier convictions that the new age of technology guaranteed that not everyone could be employed, and that therefore employment income could not generate sufficient purchasing power to keep the economy booming, disappeared. In its place came the "social conservative" philosophy that the unimpeded marketplace was indeed generally the guarantor of prosperity for the many. While the social conservative philosophy bore some resemblance to the old Social Credit philosophy—in its emphasis, for example, on devolution of power and in its opposition to socialism—it was marked more by big business economic liberalism than the anti-big-business populism that inspired the early Social Credit movement in Alberta. If the Alberta Social Credit government in the 1960s sounded less like its counterpart in the 1940s and more like George Drew's Ontario Conservatives, both in terms of its attitude to the role of the state and its hostility to federal plans in the areas of social insurance and economic growth, it is because Alberta had changed. It had become rich and could not accept that a portion of its new oil revenues was being redistributed to help provinces that remained poor. While a degree of social credit rhetoric of the early days still popped up from time to time from within the Social Credit governments after 1955, and certainly within the party, it bore no relationship to the reality of the Social Credit administration's goals. The Manning government in the 1960s felt quite alone, among provinces generally as well as among Western provinces, in its opposition to the welfare state consensus of the post-war era, a consensus that, in the pre-petroleum period of its life, Social Credit seemed to welcome. This government, I would argue, is best understood not as a government motivated by social credit ideology or western alienation, but as a government motivated by social conservative and rich-province thinking.

Endnotes

1. The notion that the post-war federal government interventions meant to address the economic problems of disadvantaged provinces constituted a second or new national policy was first discussed in Vernon C. Fowke, "The National Policy—Old and New," *Canadian Journal of Economics and Political Science* 18, no. 3 (August 1952): 271-86.

2. Their welcome of the programs can be judged by the position these provinces took at federal-provincial conferences throughout the period. Saskatchewan's presentations to the Royal Commission on Health Services also emphasized the importance of federal funding and standards for provincial medical insurance programs. National Archives of Canada (NAC), RG 33, Series 78, Hearings of the Royal Commission on Health Services, Vol. 9, File 78, "Submission of the Government of the Province of Saskatchewan," January 1962.

3. Roblin called on the federal government to make per capita grants to provinces for citizens enrolled voluntarily in comprehensive prepaid medical insurance schemes, privately or publicly operated. NAC, RG 33, Series 78, Hearings of the Royal Commission on Health Services, Vol. 8, File 48, Honourable Duff Roblin, Premier, Manitoba, January 1962.

4. Alvin Finkel, *The Social Credit Phenomenon in Alberta* (Toronto: University of Toronto Press, 1989), 63-64; Edward Bell, *Social Classes and Social Credit in Alberta* (Montreal and Kingston: McGill-Queen's University Press, 1993), 125-26.

5. Finkel, *The Social Credit Phenomenon,* 78. On the attitude of the Aberhart government more generally to the war effort, see William R. Young, "'A Highly Intelligent and Unselfish Approach': Public Information and the Canadian West, 1939-45," *Canadian Historical Review* 62, no. 4 (December 1981): 502.

6. R.M. Burns, *The Acceptable Mean: the Tax Rental Agreements, 1941-1962* (Toronto: Canadian Tax Foundation, 1980), Chapter 2.

7. See Alvin Finkel, "Paradise Postponed: A Re-examination of the Green Book Proposals of 1945," *Journal of the Canadian Historical Association*, New Series 4 (1993): 120-42.

8. See the addresses given by the various provinces in *Dominion-Provincial Conference (1945): Dominion and Provincial Submissions and Plenary Conference Discussions*, 29 April and 30 April 1946 (Ottawa: King's Printer, 1946).

9. NAC, MG 26 J13, Mackenzie King *Diaries*, 29 and 30 April 1946.

10. *Dominion-Provincial Conference (1945)*, 43-45.

11. NAC, Department of National Health and Welfare papers, RG 29, Vol. 23, File 21-2-1, W.W. Cross, Minister of Health, Alberta, to Alex Skelton, Secretary, Cabinet Committee on Dominion-Provincial Relations, 12 October 1945.

12. Public Archives of Canada (PAC), RG 29, Vol. 23, File 21-2-2, "Memorandum of Correspondence Re Dominion-Provincial Conference on Reconstruction, Proposals of the Government of Canada on National Health Program," G.B. Chisholm, M.D., Deputy Minister of Health, to A.J. Hooke, 29 December 1945.

13. *Dominion-Provincial Conference*, 7 August 1945, 188.

14. Provincial Archives of Alberta (PAA), Premiers' (Manning) Papers, File 2161, "Address to Saskatoon Canadian Club," 14 August 1946.

15. PAA, Premiers' Papers, File 1450, C.W. Lundy, Director of Welfare, Department of Provincial Secretary, Social Assistance Branch, Victoria, to George Thompson, superintendent, Civic Relief Department, Calgary, 2 February 1946.

16. PAA, Premiers' Papers, Files 1450 and 1811, contain letters from eighteen municipalities sent between 14 January 1946 and 19 February 1946, endorsing the Calgary position. Beginning with Calgary itself, the municipalities calling on the province to act were Edmonton, Lethbridge, Edson, Cardston, Macleod, Blairmore, Grande Prairie, Leduc, Vegreville, Fort Saskatchewan, Raymond, Wainwright, Coleman, Stony Plain, Magrath, Drumheller, Macleod, and Strathmore.

17. *Dominion-Provincial Conference*, 30 April 1946, 479.

18. Ibid., 444.

19. *Dominion-Provincial Conference*, 30 April 1948, 491. Manning's position reflected the general support of Prairie Canadians for the Rowell–Sirois report recommendation that the federal government distribute tax monies in a way that guaranteed residents of poorer provinces similar social services to those available to residents of wealthier provinces. As Gerald Friesen comments: "This was an important forward step, in the view of Prairie Canadians, because they were henceforth to be protected as much as possible from a disaster like that of the 1930s." Gerald Friesen, *The Canadian Prairies: A History* (Toronto: University of Toronto Press, 1987), 448.

20. *Dominion-Provincial Conference*, 30 April 1948, 495.

21. *Statutes of the Province of Alberta*, "An Act Respecting the Rights of Alberta Citizens," Chapter 11, 1946, assented to 27 March 1946.

22. PAA, Alberta Social Credit League Papers, Box 2, "An Explanation of the Alberta Bill of Rights: Your Charter of Rights and Freedoms: Radio Address by Ernest Manning," 17 April 1946.

23. Legislative Assembly of Alberta, *Journals*, 10 March 1948.

24. PAA, Premiers' Papers, File 2141A, Department of Public Welfare, "Report and Recommendations of the Departmental Committee Convened for a Review of Welfare Legislation and Policy."

25. *The Busy Bee* 1, no. 7 (December 1956): 3.

26. Ibid.

27. Finkel, *The Social Credit Phenomenon in Alberta*, 148–52.

28. *The Busy Bee* (March–April, 1963): 3.

29. Alberta Social Credit Papers, Box 2, "Report of Resolutions, Alberta Social Credit League Convention, 25 November 1964."

30. PAA, Ernest Manning Papers, Box 41, File 418, Ernest Manning to Lester Pearson, 31 December 1963.

31. PAA, Ernest Manning Papers, Box 10, File 126, "Tele-Facts," 2 November 1965.

32. PAA, Ernest Manning Papers, Box 41, File 421C, Manning to Pearson, 10 June 1965.

33. PAA, Manning Papers, Box 37, File 371c. "Premiers' Address in legislature," 23 February 1965.

34. Revelations about the Treasury Branch scandal are found in Bob Hesketh, "The Company A, Company B Charges: The Manning Government, the Treasury Branches

and Highways Contracts," MA thesis, University of Alberta, 1989. Hesketh largely demolishes the claim that Manning's Cabinet provided honest and efficient governance for the province.

35. PAA, Manning Papers, Box 41, File 418, Dr. J. Donovan Ross to Judy LaMarsh, 20 December 1963.

36. *Proceedings of Third Provincial Premiers' Conference,*Victoria, 6 August 1962 (Ottawa: Queen's Printer, 1962).

37. *Federal-Provincial Conference of the Prime Minister and Premiers,* 19-22 July 1965,Vol. 1, 25.

38. PAA, Manning Papers, Box 41, File 418, Ernest Manning to Lester Pearson, 31 December 1963; *Federal-Provincial Conference*, 19-22 July 1965,Vol. 1, 45-47.

39. PAA, Manning Papers, Box 41, File 418, Manning to Pearson, 31 December 1963.

40. PAA, Manning Papers, Box 56, File 607(a), W.O. Twaits to Manning, 12 September 1968; Manning to W.O. Twaits, 12 September 1968.

41. Bob Hesketh, *Major Douglas and Alberta Social Credit* (Toronto: University of Toronto Press, 1997), 239.

42. Hesketh devotes one brief chapter to the postwar period: "Chapter 12: Social Credit in the Postwar Era: The Expulsion of Douglasites and the Retention of Faith," ibid., 222-39. Most of the chapter deals with the unedifying debates within Social Credit from 1945 to 1957 about whether the worldwide financial conspiracy was a front for the Jews or ethnically neutral.

43. Ibid., 249.

From the Inside Out: The World of Mennonite Diaries

Royden Loewen

"THE GREAT MASS OF DIARY WRITING is poor stuff, interesting only to the antiquarian or social historian," wrote Robert Fothergill in his 1974 history of English diaries.[1] His study thus disregarded this "poor stuff" and focussed on those diaries that exhibited "marvellous richness and vitality" and were kept by "remarkable human beings [who] communicat[ed] their natures abundantly."[2] The "poor stuff" of the diary world, however, is also often outside the purview of social histories. In their attempts to recreate the social dynamic within communities, social historians have relied on less personal sources, such as demographic data, ethnic newspapers, and the reports of parochial schools, mutual aid societies, and other community organizations. One reason for the absence of personal writings is simple: as Tamara Hareven has observed, "very few ordinary men and women left behind diaries and correspondence."[3] The "linguistic turn" may represent another reason: writings that expose sentiment and offer frank evaluation are, no doubt, the most promising pages for textual analysis. Certainly, the most recent works that examine the writings of everyday life focus on autobiographies, letters, memoirs, fiction, poetry, and community histories.[4] The daily diary has been left relatively unexamined.

This essay considers the significance of personal writings that Fothergill knows as the "poor stuff" of diary-keeping and that Hareven sees as a rarity. They are the records that were abundant in one North American rural minority group: the Mennonites. The diaries contain few expressed emotions and little personal analysis. They are different from the immigrant diaries most often reproduced. Most bear little similarity to the Mennonite diaries published by other university presses. James Nyce's 1982 edition, *The Gordon C. Eby Diaries: Chronicle of a Mennonite Farmer, 1911-1913*, and Harvey Dyck's 1991 translation, *A Mennonite in Russia: The Diaries of Jacob*

D. Epp, 1851-1880, for example, are the accounts of "extraordinary" Mennonites who analyze personal relationships, comment on new technologies, evaluate social boundaries, and exhibit "intensely personal" faith experiences."[5] Most of the diaries we wish to consider record daily acts, not emotion and analysis; they reflect the contours of social units—household, congregation, and community—not the inner thoughts of the individual.

Why, then, study these diaries? For the very reason that the daily diary written by the ordinary person about everyday life turns the often hidden contours of household and community "inside out," allowing the student to see a dynamic at which census, newspaper, and parish records can only hint. These daily records reveal the nature of social relationships in rural society. They suggest the fundamental importance of the agrarian household in the community. They mirror the preoccupation of household members with work routines, food procurement, crop selection, marketing procedures, weather patterns, and seasonal change. The diaries also outline the social boundaries of the rural community, defined by kinship ties, village and district politics, and congregational life. Specifically, they include references to daily comings and goings of kin; they record the illnesses, funerals, weddings, and childbirths of neighbours; they document the worship services, revival meetings, and disciplinary actions of the congregation.

By contrasting and comparing a number of diaries, one can identify different kinds of social patterns within apparently homogeneous communities. Region, for example, was an especially important variable. Most of the diaries examined in this study include those of two Mennonite communities in Canada: the Swiss-American Mennonite community in Waterloo County, Ontario, founded between 1800 and 1812; and the Dutch-Russian Mennonite East Reserve (known later as the Rural Municipality of Hanover) in Manitoba, established between 1874 and 1879. The Manitoba and Ontario diaries show the differences among various groups of Mennonites. The Ontario diaries, for example, were located in the Mennonite archives and the homes of the diarists' descendants in Waterloo County, as well as in Pennsylvania, Indiana, and Kansas, where other Swiss-Mennonite communities were established. The Manitoba diaries were located in Manitoba Mennonite archives, but also in Nebraska and Kansas, where other Russian Mennonites lived, and in Mexico, Belize, and Paraguay, where descendants later migrated.[6] Moreover, all but one of the Ontario diaries were written in English, reflecting the decline of the German Palatine dialect, Pennsylvania Dutch, and the length of time since the early 1700s, when the first Swiss Mennonites arrived in North America. The

Manitoba diaries, on the other hand, were recorded by immigrants from Europe, and thus all but one of these diaries in this collection were kept in the German language and written in the Gothic script.

The diaries also exhibit differences in the demographic, physiological, and economic makeup of the two communities. The East Reserve was an almost homogeneous Mennonite community that comprised an eight-township land bloc set aside in 1873 for the exclusive settlement by Mennonites from Russia.[7] Here, some 2000 Mennonites from the conservative "Bergthaler" and "Kleine Gemeinde" congregations made permanent homes, while 6000 other Mennonites settled in the West Reserve, 100 kilometres to the west. Although the exclusivity of the East Reserve was lifted in 1891, and Ukrainian and German Lutheran settlers began entering the reserve, Hanover Municipality remained a predominantly Mennonite enclave. By 1901, the 2373 Mennonites of Hanover still represented fully seventy-nine percent of the municipality's 3003 inhabitants.[8] Waterloo County, on the other hand, had a polyglot population. In 1803, when Pennsylvania Mennonites acquired a 60,000-acre tract of land in the heart of present-day Waterloo County, they secured the base for an almost homogeneously Mennonite settlement. In the 1820s, when the Mennonite population reached 1500, settlements were extended westward into present-day Wilmot County. But during this time, immigration from Germany and England changed the area's ethnic composition, and by 1838, when Waterloo County was officially established by statute, Mennonites no longer comprised a majority.[9] In 1901, the 5509 Mennonites of Waterloo County represented only 10.5 percent of the county's 52,594 inhabitants.[10] Adding to the difficulty of establishing a separate, agrarian Mennonite community in Waterloo County was its urban nature. Indeed, in 1901, when not a single Hanover resident lived in a town of more than 1000 residents, almost forty percent of Waterloo County residents lived in such towns. In 1901, Hanover's largest town was Steinbach, with 349 residents (ninety-seven percent of which were Mennonite); in Waterloo County, the largest urban centre was Berlin, with 9700 residents (of which only 4.2 percent were Mennonite).[11]

Finally, Waterloo County was also more industrialized than Hanover. As early as 1856, Waterloo had been linked to Toronto by the Grand Trunk Railroad, and, in the years after 1880, steep Canadian tariffs and an aggressive board of trade transformed Berlin into an industrial city. It became known for its furniture, clothing articles, leather goods, rubber products, and sugar.[12] By 1910, this industrial march was crowned with a link to the Niagara Falls hydroelectricity plant. Hanover, on the other hand, produced primarily agricultural foodstuffs. They included wheat, oats, cheese, cream, eggs, vegetables, and meat, mostly for consumption in Winnipeg, a full day's travel away. Timber and firewood were the only other commodities of export.[13] Although a railway skirted both the east and west sides of Hanover by 1898, no railway was built through the heart of the municipality, and it was not until 1908 that a long-distance telephone connection was made to the outside. Clearly, just as Hanover was representative of a pre-industrial, agrarian society, Waterloo County was an example of a rural community that was quickly becoming industrialized and urbanized. Such regional differences revealed themselves in the two sets of Mennonite diaries discussed here.

There were other significant variables to consider in determining the nature of the Mennonite diaries. Class mattered. While the majority of known Mennonite diaries were kept by middle-aged, land-owning farm householders, others were kept by well-to-do merchants, church leaders, landless farmers, and servants. Then, too, diaries were kept by girls and women, as well as by boys and men. Clearly, religion, ethnicity, and class drew women and men to share common concerns and perceptions, but gender affected what was said and left unsaid. Generation lines cut yet another line through the genre of diary-writing. Unwed youth, middle-aged parents, and grandparents revealed outlooks specific to their particular place in the life cycle. By contrasting diaries specific to a particular region, class, gender, or generation, one can perceive in the profiles of the Mennonite diary a certain depth and clarity.

A second, and less obvious, reason for examining the daily records of common folk is that it offers a window on the writer's mindset and world view. These daily records capture the perspective of the writers as they looked "from the inside out"—out, to make sense of successive layers of social relations; out, beyond the household, to the kinship network, the local community, and to the wider society of marketplace, government, and "English" society. Even though there may be little personal reflection in the daily "household" diaries, they nevertheless suggest the subjective viewpoint of the writers. They hint at what Adrian Wilson refers to as "document genesis" and the illumination of what the diarist was attempting to achieve in the very act of writing.[14] They answer questions such as: For whom and for what occasions did the diarist intend the writings? Why did the diarist choose to record some events but exclude others? Why are some members of the household and community given more attention than others? Why did the diarist take precious moments out of a busy daily schedule to write at all? Why was it not enough to leave noteworthy events to the rich oral tradition within agrarian society? To what extent was the diary kept to ensure a common social memory and construct a sense of community in the mind of the writer? What was the purpose of this enterprise? What is the significance of diary-keeping as a social practice? Answers to these questions can do much more than identify "the biases of the document."[15] They can identify the historical process that created the diary.

Theories of literacy and speculations of its effects on the perceptions of historical actors offer some answers to these questions. Jack Goody suggests that the very act of writing is at once "more reflective [than speech] and at the same time permits [one] to . . . work out the meaning of things, to explicate more formally."[16] Walter Ong adds that the act of writing brings shape and control to the writer's world. He argues that "time is seemingly tamed if we treat it spatially, . . . mak[ing] it appear as divided into separate units next to each other."[17] This may appear especially true to the diarist because "'backward scanning' makes it possible in writing to eliminate inconsistencies," providing a sense of order that may in fact be less orderly and more elusive than the writer would wish.[18] The views of Goody and Ong recently have been challenged by scholars such as Matthew Innes, who warn about having "'orality' and 'literacy' reified into categories in their own right, as types of society or mentality."[19] Nevertheless, the ideas of Goody and Ong seem to have stood the test of time and made their way through the historiography. Scholars of immigrant literature, for example, seem to agree that writers "invent" identities by representing daily life in certain ways. They may do it by borrowing the linguistic styles and literary vehicles of the host society, in this way legitimizing and securing the immigrant presence in the new society. But then, too, immigrant or minority writers sometimes contest the understandings of the host society. Werner Sollors has argued that, where host-society writers may catalogue instances of assimilation, immigrant writers may cast the ethnic community or ethnic culture as a "'natural' and timeless category," a process that leads to the assertion of ethnic identity, or ethnicization.[20]

It is within these categories of understanding that we can assert that diary-writing was important for Mennonites, especially as they sought to replicate their closed ethno-religious communities in a Canadian society that was becoming increasingly urbanized and industrialized. Both the Ontarians and Manitobans practised an oral culture, steeped in a German dialect: Pennsylvania Dutch (or Palatine German) for the former, and Low German (or West Prussian Platt) for the latter. The dialects effectively guarded social boundaries and facilitated a community-based household economy. Yet both communities also wrote about these social relationships in a recognized literary language, either High German or English. And, by writing diaries, Mennonites created what they considered the "essentials of all time," and they did this by mapping, defining, and articulating crucial social relationships. Thus, when Mennonite diarists recorded the social outline of household, kin group, community, and wider society, they were mentally designing, even celebrating, an envisioned community. It was a community separated from the wider society, firmly rooted in an agrarian economy and anchored to the sectarian congregation. Mennonites, it would seem, joined other traditionalist societies who, according to Harvey Graff, made "use of literacy for conservative ends."[21] The daily journal of the rural Mennonite householder secured social boundaries and social networks by simply making record of them. It was a subjective enterprise without personal reflection, admissions of alienation, boasts of triumph, or solipsistic preoccupation.

A final reason for paying attention to the writing of rural people with only an elementary education is that those writings attest to the manner in which a rudimentary literacy develops within rural society. Linking the history of the Mennonites and literacy provides at least one set of conditions that gave rise to a general ability to read and write in rural society.

Important for literacy among Mennonites was their status as a religious minority. Like other groups outside recognized state churches, Mennonites used literacy to defend themselves against persecuting state authorities and to create a common set of understandings within the minority group.[22] Indeed, the diaries illuminate a mechanism that allowed Mennonites to develop into an ethnic group. Widespread literacy among Mennonites had developed soon after their genesis during the sixteenth century. Mennonite historian Arnold Snyder has observed that "communication by handwritten epistle, confessions, accounts of martyrdom and exhortation was common among the early Anabaptists, whose leaders at least were generally literate in the vernacular."[23] Literature became even more important than before, as moderate Anabaptists, who had rejected the authority of state churches and seditiously preached "rebaptism," began to argue that they were not part of the mystical or the fanatically militant branches of Anabaptism. Thus, literacy was used by Anabaptist leaders to aid the movement to coalesce into a stable, even conservative, sectarian community. The very denotation of "Mennonite" rose after the Dutch-Anabaptist leader Menno Simons became the most prolific of the Anabaptist writers. In later centuries, his devotional writings and apologias were linked with a voluminous 1660-page martyrology, the *Martyrs' Mirror*, and several catechisms and hymnals to create a literary corps that served to energize and direct a highly self-conscious, migrating people.[24] These books were carried by Mennonites from one country to another, and in time they became the very symbols of group identity. A sign of the importance that Mennonites placed on literacy was not seen in their ownership of the books, but in their practice of reading them. Indeed, reading the lyrics of martyr hymns in worship and reading catechisms in preparation for baptism were mandatory exercises for all Mennonites. Arguably, not only baptism, but also the recitation of the catechism, a piece of writing, became a rite of passage into full adult membership in the community. Its direct consequence was a rudimentary, but universal, literacy within the Mennonite community.[25]

This level of literacy also reflects the history of Mennonites as "free peasants." This status meant that they negotiated with local sympathetic lords to make deals that secured special privileges and land rights. This was a crucial feature of their successive migrations—of Dutch Mennonites to Polish Prussia, New Russia (present-day Ukraine), and Manitoba, and of Swiss Mennonites to southern Germany, Pennsylvania, and Ontario. And arguably, this status may have spurred the transformation of Mennonites from readers to writers.[26] As free peasants, Mennonites also engaged in an early market economy, the very act noted by François Furet and Jacques Ozouf to have contributed to a rudimentary literacy among French farmers. To participate in a national-based economy required the act of reading in order to transcend the bounds of the local community that orality imposed. Numeracy, that is, a preoccupation with quantifying daily life (or, calculating rationally the extent of yield, profit, and advantage), was another exercise that a market economy encouraged.[27] And, as "free peasants," Mennonites were also often required by the state to keep records.[28] The Dutch Mennonites who migrated to the Russian Empire at the close of the eighteenth century, for example, encountered a bureaucratic state that was intent on compelling foreign agricultural colonists to "become integrated into the rapidly developing rural economy of southern Russia" and to demonstrate that integration through the submission of annual village and district records. For Swiss Mennonites who migrated westward from the German Palatinate to Pennsylvania at the same time, the demands of a market economy required negotiations with colony officials, close attention to the particulars of "partible" inheritance, and knowledge of the economic opportunities in different parts of the colony.[29] Each of these activities also encouraged a rudimentary literacy.

Literacy may also have risen as a result of migration itself. Not only did migration force negotiation with government, encourage the reading of land-sales agent reports, compel the writing of letters across distances, but it also took Mennonites outside the confines of local communities into wider worlds. At least one historian has argued, "It is much easier when travelling to perceive one's life as a progression by stages than when fixed in one place, in one occupation."[30] Diaries sometimes commenced at migration, when the farmer was introduced to a new terrain and new climate; seemingly the passage from one space to another was linked to an increased awareness of the passage of time. By the nineteenth century, when both Dutch and Swiss Mennonites arrived in Canada after successive migrations, diary-writing was widespread.[31]

The writers of the daily Mennonite diary were not "remarkable human beings." They were ordinary rural folk—young women and grandmothers, teenaged boys and old men, husbands and wives, farmers and merchants, rural preachers and landless householders. They wrote to record their everyday lives, quotidian drudgery to some, miracles of life and community for others. In the process, they provided glimpses of their lives, their mindsets and their history as a people.

The method by which the rural Mennonite householder sought to affect the immediate world, then, was to simply record life's social profile. For most Mennonites, the notion of household, community, and social boundary was so pervasive that little else was recorded—these were rural household journals.

There were, however, two kinds of diary-writing that skirted these issues: one was the travelogue; the other was the highly individualistic, private diary of Mennonites who lived in more urbanized worlds. Both the travelogue and the private diary reflect the life world of a Mennonite who stood aside from the everyday life in the rural community. Fothergill's suggestion that diaries can be seen on a scale that measures the intensity of individualism—that is, degrees of "evolution towards literary self-consciousness"—may be useful in understanding these two diverging types of Mennonite diary.[32] It may be argued that the travelogue and the private diary stand on either side of the rural household journal on this scale. Clearly, the private diaries of Mennonite town-folk and pietists reveal the greatest degree of "literary self-consciousness," while the travelogues of Mennonite farm migrants show such consciousness as only emerging. The travelogue demonstrates that migration can change one's sense of time and space; the private diary indicates a growing individualism when sectarian community and rural household lose their hold on one's life.

The Mennonite travelogues, usually recorded by men, illustrate how journeying from familiar environs could stimulate a literary awareness. One such diary, written by farmer Cornelius Loewen in 1874, incorporates a sub-diary into a sketchy, daily logbook. Loewen, who migrated from the Borosenko Mennonite Colony, New Russia, to settle in Gruenfeld, Manitoba, popularly known as the first Mennonite village in western Canada, kept a diary that contained only sporadic accounts of his household's market transactions. Then, on 1 June 1874, the diary abruptly takes on a new style, suggesting that it may have been written by someone else and copied into Loewen's notebook. The first words—"here is the trip from Russia to America written up"—head a detailed daily description of the transoceanic voyage. The succession of cities—Odessa, Berlin, Hamburg, "Lieverpol," "Halifaks," "Qaebek," Toronto, Winnipeg—ties the new and old worlds together. The careful documentation of the method of travel—by wagon, riverboat, train, ferry, ocean liner, lake-size steamboats, and ox cart—and the hours spent at train stations and seaports, complete the map. References to the icebergs and whales off the coast of Newfoundland, to "walk[ing] on dry earth" at Halifax, to meeting "Canadian Mennonite brothers [in Toronto, who] gifted us with meat, lard, butter and dried apples" were the signposts of a new land. Loewen's immediate world was awry; the diary, however, provided a sense of control and order.[33]

A similar pattern characterizes the migration account of Ezra Burkholder, a nineteen-year-old Ontario youth of Mennonite heritage who travelled to Kansas in 1976 to join his family, who had migrated earler. Despite the fact that Burkholder was a University of Toronto student when he wrote his diary, his record is similar to the travelogue within Loewen's. Burkholder pays special attention to the details of the trip. In fact, his diary seems to begin on the day he left home: "July 7th, 1876, started from Floradale in company of Jesse Snyder in a big wagon."[34] After boarding the train in Berlin and being whisked out of Waterloo County, he soon began describing the unfamiliar—the landscape and farmland, strangers on the train, and the passage of time. His entry for 10 July, the third day of travel, was typical: "It commenced to rain at 12:45. . . . Got a glass of pop at Chatham, .5 cents. West of Chatham, prairie to the right and brush to a certain space to the left. I was informed by a gentleman that there is a space west of Chatham all marsh." Here was a young man, it seems, who sensed, as never before, the passage of time and space. Clearly, travel for both Loewen and Burkholder resulted in an unprecedented mapping of time and space outside familiar boundaries.

At the other end of the continuum of Mennonite diary-writing are the most personal of the diaries. These provide accounts of introspection and religious conscience, and often of social analysis. Sometimes the personal reflections are almost solipsistic, nearly absolute self-absorption.

The most intensely personal diary in our collection was kept by Margaretha Jansen, the twenty-four-year-old daughter of Russian Mennonite immigrant leader Cornelius Jansen and his wife, Helena Friesen, who temporarily lived in Waterloo County between August 1873 and June 1874. Margaretha Jansen was a woman in a strange land, responsible for her ailing mother and younger siblings during her father's and brother's lengthy land-scouting trips in the United States. If these events provided her with a strong self-awareness, her subjective religiosity, rooted in the urban Mennonite church of Berdyansk on the Sea of Azov, heightened that awareness.[35] Her diary frequently described doubt, fear, and religious calling. Her moods shifted from great gaiety when she "laughed so much" to times when she thought about the future and had "not been so afraid … for a long time." She feared for her travelling father, her former servants in Russia, and her relatives in Prussia. And she was ecstatic, especially when she could hear revivalist Daniel Brenneman and realize "a strong love for Jesus." Through all this she had an expressed literary consciousness, wondering, for example, whether deriding an acquaintance, Heinrich, as tedious, and a visitor, Mr. Albert, as "avaric[ious]," in her diary was right; that is, "think[ing] this way about a person and then to writ[e] it also." Here was a diarist with a full "literary self-conscious."

The personal nature of Margaretha's diary is made especially apparent when it is contrasted to another diary of an immigrant woman, Maria Klassen of Manitoba. In her records, Klassen reflects the outlook of a woman in very different circumstances from those of Jansen in Waterloo.[36] Klassen's diary, for example, recorded little emotional contemplation. Within it is a letter from a brother in Russia who denounced her for having joined the migration and boasted of his own liberation from the Mennonite community. But the diary itself was a household account, with careful detailing of the daily activities of all family members, the comings and goings of neighbours and kin, and the events in the community, especially within the Bergthaler congregation. Especially important for Klassen was the economic strength of the household. Interwoven in the description of work and weather were the numerical aggregates; that is, numbers that marked the economic strength of the farm. Labour costs, harvest yields, and market prices were recorded with precision. Maria Klassen, for example, noted that, on her husband's 4 October trip to Winnipeg, he "went … at 5 in the morning with 14 bags of wheat." And she noted that upon his return he had received "54 cents" a bushel for the wheat. She noted that on 18 October the Klassen household sold to Gerhard Unger a half share in an old stove, but she added that he paid for it with two sheep, which should be compared to the ten dollars that "Penner" received for his half. When, on 21 November, the Klassens slaughtered a cow with neighbours "Hiebert and J. Rempel and Mrs. Peters," she noted that the animal "was nice and fat," measured by the fact that from it they "got two pounds tallow." Thus, although both women were immigrants who lived in Mennonite communities, Klassen was a group immigrant, a member of an immigrant unit that included transplanted household, kin, and congregation. Life in a new land was marked by relatively little upheaval. Household activities and social ties differed little from those in Bergthal Colony in New Russia.

The same degree of difference in perception apparent in the diaries of Margaretha Jansen and Maria Klassen can be seen in the diaries kept by religious leaders. Intense introspection pervades the diary of Pennsylvania evangelist Levi Jung during an 1863 whirlwind preaching tour of the Niagara and Waterloo Mennonite settlements. This was no ordinary travelogue. Rather, it was a highly self-conscious exposé of how Jung, against his father's wishes, "resign[ed his] heart to Christ" and travelled north to engage in a seemingly endless cycle of emotionally charged public meetings and private visits. He preached with "assist[ance] from on high" in one part of the day and met with young "souls, deeply distressed about their … salvation" in another; he experienced "spiritual darkness" in one hour but had a sense of having his "soul … refreshed" the next.[37] The whole episode was a spiritual journey where Jung constantly analyzed his own relationships with other people and his personal encounters with God.

Juxtaposing Jung's diary to that of *Aeltester* (Bishop) Peter Dueck of Steinbach, Manitoba, illuminates a sharp difference in the way that spiritual leaders perceived their missions. Like Jung's diary, the journal of Dueck served as a running social commentary by a religious leader. Peter Dueck, however, recorded no personal spiritual reflection. Rather, he reported on the *Bruderschaft*, the Brotherhood, or church business meetings. His records continue from 1901, when he was elected *Aeltester*, to 1919, when he died. Throughout these years he commented on the "sins" in the community, naming those caught in theft, assault, adultery, and drunkenness. He held his sharpest criticism for those who "assimilate to the ways of the world"; that is, those who purchased "ostentatious" cars, welcomed an ever-encroaching government with its public schools and military campaigns, and embraced "evil businesses that grow larger every day." The diary records a growing concern with rowdy youth who dressed in stylish clothes, participated in "worldly" wedding celebrations, and drove the "costly" cars. Particular concern was directed to those parents who seemed powerless to stop these activities and even seemed linked to them by their own support for a public school in Steinbach and a growing openness to a consumer culture. Peter Dueck's diary describes a congregation's attempt to contest the fracturing of an Old World community in the face of growing consumerism and individualism.

Dueck's diary is similar to the records of two Mennonite entrepreneurs, merchant Klaas R. Reimer of Steinbach, Manitoba, and miller Elias Eby of Waterloo, Ontario. These well-to-do community members were unusually candid in offering their opinions on the merits and moral nature of their fellows. It was a practice made possible, one might speculate, by their position in the Mennonite community. David Blackburn documents the manner in which shopkeepers stood between classes in Germany, and Clifford Geertz documents the way in which entrepreneurs in Indonesian villages "stand outside the immediate purview of village social structure ... insulated by ... rank from the localized bonds of village society."[38]

Both Reimer and Eby reflected this kind of social distance. They both offered evaluations of their fellows with unequivocal paternalism. Eby was the second son of Bishop Benjamin Eby, the founder of Berlin, Ontario; like his father, Elias became a noted miller and merchant. His diary reflects this elitist position, as he readily lauds some and denounces others. The Russian Mennonite immigrants who passed through Waterloo County in 1874 en route to Manitoba are noted as an "innocent, peaceful and modest people"; young Susanna Brubacher, who died in March 1876, is described as "this once blossoming virgin"; "old Jonathan Bauman," who died a month later, as "an obliging citizen, a good neighbour and an active reformer." But a neighbour who died in June 1876 is described as "a squanderer, wasting his own and the children's money," and another, who died in July 1876, as a "clever doctor, but [one who] lost the confidence of many of his friends through heavy drinking."[39]

In Manitoba, the well-to-do Steinbach merchant Klaas Reimer, the grandson of *Aeltester* Klaas Reimer, founder of the Mennonite Kleine Gemeinde, kept a similar record. Although the medium shifted from memoir to autobiography to diary and then to descriptions of his correspondence, Klaas seemed always ready to assess the behaviour of his acquaintances. The notes of his correspondence describe his religiousness and his deep bonds to family and community; they also offer frank appraisals of the behaviour of his clientele, kin, and congregational leadership. In February 1890, Reimer noted that, in a letter to the recently remarried Isaac Harms of Nebraska, he asked him how he found "such a marriage in his old age, in his 80th year [to] a wife of 38"; in his own notes, Reimer commented freely that "it is often not good when this happens." Reimer was also quick to denounce his foes. In 1895, when ministers from the conservative Kleine Gemeinde Mennonite church wrote to oppose the size of his "business deals," suggesting a motivation of "greed," Reimer noted that he had written back to complain that the leaders "[kept] on forgetting how much unrighteousness occurs because of poverty" and added frankly, "That does not seem right to me."[40] Reimer and Eby, unlike most farm householders, were able to disengage themselves from the immediacy of community affairs and to analyze their social intercourse.

Most Mennonite diaries contain neither personal reflection nor social commentary. They are household journals, offering records of those patterns of life that were the most important to the domestic unit: weather, seasonal changes, community networks, work routine, and, most important, household relationships.

These are the concerns found in the most common of Mennonite diaries, those kept by married, male, farm householders. The diaries of Heinrich Friesen, a farmer of medium wealth from Hochfeld, Manitoba, and Ephraim Cressman, a young farmer from Breslau, Ontario, differed in several significant ways.[41] Their families were at different points in their life cycles, their farms were located in different physical environments, and they operated in markedly different economic and cultural environments. Ontario's Cressman, for example, lived in a relatively temperate physical environment, within a highly commercialized milieu and in a township that was highly integrated into provincial and regional politics. Manitoba's Heinrich Friesen lived in a setting sharply divided by the seasons, shaped by a simple agrarian economy, and a community that was almost homogeneously Mennonite. Cressman, thirty-five in 1890, had a small and young family (he had three small children, one an infant); Friesen, fifty-six in 1898, had seven children and one foster child, aged twelve to twenty-eight, two of whom were married. Despite these differences, Cressman and Friesen recorded similar concerns. The locus of both diaries, after all, was the household, its economic concern, and its internal and external social relationships.

The work described in Cressman's diary records the tasks required by a farmer in an Ontario milieu. Its array of markets, advanced technology, mixed economy, proximity to urban centres, and moderate climate shaped Cressman's strategies. Each day during January, Cressman worked with the farm's swine and cattle, but he also travelled frequently to nearby Breslau to purchase "bran and shorts" or to Berlin to sell "wood, logs and stakes." By early April, Cressman began working the land, "spreading manure," and "gangploughing" the seedbed. He then seeded the wide variety of crops that Ontario's moderate climate sustained and diversified economy demanded: clover, wheat, barley, oats, peas, sugar beets, carrots, and turnips. No sooner were these crops planted than Cressman focussed his energies on his livestock, selling the first cattle and swine, and shearing the sheep and washing wool. By July, Cressman cut the first hay and "cradled" the winter wheat. After the crops had dried in the fields, they were hauled to Cressman's huge bank-barn for storage until the early winter "thrashing." In the meantime, Cressman reploughed the fields and by September began seeding winter wheat and rye. In autumn, too, Cresman began the "pulling" of the apples, the harvest of the feed roots (the turnips and the carrots), and once again marketed swine in Berlin. December reintroduced the routine of winter; the endless days of hauling wood to Berlin, broken only by the hog-butchering bee and the repayment of a loan at Waterloo's Molson Bank. Each day brought a task toward building the economic strength of the household within a highly commercialized setting. It was a routine so unyielding that not to work the field or not to market a product was an unusual day, duly noted with the words "tinkering around."

The routine of work on the Heinrich Friesen farm in Manitoba was similar to the routine at Cressman's, differing only in its adaptation to a simpler economy and a more extreme continental climate, with more arid conditions and a shorter growing season. January and February marked the time on the Friesen farm when the adult males hauled hay, not from bank-barns as in humid Ontario, but from the fields, where Manitoba's dry climate allowed storage of hay. But usually even more time was devoted to hauling wood—firewood and lumber—from the forests to the east of the East Reserve. In March, the last of the previous year's crop was marketed, in large part to make use of the last of the winter sleigh trails. In April, once the water was low at the dam near Bergthal and the boys had drained water from the ploughed fields, the next season could begin. The lambs were branded and the seed wheat was cleaned, and a short time later the sheep were let out onto the pasture and the seeding of wheat, peas, oats, and rye was started. After the garden, too, was seeded, the Friesens turned their attention to fencing and renovations. By July, it was time to pull the mustard and thistles from the grain field. August saw the entire Friesen family cut the hay on the newly purchased Métis lands and stook the wheat sheaves on the cultivated village land. September brought out the ploughs and even offered a forage into the nearby bush for wild fruit. October was the month of the harvest; the jointly owned threshing machine moved in succession in 1898—to the Falks', the Hieberts', then to the Friesens', and after that to the farmyards bearing the names of Wiebe, Kehler, Gerbrand, Schultz, Krause. November was the month at the Friesens' and at other village households for successive days of hog butchering. By December, it was time to haul more of the wheat to the elevator in Niverville or Ste. Anne.

These records clearly indicate the range of opportunities and restrictions that shaped the world of the average male householder. Of the various restrictions, weather was the most immutable to human agency. The whole of life was shaped by temperatures, wind velocities, precipitation, and degrees of sunniness. Daily weather entries were not simply records maintained by idle minds; they were a crucial feature of all household diaries because they were critical aspects of life. A second signal of opportunity and restriction was the economic strength of the household. Like the diary of Maria Klassen, those of Cressman and Friesen were records of the attempt to manipulate and secure the fruits of nature. By recording yields of produce and market prices, these diarists sought to objectify life in the household.

The diary enabled its authors to secure a measure of control over their lives by recording the events of the household and noting its social links with the wider community. In substance it was a fundamental cultural expression deeply rooted in Mennonite society. The diary demonstrated the remarkable degree to which this farm community was actually a culture of literacy. And a measure of this was the fact that diary-keeping crossed any lines of generation that may have existed. The married male's diary may have been the most common daily record, but married and unmarried, male and female, elderly and young diarists alike focussed on the everyday life of household work routine, kinship ties, and church congregation. Where they differed in descriptions of these community features, the diaries provided a unique glimpse of Mennonite society from the perspective of a specific age.

The diaries of Moses Weber, who was seventeen in 1865, and of Heinrich Kornelsen, who was fifteen in 1875, reveal just how early Mennonite youths began acquiring a sense of time and space. The possibility of shaping everyday life is apparent from the diaries of both boys.[42] The diaries of Weber and Kornelsen offer glimpses into the lives of rural youths of strikingly different settings. Weber was a third-generation Canadian in 1865; he lived in a highly commercialized milieu, attended high school, and wrote in English (only his spelling, such as rendering sugar trough as "shugar trauf," and his syntax, apparent in "Jacob went behind Berlin working," signalled his German background). Kornelsen was an immigrant who wrote in German, lived in a closed, agrarian community, and recorded his fascination with the physical features of his new home. True, there are differences in the Weber and Kornelsen diaries, but there are also important parallels. Each describes a world that, while separate from the world of adults, is nevertheless similarly defined—by the household economy bound by nature and the local economy, and by the social ties of kin and Mennonite community.

Moses Weber's diary does not readily reveal his youth. The daily diary entries began, as all other household records did, with a description of weather; "a midlen clear day" or "a rough day" were typical entries. He described his daily work: "We did begin to plough" or "we did begin hauling dung." He identified closely with the household, noting, for example, that his father received "$1.04 for springwheet and $1.09 for faul wheet" in Waterloo or that "father [drove] to David Martins and did get five young pigs." When Moses recorded visits, it included all comings to and goings from the Weber household; his entry for 22 January was not only that he and his sister Susan "went to the meeting at Gressman's, and to John Webers' for dinner," but also that his father, who was a Mennonite preacher, and mother "went to the meeting at Martins." And his was clearly a mind in tune with the Mennonite community, noting the deaths and funerals of community members and the occurrence of special church meetings when "strange preachers" from either Pennsylvania or Ohio came calling. In 1865, the only entry that broke the routine of recording household and community life was the one for 14 April marked by six asterisks and noting that "President of the U.S. . . . . was killed by another person."[43]

The diary of young Heinrich Kornelsen represents a somewhat different point of view. Heinrich was a young immigrant and a member of a stem family, with a father, stepmother, and half-siblings. His life, thus, was more independent than Moses's. Because the 1870s marked the beginning of the settlement period in Manitoba, Heinrich lived on a frontier and was clearly engrossed by his new physical environment. Besides listing weather patterns, he made special note of wildlife: on 28 December he "caught a rabbit … and found a wolf." But as a teenager he was also expected to work as a servant in neighbouring households, in his case in the households of his sisters or uncles. And he knew his rights under the unusual Mennonite inheritance system that stipulated an equal division of all land between boys and girls; thus, in the sections of the diary for 1876 and 1877, he recorded the visits of the Waisenmann, the estates administrator who came to calculate the exact size of his mother's estate—that is, exactly half of the household's net worth—and Heinrich listed the amount of the inheritance owing him at the age of majority. Still, his was not an isolated world; like the adult diarists, he carefully recorded the social ties that defined his wider world. He noted not only his visitors, but also the visitors of his father and stepmother, and the location of the Mennonite worship service for any given Sunday.[44]

A similar pattern of record-keeping pervaded the diaries of the community's elderly. Manitoba's Abraham Reimer, who turned seventy-one in 1879, lived the life of a poor elderly grandfather who witnessed[45] the dynamic households of his sons and daughters, who were among the wealthiest merchants, millers, and farmers in the district. Having been a ward of the church mutual aid society in the past and relying for much of the household income on his wife's work as a seamstress, he earned the dubious nickname "Foula Raema," that is, "Lazy Reimer." One reason for the designation is clear; he got little work done because he spent so much time observing others at work. And this habit was at least partly because of his age. This is the record not only of a poor man, but also of an old man. His concern was not with the nuclear family, but with the extended family, which included the households of his seven married children. In fact, few days passed when Reimer did not leave his cottage, visit one of his married children, and comment on their household activities. In a single week in April 1879, for example, Abraham Reimer recorded that son-in-law Abram Penner was building a barn at Peter Friesen's, that the "Abraham Reimers and Peter Reimers walked" the seven muddy kilometres to Steinbach to attend church, that both son-in-law Peter Toews and son Abram began ploughing, that son Klaas sold him thread and coffee from his store, and that both daughter-in-law Maria Reimer and daughter Margaretha, or "Die Abram Pennersche" as he calls her, offered him six eggs for hatching. During the same week, Reimer visited—sometimes staying for a meal or for a night—each of his six children, two in his own village, Blumenort, and four in Steinbach, seven kilometres distant. During the course of the year, Reimer also detailed the household economies of his married children, recording the acres planted to various crops, their yields, and the prices they earned in Winnipeg.

Ontario's Moses Bowman was more well-to-do than Reimer, and as a gifted preacher he held an important office in the church.[46] His life was an endless routine of church meetings, funerals and baptisms, speaking engagements, and consultations with other ministers. Despite his public profile, the greater part of his world was shaped by his eleven sons and daughters, ten of whom were married by 1890. Like all Mennonite ministers, Bowman spent most of his time "at home," and at age seventy-one his overriding concern was with the last details of generational succession. He had already distributed his 200 acres of land to his children and sold the family farm to one of his sons, Aaron. But he still needed to make some adjustments to ensure equality within the complex partible inheritance system; one day in May he mailed son Samuel in Michigan $800 and two days later collected $700 from another son, Moses Jr. His social life involved frequent visits to the households of both his sons and his daughters, and his social space incorporated the farms of his sons. His diary revealed a mental mapping that designated a layer of kin identity over the Waterloo community; thus on 13 February 1890 when Bowman drove to Berlin, it was via the "middle Street throu [son] Aaron's Road, [and] came back through [son] Noah's Road." But the importance of his children's households in his life was most visible in his own work routine. It frequently involved working for one of his sons, especially Aaron, on whose farmyard he lived. He helped Aaron "tap ... sugar trees" in March and "lay ... his barn floor" in July; he stayed home to "help Aaron thrash" in August and "dig ... Aaron's potatoes" in October. Bowman's diary reveals the viewpoint of a community church leader but also of an elderly agrarian householder.[47]

Like young Moses Weber and Heinrich Kornelsen, the elderly Abraham Reimer and Moses Bowman were not at the centre of a farm household, yet both the young and the old saw it as their role to comment on the households to which they were linked directly or indirectly.

The diaries discussed earlier in this essay, those by Margaretha Jansen and Maria Klassen, indicated that the tradition of diary-keeping among Mennonites crossed not only lines of region, class, and generation, but of gender, too. The diaries of several established Mennonite farm women reveal a common perspective among women farm householders. At various points in their life cycles, women, like men, kept journals that dispassionately documented the daily work routine within the household, as well as the social network in which the household was set. Seemingly, as long as the farm economy was rooted in a household mode of production, women diarists were preoccupied not with self but with family—both the household and kinship social networks. Studies of women diarists have sometimes demonstrated the usefulness of diaries in asserting the separate identity of women in a male-dominated world. Judy Simons has argued that, "dogged by conventions of femininity," literary women through the centuries were "able through their diaries to break with those conventions."[48] Margaret Conrad's study of rural Canadian east-coast women—women with "few literary pretensions"—makes a different argument: the diaries of women in her study reflected "the real power of women in rural families"; they revealed a "remarkable . . . sharing of jobs" with men and a set of social concerns "often shared by the men in their lives."[49] Mennonite women lived less idyllically, but their diaries, too, reflected the social setting of the rural community and farm household that drew women and men to a common pursuit, and often to similar life perspectives.

To a degree, the diaries of Mennonite farm women reflect marriage status, region, proximity to a town, and class. Four different women represent four worlds: Margaretha Plett Kroeker, who was forty-nine in 1892, came from a prosperous farm located within the boundaries of the bustling town of Steinbach, Manitoba; Laura Shantz, who was thirty-four in 1918, was a single woman who lived with her parents, the owners of a well-established Waterloo, Ontario, farm; Maria Reimer Unger, who was forty-three in 1919, came from a similarly successful farm in the rural district of Blumenhof, Manitoba; Judith Klassen Neufeld, who was fifty-three in 1922, represented a Manitoba household that was forced to leave the farm during a year of depression.[50] Despite the marked difference in their worlds, these four women perceived society in similar ways. For each of these women the household was the primary social unit, and kinship and congregation marked its social tentacles.

Remarkably, Kroeker's 1892 diary sheds little light on the commercial and social dynamic of Steinbach. And only indirect evidence reveals the Kroekers' social standing in town. The diary, for example, reveals that although in 1892 the Kroekers had no children living at home, they relied on help from servants (including a Ukrainian and a German Lutheran) and were in a position to care for a foster daughter and an older woman with disabilities. Clearly indicating the spaciousness of their house are the notes that the Kroekers regularly hosted the worship service of the town's largest church; and inevitably this was a time, too, when at least some of Margaretha's brothers and sisters, the Pletts of Blumenort and Blumenhof, and other church friends from neighbouring villages would stay for lunch and perhaps for Faspa. But there is no evidence of ostentatious living and no reflection on the relative wealth of any of the Kroeker neighbours.

Like the diaries of men, the works by women farm householders usually omitted personal reflection. Even during times of obvious emotional pain or moments of ecstasy, there is a stoic tone in the female diaries. When Judith Klassen Neufeld noted that she and her husband were forced to leave a rented farm that they had hoped to purchase, and only after considerable search rented a house that required cleaning, she offered no utterance of despair or fatigue or disappointment, just the short quip that on 22 June, a day on which it was "very hot," "we moved from our farm."[51] Her tone did not change, even in times of shock, joy, or impatience. A tragedy in

June was recorded as a matter of fact:"Peter K. Friesen was killed in Steinbach while cutting down a tree. A piece of iron struck his head." A moment of obvious joy in January received the same short shrift: after the opening note on this day, she wrote, "Papa and Johan went to the river to get wood," followed with the simple phrase, "in the p.m. the children were blessed with a infant son." On 30 October, Judith recorded a moment of youthful indiscretion on the part of her unmarried son, Jacob, who slept "until noon, as he attended the wedding last evening [and] came home at 6 a.m.," but she recorded no judgement.

Like the diaries of the men, too, women's diaries carefully documented the economy of the household and the social events in the community. In 1918, Ontario's Laura Shantz, for example, recorded a range of work outside the house. Shantz secured her household's economic strength by working both the farmyard and garden. Records such as "Buzzard cow, calf" or the "Mooly heifer, calved," indicate her central role in the dairy barn. References to "set three hens in the corncrib" or "sow has eight pigs in sheep pen" place her in other corners of the farmyard. Notes such as "Eph's butchered five pigs, one for Mother Shantz" or "took up potatoes in truck patch" also link her to food procurement. But she also identified with the entire household economy, including the parts dominated by men. Thus, she documented when "men worked on land," the day that "Walter . . . took load of pigs out to Baden," and the time that "Pa fetched [the] new Ford." And these household records extended easily into community and kin records. In October she noted how neighbour "Rosenbergers filled silo," and in other months she wrote about land transactions, auction sales, barn fires, and barn-raising bees within the community. She mentioned special church services, Bible conferences, baptism instruction meetings, singing hour, and successive protracted revival meetings, led by Ed Hess at the Geiger Church, David Garber in Blenheim, and C.F. Derstine in Kitchener. True, there are references to the invading outside world: the notes of "the death of Pte. Elgin Eby in Action overseas, 71 Battalion, machine gun section" or even of "young Howling [who] stole cigars ... at Kavelmans store" were signs of a Mennonite community tied to a wider world. Still, Laura Shantz's diary was a record of the social ties and boundaries that allowed a Mennonite community to survive a time of rapid urbanization.

If the tone and subject of women's diaries are the same as those of the men, it is still true that men and women exhibited different perspectives on the household, based on gender. Unlike men, women seem to have viewed the farm from within the house. Laura Shantz's diary mentioned children, health, the comings and goings of other women, and the domestic duties of cleaning and baking. In the women's diaries there are fewer references to weather and season. When Shantz noted weather patterns, they were the views of someone on the inside of the house: the blizzard in January 1918 was so harsh that "Joe Shantz ... couldn't get home," the February cold snap so extreme that it froze the "water pipes ... from tank to house," the "ice storm" of March so severe that "tellphone wires broke." Like the men, she made reference to life-cycle events—deaths of children and of elderly neighbours—and to such tragedies as murder, suicide, and accidental death. Unlike the diaries of most men, however, Laura Shantz's more frequently referred to birth, marriage, and especially to health. Typical were entries such as the February notes, "Elvin Shantz has mumps and Moses B. congestion of the lungs" and that "Mary Tohman had operation for appendicitis was burst [and] Wesley Battler [ha]s scarlet fever." She showed even greater concern for the health of immediate family members with records such as "Walter had sore ear" and "Dr Gillespie put me to bed," and with weight statistics for each of the women in the house: on 17 March it was "Grandma ... 118, Ma 154, Nurse 161, Laura 144."

There are many similarities between the Ontario and Manitoba women's diaries. Middle-aged mother Maria Unger, who lived in Manitoba, lived in a more closed, less commercialized society and in a harsher physical environment than her Ontario counterpart. Still, the Shantz diary and the Unger diary show a common preoccupation with daily work in a farm household and a social network marked by kin and congregation. Maria Unger's diary also depicted a woman's world with references to female social networks, childbirths, and quilting bees, and to interactions between mothers and daughters. Her diary, too, was written from the perspective of inside the farmhouse; there were few details of weather but many mentions of such domestic work as "whitewashing the kitchen," "mangling the wash," "baking bread," "spinning, knitting, and sewing," and caring for the small children. Yet, like Laura Shantz's diary, Maria Unger's was a farm household journal. The daily work activities of each member of the family, female and male, was described. Maria Unger's entry for 17 March 1919 was typical: "Papa and Johann drove to Giroux for wood and I wove. The girls patched and dyed wool." And, like that of Laura Shantz, Maria Unger's world included the farmyard, where calves were born, brooding hens were set on eggs, and gardens were harvested. The only difference in the work pattern of Shantz and Unger was that, in the context of Manitoba's short growing season, Unger and her teenaged daughters spent more time in the fields, especially piling wheat sheaves into stooks to dry in Manitoba's hot, arid July.

Three final diaries, written in the 1920s, reveal how the degree of security on the farm, without regard to gender or region, ultimately shaped one's perspective. These diaries reveal that advancements of urbanization and technology in the host society did not homogenize society, that conservative ways could continue in a changing and heterogeneous world in Ontario, and that upheaval could visit a well-established farm in southern Manitoba.

Marie Schroeder, nineteen in 1926, lived on a farm but, as a stepdaughter of the male household head, she faced an uncertain future.[51] Schroeder's parents, who had migrated from the East Reserve to the West as children, migrated again shortly after Marie's birth, when her youthful father suffered a serious accident. Her parents were forced to leave their rented farm and move to church property in the town of Lowe Farm, where they lived until her father died. Later, when her mother remarried, this time to a well-to-do farmer, the family moved to his farm, north of the town of Morden. But Marie was a stepchild in a blended family of eighteen children, and she faced the promise of only a small inheritance. The Schroeder diary reflects that of a woman who had cast her eyes beyond the homestead. Although she had much work to do on the farm, she had taken the opportunity of studying beyond the mandatory seventh grade, and thus when she milked the cows she thought poetically, and when she wrote her diary she did it in English and with frankness and introspection. Her descriptions are among the most literary in this collection. She recorded moments of heartfelt joy, even giddiness, and of self-doubt. She offered her resistance to joining the church, her fascination with young men browned by the Mexican sun, her joy at capitalizing on the one-cent sale in Morden, and her antipathy to the "Plum Coulee girls." But most telling is her "secret hope that [she might] write things that have a real worth someday; things that are worth printing, and things that other folks would love to read and pay for." Marie Schroeder was a farm woman but, finding little prospect of farming, she looked past the farm, into her own soul and out beyond the homestead. Specific mixes of gender, class, and generation produced specific worlds of Mennonite diarists.

The 1927 diary of sixty-seven-year-old Cornelius T. Friesen reveals a life in turmoil. Friesen had been a local community leader, head of the local estates and credit organization called the Waisenamt.[52] Now, in the late 1920s, the Chortitzer Mennonite community of Manitoba's East Reserve was splitting. Many of its members were prepared to contest Manitoba's 1916 School Attendance Act, which compelled Mennonite children to attend publicly inspected, English-language schools. These Chortitzer

Mennonites sought to maintain their German-language parochial schools by leaving Canada and re-establishing themselves in distant Paraguay's Chaco region. An emotional intensity and social dislocation reveal themselves in Friesen's account as members took their farewell, often with a sense of permanent separation. And those Chortitzers who remained in Canada redoubled efforts to revitalize the old foundation of the church: they met to establish moral guidelines for the community, they welcomed ministers from other regions to strengthen a community weakened by emigration, and they made way for new Waisenmänner to fill in for Friesen, who had retired, and for others who had joined the emigration.

The 1929 diary of thirty-five-year-old Ontario farmer Ishmael Martin provides some information on the introduction of new crops and the shift from selling cream and butter to whole milk. Yet this is no new world. Martin's life continued to revolve around the triad of household, kin group, and church congregation.[53] His traditionalist life seems to be safeguarded by his farm and his Old Order Mennonite roots; there are no references in his diary to any life-transforming technology, whether car or tractor, telephone or electricity. More important in bringing a change to the tradition of Mennonite diary-keeping than the simple passage of time from one century to another was the social setting of the diarist. Martin may have written his diary during the 1920s, but he reflected a less individualistic and introspective mindset than those diarists of the nineteenth century who lived in more heterogeneous settings. The diaries of Margaretha Jansen and Levi Jung reflect a growing individualism associated with a more sub-jective religiosity; the diaries of miller Elias Eby and merchant Klaas Reimer suggest their writers' ability to distance themselves from the immediate community and reflect on its nature. The diaries of Ontario and Manitoba farm women and men, however, reveal a different perspective. They reflect a preoccupation with the household's economy and an inveterate depend-ence on a local social network. The deeply rooted nature of this kind of diary is reflected in the fact that old men and teenaged boys, married and unmarried women, and farmers of the 1890s and the 1920s kept diaries of a similar nature.

This "poor stuff" of Mennonite diary-writing provides few direct glimpses into Mennonite consciousness and few analyses of the development of Mennonite community. Except for occasional references to community tragedies, church upheavals, or weather aberrations, these diaries contain little sensation. But this very absence offers an invaluable glance into the everyday worlds of rural Mennonites in Canada. More important than even the content, however, is the medium of diary-writing itself. To know what they chose to record is also to know something of their culture; that is, the symbols and systems of meaning constructed by ordinary people in their everyday lives to make sense of life, and particularly to make sense of changes and inconsistencies of life.[54] Here was an attempt to order one's life in the face of the immutability of physical forces, the uncertainty of the market economy, the vulnerability of the social boundaries, and the ambiguous circle of friend and foe within the community. Here was an attempt by members of a cultural minority to survive in a rapidly changing, wider society. The diaries themselves reflect their authors' determination that, within their households, kinship networks, and church congregations, Mennonites might continue to fashion a sense of order in their worlds.

*I wish to offer my deep gratitude to Reg Good and Lorna Bergey of Waterloo, Ontario, and Irene Enns Kroeker and Dave K. Schellenberg of Steinbach, Manitoba, who offered invaluable assistance in the translation or transcriptions of the diaries analyzed in this essay and in obtaining crucial background information on the dairists.

Endnotes

1. Robert Fothergill, *Private Chronicles: A Study of English Diaries* (London/New York: Oxford University Press, 1974), 2.

2. Ibid., 2, 10.

3. Tamara Hareven, "The History of the Family and the Process of Social Change," *American Historical Review* 96 (1991): 116.

4. Brian W. Beltman, *Dutch Farmer in the Missouri Valley: The Life and Letters of Ulbe Eringa, 1866-1950* (Urbana, IL: University of Illinois Press, 1997); William Boelhower, "Dutch-American Fictions: Learning to Read the Signs," *European Contributions to American Studies* 17 (1990): 131- 53; Charlotte Erickson, *Invisible Immigrants: The Adaptation of English and Scottish Immigrants in 19th Century America* (Ithaca, NY: Cornell University Press, 1972); Walter D. Kamphoefner, Wolfgang Helbich, and Ulrike Sommer, eds., *News from the Land of Freedom: German Immigrants Write Home*, trans. Susan Carter Vogel (Ithaca, NY: Cornell University Press, 1991); Wolf D. Kindermann, "Asian-American Literary Perception of the United States, 1930-1940s," *European Contributions to American Studies* 17 (1990): 243-72; Robert Orsi, "The Fault of Memory: 'Southern Italy' in the Imagination of Immigrants and the Lives of Their Children in Italian Harlem, 1920-1945," *Journal of Family History* 15 (1990): 133-47; Tamara Palmer, "Elements of Jewish Culture in Adele Wiseman's *Crackpot*: A Subversive Ethnic Fiction Female Style," *Prairie Forum* 16 (1991): 265-85; Ira Robinson, Pierre Anctil, and Mervin Butovsky, *An Everyday Miracle: Yiddish Culture in Montreal* (Montreal: Vehicule Press, 1990); Regine Rosenthal, "The Cultural Work of American

Jewish Immigrant Autobiographies," *European Contributions to American Studies* 17 (1990): 152-75; Roshan Roshan, "In Quest of a Habitation and a Name: Immigrant Voices from India," *International Journal of Canadian Studies* 6 (1992): 87-98.

5. James M. Nyce, ed., *The Gordon C. Eby Diaries: Chronicle of a Mennonite Farmer, 1911-1913* (Toronto, ON: Wilfred Laurier University Press, 1982); Harvey L. Dyck, ed. & trans., *A Mennonite in Russia: The Diaries of Jacob D. Epp, 1851-1880* (Toronto: University of Toronto Press, 1991).

6. The various archives in Ontario and Manitoba include: the Mennonite Archives of Ontario, Waterloo, ON; Doon Heritage Crossroads, Kitchener, ON; Manitoba Genealogy Inc., Winnipeg, MB; Evangelical Mennonite Archives, Steinbach, MB; Mennonite Heritage Village, Steinbach, MB; Mennonite Heritage Centre, Winnipeg, MB.

7. For a history of Hanover, see: Lydia Penner, *Hanover: One Hundred Years* (Steinbach, MB: R.M. of Hanover, 1982); Abe Warkentin, *Reflections on Our Heritage: A History of Steinbach and the R.M. of Hanover from 1874* (Steinbach, MB: Derksen Printers, 1971); John Dyck, ed., *East Reserve Village Histories, 1874-1910* (Steinbach, MB: Hanover Steinbach Historical Society, 1990). See also relevant sections in E.K. Francis, *In Search of Utopia* (Altona, MB: D.W. Friesen and Sons, 1955); John Warkentin, "Mennonite Settlements in Southern Manitoba: A Study in Historical Geography," Ph.D. dissertation, University of Toronto, 1960; Royden Loewen, *Family, Church and Market: A Mennonite Community in the Old and the New Worlds, 1850-1930* (Urbana and Chicago: University of Illinois Press, 1993); Dennis Stoesz, "A History of the Chortitzer Mennonite Church of Manitoba, 1874-1914," M.A. thesis, University of Manitoba, 1987.

8. *Census of Canada, 1901*, Table X.

9. For histories of Waterloo County see: Elizabeth Bloomfield, *Waterloo Township through Two Centuries* (Kitchener, ON: Waterloo Historical Society, 1995); John English and Kenneth McLaughlin, *Kitchener: An Illustrated History* (Waterloo, ON: Wilfred Laurier University Press, 1983); J. Winfield Fretz, *The Waterloo Mennonites: A Community in Paradox* (Waterloo, ON: Wilfred Laurier Press, 1989). A.G. McLellan, ed., *The Waterloo County Area: Selected Geographical Essays* (Waterloo, ON: 1971); Kenneth Cressman, "A Descriptive Summary and Analysis of the Changing Settlement and Occupational Patterns of the Mennonites and Amish Mennonites of Wilmot Township," M.A. thesis, Waterloo, 1988; Ezra Eby, *A Biographical History of Early Settlers and their Descendants in Waterloo Township, 1895* (Waterloo, ON: 1984).

10. *Census of Canada, 1901*, Table X.

11. Ibid.; Hanover Municipality Tax Rolls, Rural Municipality of Hanover (hereinafter RMH), Steinbach, MB. Winnipeg, possessing some 42,000 inhabitants by 1901, lay a full day's travel by horse from the centre of the municipality.

12. English and McLaughlin, *Kitchener*, 53ff.

13. Royden Loewen, "Ethnic Farmers and the Outside World: Mennonites in Manitoba and Nebraska," *Journal of the Canadian Historical Association* 1 (1990): 195-214.

14. Adrian Wilson, "Foundations of an Integrated Historiography," in *Rethinking Social History: English Society 1570-1920 and Its Interpretation* (Manchester: Manchester University Press, 1993): 293-35.

15. Ibid., 314.

16. Jack Goody, *The Interface between the Written and the Oral* (New York: Cambridge University Press, 1987), 300.

17. Walter Ong, *Orality and Language: The Technologizing of the Word* (New York: Methuen, 1982), 42.

18. Ibid., 104, 81.

19. Matthew Innes, "Memory, Orality and Literacy in an Early Medieval Society," *Past and Present* 77 (1998): 3-36.

20. Werner Sollors, Introduction to *The Invention of Ethnicity* (New York: Oxford University Press, 1989), xiv; see David Gerber, "You See i Speak Wery Well English," *Journal of American Ethnic History* 12 (1993): 56-65, in which he reviews Walter D. Kamphoefner et al.; Betty Bergland, "Postmodernism and the Autobiographical Subject: Reconstructing the 'Other'," in *Autobiography and Postmodernism*, ed. Kathleen Ashley, et al. (Amherst: University of Massachusetts Press, 1994).

21. Harvey J. Graff, Introduction to *Literacy and Social Development in the West: A Reader* (New York: Cambridge University Press, 1981), 4.

22. Mark Zborowski and Elizabeth Herzog, *Life Is with People: The Culture of the Shtetl* (New York: Schocken, 1952), 32; Ira Robinson et al., *An Everyday Miracle: Yiddish Culture in Montreal*, 11; C.A. Dawson, *Group Settlement: Ethnic Communities in Western Canada* (Toronto: Macmillan, 1936).

23. Arnold Snyder, *Anabaptist History and Theology: An Introduction* (Kitchener, ON: Pandora, 1995), 108; see also Arnold Snyder, "Orality, Literacy and the Study of Anabaptism," *Mennonite Quarterly Review* 65 (1991): 371-92.

24. Robert Friedmann, *Mennonite Piety through the Centuries: Its Genius and Its Literature* (Goshen, IN: The Mennonite Historical Society, 1949).

25. James Urry, *None but Saints: The Transformation of Mennonite Life in Russia, 1789-1889* (Winnipeg: Hyperion, 1989), 154.

26. Leo Driedger, *Mennonite Identity in Conflict* (Lewiston, NY: E. Mellen Press, 1988); Urry, *None but Saints*; Peter J. Klassen, *A Homeland for Strangers: An Introduction to Mennonites in Poland and Prussia* (Fresno, CA: Center for Mennonite Brethren Studies, 1989); James T. Lemon, *The Best Poor Man's Country: A Geographical Study of Early Southeastern Pennsylvania* (Baltimore and London: John Hopkins University Press, 1972); Richard MacMaster, *Land, Piety, Peoplehood: The Establishment of Mennonite Communities in America, 1683-1790* (Scottdale, PA: Herald Press, 1985); Aaron Spencer Fogleman, *Hopeful Journeys: German Immigration, Settlement and Political Culture in Colonial America, 1717-1775* (Philadelphia: University of Pennsylvania Press, 1996).

27. François Furet and Jacques Ozouf, *Reading and Writing: Literacy in France from Calvin to Jules Ferry* (New York: Cambridge University Press, 1982), 190. See also Keith Thomas, "Numeracy in Early Modern England," *Transactions of the Royal Historical Society* 37 (1987): 103-32. I thank James Urry for bringing this article to my attention.

28. Urry, *None but Saints*, 138; Ingrid I. Epp and Harvey L. Dyck, *The Peter J. Braun Russian Mennonite Archive, 1803-1920: A Research Guide* (Toronto: University of Toronto Press, 1996).

29. See Fogleman, *Hopeful Journeys*. Partible inheritance practice among Mennonites required equal division of property among all children, both male and female. Impartible inheritance prohibited division of property.

30. Fothergill, *Private Chronicles,* 14.

31. For standard accounts of the history of Canadian Mennonites see: Frank H. Epp, *Mennonites in Canada, 1786-1920: The History of a Separate People* (Toronto: University of Toronto Press, 1974). For sociological analyses of the Waterloo County and East Reserve communities, see: Fretz, *The Waterloo Mennonites*; Francis, *In Search of Utopia.*

32. Fothergill, *Private Chronicles,* 35.

33. Cornelius Loewen, "Tagebuch, 1863-1892," Mennonite Heritage Village, Steinbach, MB. For other travelogues by East Reserve Mennonites describing the transoceanic voyage, see: Gerhard Doerksen, "Tagebuch, 1876," Bernard P. Doerksen, Blumenort, MB; David L. Plett, "Tagebuch, 1875," Betty Plett, Blumenort, MB; Peter Loewen, "Tagebuch, 1874," Evangelical Mennonite Conference Archives, Steinbach, MB.

34. Ezra Burkholder, diary, 1876, Mennonite Archives of Ontario (hereinafter MAO), Waterloo, ON.

35. Margaretha Jansen, diary, 1873-1874, trans. Anna Linscheid, Mennonite Historical Library, Newton, KS. For a history of the Jansen family, see: Gustav Reimer and G.R. Gaeddert, *Exiled by the Czar: Cornelius Jansen and the Great Mennonite Migration, 1874* (Newton, KS: Mennonite Publication Office, 1956).

36. Maria Stoesz Klassen, "Tagebuch, 1887," trans. Irene Enns Kroeker, Steinbach, MB; Margaretha Plett Kroeker, "Tagebuch, 1892-1911," trans. Ben Hoeppner, courtesy Ben K. Plett, Landmark, MB.

37. Levi Jung, "Excerpts from the Diary of Levi Jung, 1863," edited by Richard E. Taylor, Schwenkfelder Library, Pennsburg, PA.

38. David Blackburn, "Between Recognition and Volatility: The German Petite Bourgeoisie in the Nineteenth Century," in *Shopkeepers and Master Artisans in Nineteenth Century Europe,* ed. Geoffrey Crossik and Heinz-Gerhard Haupt (London: Methuen, 1984); Clifford Geertz, *Peddlers and Princes: Social Change and Economic Modernization in Two Indonesian Towns* (Chicago: University of Chicago Press, 1963), 142. See also James Urry, "Prolegomena to the Study of Mennonite Society in Russia, 1880-1914," *Journal of Mennonite Studies* 8 (1990), who notes that in turn-of-the-century Mennonite colonies in Russia "new ways of relating to various sectors of the community developed, with a degree of solidarity emerging among those who shared the same education standard, wealth, occupation and status" (64).

39. Elias Eby, diary, 1876, trans., n.n., MAO.

40. Klaas R. Reimer, account of letters written, 1885-1896, trans. Peter Dueck, EMCA.

41. Ephraim Cressman, diary, 1892, MAO; Heinrich Friesen, "Journal 1896-1898," trans. Irene Enns Kroeker, *Historical Sketches of the East Reserve, 1874-1910,* ed. John Dyck (Steinbach, MB: 1994), 477-501.

42. Moses Weber, diary, 1865, MAO; Heinrich Kornelsen, "Tagebuch, 1875," trans. Dave Schellenberg, EMCA.

43. Weber, diary.

44. H. Kornelson, "Tagebuch." Mennonite churches in both Manitoba and Ontario rotated their worship services during the course of the year from one village to another within the district.

45. Abraham F. Reimer, "Tagebuch, 1879," trans. Ben Hoeppner and Royden Loewen, EMCA.

46. Moses Bowman, diary, 1890, MAO.

47. Ibid.

48. Judy Simons, *Diaries and Journals of Literary Women: From Fanny Burney to Virginia Woolf* (Iowa City: University of Iowa Press, 1990), 196.

49. Margaret Conrad, "Recording Angels: The Private Chronicles of Women from the Maritime Provinces of Canada, 1750-1950," in *The Neglected Majority: Essays in Canadian Women's History*, ed. Alison Prentice and Susan Mann Trofimenkoff (Toronto: McClelland and Stewart, 1985), 52, 58.

50. Margaretha Plett Kroeker, "Tagebuch, 1892" ; Laura Shantz, diary, 1918, in the possession of Lorna Bergey, Kitchener, ON; Maria Reimer Unger, "Tagebuch, 1919," trans. Margaret Toews and Royden Loewen, in the possession of Peter U. Dueck, Steinbach, MB; Judith Klassen Neufeld, "Tagebuch, 1922," trans. Mary Enns, in the possession of Mary Enns, Steinbach, MB.

51. Marie Schroeder, diary, 1925, in the possession of Susannah Schroeder Janzen, Steinbach, MB.

52. Cornelius T. Friesen, "Tagebuch, 1925," trans. Ben Hoeppner and Royden Loewen, in the possession of Irene Enns Kroeker, Steinbach, MB; Ishmael Martin, diary, 1929-1935, trans. Paul Hunsberger, Kitchener, ON.

53. Ishmael Martin, diary, 1929-1935, Paul Hunsberger, Kitchener, ON.

54. See: Clifford Geertz, *After the Fact: Two Countries, Four Decades, One Anthropologist* (Cambridge, MA: Harvard University Press, 1995); Hans Medick, "'Missionaries in a Rowboat'? Ethnological Ways of Knowing as a Challenge to Social History," *Comparative Studies in Society and History* 29 (1987): 76-98; Fredrick Barth, Introduction to *Balinese Worlds* (Chicago: University of Chicago Press, 1993).

Making Modern Citizens: The Construction of Masculine Middle-Class Identity on the Canadian Prairies, 1890-1920

R. Rory Henry

PRAIRIE IDENTITY DID NOT SPRING FORTH from the mere process of settlement, from some Ontarian continental drift, from the great strike, or as the result of some spasmodic reaction to tariff policies or federal disallowances.[1] Identity was formed in the cultural interaction, and the cultural reactions, of the people who lived in the West. Consequently, much of prairie history since the late 1960s and 1970s has focussed on the inter-actions of marginalized groups, primarily the working class and eastern European immigrants. The middle class has received little attention from historians, despite the fact that it proved to form the dominant identity. Without a more developed understanding of middle-class identity and culture on the prairies, much of what we say about any other social groups will be incomplete, as the context in which they operated was very much set by middle-class discourse.

Historians have not developed the history of the middle class in the period from 1890 to 1920 because on the surface the story looks fairly straightforward: western Canadians were at the forefront of the expansion of the British Empire, and a society was arising that promised to improve on the great British culture that had created it. Such improvements would take the form of social equality and democracy. As Gerald Friesen argues, this combined "to create a powerful new regional image."[2] This happily growing society was threatened by the arrival of thousands of immigrants who were neither part of the British parent culture, nor part of the Anglo-Canadian culture, and were certainly not part of the "new regional image." Yet a "social calm" prevailed, due to the "prairie leaders' confident assump-tion that they could 'Canadianize' the newcomers."[3] The rapid economic and social expansion that was simultaneously occurring also caused little consternation. "Rather," in Friesen's words again, "the leaders of the prairie west became even more conscious of the region's identity and increasingly aware of its mission to the nation."[4] With the chaos of the Great War and its aftermath, "ideals of social reform and majoritarian democracy ... moved ever closer to repression and nativism."[5] By 1919 it was time to contain the challenge from below, and non-Anglo-Canadians and the working classes have been suffering the consequences pretty much ever since.

The consequence of this belief in the happy, confident, and stable middle class is that historians have tended to concentrate on the ways in which the middle class mobilized ideology and the state to affect the development of the identity of Native Canadians, immigrants, and radical labour. The middle class itself is viewed as a static grouping that did things to the identities of other people while their own identity remained unchanged. While making others in their own image, however, middle-class educationalists, and social and moral reformers, were also self-consciously seeking to reshape the identity of the middle class itself in order to suit the changing conditions of modern life. Certainly, prairie regional identity did develop out of a belief that the new land offered the opportunity for an important social and political mission. Perhaps more important, however, were the changes many in the middle class hoped would be effected in the personal and cultural identity of all western Canadians.

By looking at the formulation and reformulation of the identity of the dominant cultural group, we can begin to fill out our understanding of prairie history and the development of regional identity. To further this process, this paper examines education in Manitoba and concentrates on two of the main methods that were thought to shape the identity of the male citizen and hence the class and the nation. The first method is the widespread desire to reshape the character of the individual, and the second is the related concern with the promotion of manliness.

First of all, however, the context in which this middle-class identity was being formed was far from rosy, regardless of geographical and economic growth and the associated ravings of boosters. The standard interpretation of middle-class identity on the prairies often ignores the fact that the middle class was engaged in a process of redefining itself long before the immigrants and the industrial working class appeared as a viable threat. The Prairie West was undergoing dramatic social, cultural, political, and economic changes. The growth and expansion of the period from the 1890s to the 1920s is a familiar story, perhaps so familiar that the effect of such changes is lost on late-twentieth-century observers—though it certainly was not lost on members of the middle class in this period. There was an intense awareness that society was becoming modern, and that life in this

modern world would be very different from that which had been lived
before. As Marshall Berman has noted, the social and cultural consequences
of becoming modern are profound. Industrialization, urbanization, immigration, and fundamental advances in science and technology, for instance,
created "new human environments" while largely destroying the old ones.[6]
From the 1890s onwards, there were changes in economic systems, with
the increase in industrial enterprises and the beginnings of the managerial
and professional revolution. There were continuing changes in the size and
composition of the state, and changes in democratic participation. Socially
and culturally, there were fundamental changes in the provision of schooling and new concerns about economic, social, and sexual relations. These
pressures were felt more strongly on the prairies, which lacked many of the
stabilizing institutional and social supports that existed in the Old World, or
even in eastern Canada.

As far as the middle-class educationalists and reformers, who set much
of the cultural agenda through the schools, were concerned, the central
problem in western Canada was confronting the modern world. Urbanization, industrialization, and class and racial conflicts were dependent variables. The solution for key portions of the middle class was to change the
identity of the middle class itself.[7] The goal was not what we have been
comfortably calling "Canadianization" or "Anglo-Assimilation" or even
"Anglo-Conformity," because in many ways these identities were not sufficient in and of themselves to meet the conditions of the West. The pace of
change was too great, and the lack of institutional and cultural bulwarks
too profound. Middle-class identity, and hence ultimately the dominant
portion of the prairie identity, was formed in this environment—an environment where it was feared, to use the catch phrase, that "All that is solid
melts into air."[8]

The middle-class identity that was thought to be required to cope in the
modern world was one that was to some degree flexible and adaptable.
Moreover, it was an identity that emphasized self-control and the virtues
and values that would allow continued success and progress in the changing conditions of life. The values that were usually listed are familiar ones:
citizenship, duty, democracy, honour, reputation, morals, manners, integrity,
and manhood, for instance.[9] Such values were necessary to deal with the
unprecedented temptations of the modern world. In order to ensure that
these values became part of the modern identity, the goal of many in the
middle class was to develop the individual character of each citizen, regardless of ethnic or class background. As one prairie commentator defined it,
character was "a completely formed will."[10] A citizen of character was one

who had the ability to act in the proper manner, regardless of difficulties or temptation.

Character meant fighting temptation and self-interest, two threats that were in abundance on the prairies. W.J. Sisler, a prominent member of the educational establishment in western Canada, promoted the motto "He who conquers self succeeds" in the many schools he influenced. Only by controlling selfish desires could the individual, and hence the West, hope to overcome the modern problems that were believed to be connected to the failure of the will. Such problems included industrial conflict, poverty, prostitution, falling birth rates, allegedly rising insanity and venereal disease rates, false patriotism, materialism, and any number of other bugbears. It is important to note that character was about self-discipline and self-regulation. Attempts to legislate or otherwise consciously to regulate an identity that could cope with modern life were considered futile. The dominant philosophy and pedagogy of the time was that such changes could only be internalized by the individuals themselves—the values of character, and the identity that would result, had to be self-imposed.[11]

All around the English-speaking world there were continued claims that the only hope for the future was to develop character. As an article in the *Western School Journal* claimed, "The supreme question of the century is the question of personal character. The nation that can grow a worthy manhood and womanhood can live. It is immortal. The nation whose personal life deteriorates is already smitten with death. Character is the only conserving and conquering power."[12] In western Canada in particular, the education system was the central, and sometimes only, means at the disposal of the middle class to build character.[13] Character building as an explicit belief and goal can be found at all levels of the educational system, voiced by inspectors, school administrators, politicians, parents, and teachers alike. Promoting character building was not merely rhetoric. George Best, a school inspector for almost all of the period under discussion, claimed that teachers knew their objective and had the freedom to reach it. As Best put it, the teacher adored scholarship, "but in his code, citizenship, character, manhood, came first."[14] Education was about what Best termed "freedom, self-control, co-operation and sympathy."[15]

These goals were in large part accomplished using the Manitoba curriculum, which was called the "Programme of Studies." In an address to the Western Manitoba Teachers' Association convention, J.T. Yemen, a female teacher, was entirely untroubled in saying that the practical aim of education was to suit students for the modern world by developing their characters. As Yemen put it: "Under the names of hygiene, physical culture, manners, and morals is what is to be taught to twentieth century children so that they may be a people of vigorous health and fine physique, a people pure in heart, courteous in manner, respectful to parents, fulfilling all the duties of citizenship, patriotic, merciful, and obedient to the Moral Law."[16]

The 1889 "Programme of Studies" (in this case for the Protestant schools) included in the teacher's responsibilities lessons on cleanliness and temperate habits of all kinds. The teacher was directed to inculcate identity under four categories: duties to self, to others, to the State, and, strangely, to animals. Duties to self, for example, included "self-culture, self-respect, self-control; purity in thought, word and deed; industry, economy; truthfulness, courage, etc." Duties to the state included civil duties, including respect for the law, tax paying, patriotism, and support of the government, and political duties, such as voting and viewing public office as a sacred trust.[17]

Character education also occurred outside the curriculum, through the influence of the teacher and schoolmates, through imperialism, through sport, through gender relations, and various other formats.[18] All these methods were actively promoted in western Canada. It was important to promote character whenever possible, as it was thought that there was also a physiological connection and that character could thus be acquired through force of habit. After a scientific discussion of the nervous system, the author of the approved health text in Manitoba pointed out that the nervous system depends largely on habits that make actions second nature. This, he claimed, was true physically and morally. The moral habits that were formed while individuals were young would follow them through life, and by the time people reached their mid-twenties, such habits were almost impossible to lose.[19] Here, again, is another reason legal regulation was intended more for affecting the environment of the young, than for effecting changes in their parents' identity. One critic claimed that those desiring reform should give up on the rest of society and just concentrate on students for ten years or so, and then the students would graduate and take care of everything.[20]

The opportunity to affect the identity of the young in the absence of many of the temptations of the Old World and Ontario was a significant element in middle-class identity in the West. The newness of their society made the potential and the risk of their character-building enterprise all the more dramatic. Western Canadian society was thought to be distinct, both in terms of the lack of initial problems and in terms of the speed of change.

Another reason why the western Canadian use of character was different was the commitment to the belief that character could be obtained by

all, regardless of social position. Here the social and political regional identity interacted with the cultural. For example, school inspector C.K.
Newcombe described the goal of the high school in Manitoba as being "to
give students some ability to weigh facts and make deductions; they aim at
creating a body of men and women whose function it will be to mould
public opinion and keep it pure, a body from whose ranks will be drawn
the leaders of the various movements which tend towards the betterment
of the community and the race."[21] No one vision was set, nor any one put
forward, as long as the race in the West continued to better itself. Commentators on character were unanimous that society had to become "a
self-governing community." As a result, students had to be allowed the freedom to discover their own views. The modern citizenship connected with
character did not require a submissive mind, but an inquiring and independent one.[22]

Similarly, modern citizenship also required manly minds and bodies. As
Morris Mott has argued, sport and games were used to confront the health
problems that were believed to be connected to the modern world. The
pace of modern life, and its sedentary and urban environment, were thought
to sap both physical and moral energy, both of which were vital to modern
existence. As the Manitoba Health Reader proclaimed, "The man with a
clear and unimpaired brain, with a healthy, well-cared-for body, with body
and brain controlled by a determined, resolute will—he is the man who
will make a success in the coming years of the twentieth century."[23] While
physical education was certainly in part an attempt to respond to fears of
physical and moral decline, a more profound reason for the promotion of
physical education was the middle-class desire to redefine masculinity.

As an editorial in the *Western School Journal* claimed, those who argued
for practical education solely suited to making a living are doing damage to
themselves, to their children, and to the state. There was much more to
education. The state had a duty to protect itself and its citizens from degra-
dation, ignorance, vice, and crime, and the state could do this by teaching a
student how to be a man or, rather, how to be a certain type of man. The
Journal claimed that through education a student should "learn what is
becoming to him as a man who is to build up a mighty nation in the
West."[24] Indeed, this was another area in which the West should find its
own way. Another editorial in the *Western School Journal* claimed that the
West did not want teachers from back East, those whom the editors referred to as "our enslaved brethren of the 'effete' provinces."[25]

The form of masculinity promoted in the schools of Manitoba is generally referred to as manliness. Manliness, as J.A. Mangan and others have

demonstrated, was "a distinctive and powerful moral code" in the English-speaking world.[26] Manliness was a guide to conduct, which became a powerful cultural representation in the tumultuous decades before the Great War and was promulgated by a wide variety of means—from teachers, professors, preachers, and writers to politicians and sporting figures.[27] Coolness, discipline, and leadership were all components of manliness, and each would help the new generation of manly citizens control themselves and others in the face of seeming social and moral decline. Central to the ideal of manliness was a combination of vitality and self-control.

The vitality of the modern citizen was a prevalent concern for the middle class from the 1890s onwards. The feared lack of vitality was even more pronounced in the settler dominions of the British Empire. Away from the cradle of the race, many Britons feared that instead of progressing, they would degenerate and lose the characteristics that underlay their claim to political, imperial, and social dominance. The display and measurement of energy was an essential means of determining the present and future of the race. These concerns were tied directly into the emergence of a national identity in western Canada and concomitantly in the emergence of a modern identity too. David Walker has noted in the highly similar Australian context, "The display of energy ... was a critically important ritual which became thoroughly enmeshed in debates about the nature and meaning of nationality."[28] As W.L Morton commented, "The man who was a good sport, good shot, and good horseman was sure of esteem from young and old, and the ideal within its limits was a proud and manly one."[29]

Particularly problematic, especially in the West, was the fact that while education was one of the few agencies that could be used to promote character and manliness, education itself was seen as enervating, and hence unmanly. One teacher claimed, "Our education, rural and urban, is altogether too bookish as it is." Indeed, "It is better a hundred times that a boy should be hardening his muscles, moral and physical, in overcoming some practical difficulty, in accomplishing some real objective aim, than that he should be allowed to acquire pottering, idle habits in a distasteful atmosphere of books and abstract figures and hazy ideas that lead nowhere."[30]

One so-called medical expert termed the school "the greatest sedentary institution." The school was a distinct danger to manly identity as it contained society's future citizens and "because it affects the child during the growing and developing period of its life." The child was kept inactive when it should have been active. The result, claimed a US-based doctor, was "a great many physical disorders. Disturbances of digestion, of metabolism, of physiological function result." Schooling also affected the "play instinct," which was bad, because "adults who have lacked a normal and energetic play experience in youth never display the vigour and vitality of those who have had such expression. They also lack in spontaneity, enthusiasm and wholesouledness because these characteristics are acquired in youth and not in later life."[31] As a result, western Canadian educators became even more obsessed with physical education: their window of opportunity was closing rapidly.

Influenced by the vitalist physiology of the period, another important aspect of manliness was self-control, which was meant as both a physical and mental attribute. Stimulation and intemperance, with respect to sex or alcohol or whatever, were thought to lead to a dehabilitated system; and conversely, health stemmed from an ascetic lifestyle. The connection between individual and social decline and masturbation is one of the more popularized aspects of self-control in this period, though various other intemperate acts fit in here too. As the health text *Elementary Physiology and Hygiene* told a generation of children, "The value of the human body as a machine is lowered by every form of *overindulgence* [original italics]." This included talking, playing, studying, working, and intemperate behaviour of all kinds.[32]

W.A. McIntyre, the head of the normal school, and hence the teacher of the teachers, claimed that manliness did away with the dissipated type in the schools. In his words, "Where good bodily health, graceful carriage, manly bearing are found, it is difficult for criminal tendencies to develop. The boy who slouches, who tips his hat over his left ear, and who persistently keeps his hands in his pockets, is in a fair way to harbor those thoughts which make for unrighteousness."[33] The symbolism was clear, and it was also a classic description of the degenerating masturbator.[34] By making students sit up straight and take their hats off indoors, teachers were not simply impressing middle-class habits of respectability—they believed they were saving society from collapse.

While middle-class and prairie identity in this period stemmed from the attempt to redefine the identity of individual citizens to meet the demands of modern life, such attempts were clearly not unique to the prairies. What was distinctly prairie was that this project was deemed both possible and likely to succeed. As Gerald Friesen has previously argued, the West allowed the potential for a new society; democracy, egalitarianism, cooperation, virility, opportunity, and progress, for example, were all possible. However, they entered the western identity not as social or political goals in and of themselves, but through the worldwide Anglo-Celtic concern with personal character.

The distinctive regional identity was due not only to political and social ideas of potential development, but more to the potential for individual and cultural development. In other words, it was not only the political and social aspects of society that could be improved, but the individuals themselves. Indeed, in the idealist or New Liberal thinking that pervaded much of the middle class, improving the individual was the point behind improving the state and society. Middle-class identity in western Canada between 1890 and 1920 was premised not on being Canadian or British Canadian, but on the possibility of surpassing both. The defining principle of the Anglo-Celtic identity, regardless of its location, was the belief that character made the man, and through him the nation—and character was not fixed. Character in the prairie West could change, and the possibility that such changes could advance the inhabitants of the West farther than any people before them gave the West a distinct identity. We need to take seriously middle-class claims that a new race was emerging in the West. The most famous example, perhaps, is Ralph Connor's much maligned preface to *The Foreigner*.[35] Such a belief was fundamental to the educational project of the West, and to much of middle-class identity. The middle class needs to be examined as something other than a cultural monolith. To do so will enhance our understanding of such things as imperialism, nationalism, class, secular social and moral reform, gender, and ethnicity in western Canadian history.

Endnotes

1. For a historiography of the development of regional identity in western Canada, see R. Douglas Francis, "In Search of a Prairie Myth: A Survey of the Intellectual and Cultural Historiography of Prairie Canada," *Journal of Canadian Studies* 24, no. 3 (Fall 1989).

2. Gerald Friesen, *The Canadian Prairies: A History* (Toronto: University of Toronto Press, 1987), 340.

3. Ibid., 345.

4. Ibid., 343.

5. Ibid., 355.

6. Marshall Berman, *All that Is Solid Melts into Air: The Experience of Modernity* (New York: Simon and Schuster, 1983), 16.

7. Valverde discusses this process of change but tends to describe it as almost incidental—if not accidental—to the desire to "reshape the ethical subjectivity of the nation."

Mariana Valverde, *The Age of Light, Soap, and Water: Moral Reform in English Canada, 1885-1925* (Toronto: McClelland and Stewart, 1991), 17.

8. Berman, *All that Is Solid*, 15.

9. For an excellent brief discussion of the definition of the term *character*, see Stefan Collini, "The Idea of 'Character' in Victorian Political Thought," *Transactions of the Royal Historical Society* 35, 5th series (1985); see also his *Public Moralists: Political Thought and Intellectual Life in Britain, 1850-1930* (Oxford/New York: Clarendon Press/Oxford University Press, 1991).

10. L. Seeley, "Character as an End of Education," *Western School Journal (WSJ)* 8 (October 1906): n.p.

11. For a classic exposition of self-regulation and character in the Canadian context, see Sir Robert Falconer, *Idealism in National Character: Essays and Addresses* (London: Hodder and Stoughton, 1920).

12. Seeley, "Character."

13. Education was not only important in building modern citizens in the West because it was a surviving institution, but also because its increased importance was in itself a modern phenomena. As an editorial on "Our Schools and their Critics" argued, "The exactations of business and society are making the home less and less a factor in the education of the child and thrusting more and more of this all-important duty upon the school. No fact in modern life is more to be deplored than this tendency." *WSJ* 2 (February 1906): n.p.

14. Edward E. Best, "Memoirs of a School Inspector, 1888-1932," Public Archives of Manitoba (PAM), MG 9 A-95-1, 38.

15. Best, "Memoirs," 84.

16. Printed in *WSJ* II, no. 4 (April 1907): n.p.

17. *The School Times* 1, no. 12 (July 1889).

18. *WSJ* I, no. 8 (October 1906): n.p.

19. H.W. Conn, *Elementary Physiology and Hygiene* (Toronto: Copp, Clark, 1903). Authorised by the Advisory Board for Manitoba. Such ideas were still promoted in the 1940s. See J.W. Ritchie, rev. W.J. Dobbie, *Human Physiology* (Toronto: Gage, 1940).

20. W.J. Gordon Scott, "Democracy in the Classroom," *WSJ* XV, no. 6 (June 1920): n.p.

21. Chas. K. Newcombe, "The High Schools and their Relation to the Community," *WSJ* I, no. 4 (April 1906): n.p.

22. *WSJ* III, no. 10 (November 1908).

23. Conn, *Elementary Physiology and Hygiene,* 186.

24. *WSJ* IV, no. 5 (May 1909): n.p.

25. *WSJ* I, no. 8 (October 1906): n.p.

26. J.A. Mangan and James Walvin, *Manliness and Morality: Middle-Class Masculinity in Britain and America, 1800-1940* (Manchester: Manchester University Press, 1987), 2.

27. John Tosh, "What Should Historians Do with Masculinity? Reflections on Nineteenth-century Britain," *History Workshop Journal* 38 (1994); see also Michael Roper and John Tosh, "Introduction: Historians and the Politics of Masculinity," in

Manful Assertions: Masculinities in Britain since 1800, ed. Michael Roper and John Tosh (London: Routledge, 1991).

28. David Walker, "Energy and Fatigue," *Australian Cultural History,* no. 13 (1994): 165.

29. W.L. Morton, *Manitoba: A History* (Toronto: University of Toronto Press, 1967), 262.

30. S.E. Lang, "Better Organisation of Educational Agencies," *WSJ* I, no. 5 (May 1906): n.p.

31. *WSJ* 2, no. 1 (January 1907): n.p.

32. Conn, *Elementary Physiology and Hygiene,* 186.

33. *WSJ* I, no. 4 (April 1906): n.p.

34. See David Walker, "Continence for a Nation: Seminal Loss and National Vigour," *Labour History* 48 (1985); see also Michael Bliss, "'Pure Books on Avoided Subjects': Pre-Freudian Sexual Ideas in Canada," *Historical Papers* (1970).

35. "In Western Canada there is to be seen to-day that most fascinating of all human phenomena, the making of a nation. Out of breeds diverse in traditions, ideals, in speech, and in manner of life, Saxon and Slav, Teuton, Celt and Gaul, one people is being made. The blood strains of great races will mingle in the blood of a race greater than the greatest of them all." Ralph Connor (C.W. Gordon), *The Foreigner: A Tale of Saskatchewan* (Toronto: Westminster Co., 1909).

Who's from the Prairie? Some Prairie Self-Representations in Popular Culture

Alison Calder

FOR THE FIRST FEW MONTHS after I moved to Ontario from Saskatch-ewan, I woke up to the same advertisement on the radio. The ad, for a real-estate company, stressed the great bonuses available to consumers who chose that company to represent them. It worked by mocking the bonuses of-fered by another, fictitious company. These bonuses started out small (a calendar with pictures of kittens wearing cute outfits) and progressed to the increasingly comic and useless, finally reaching the nadir of all bonuses: a framed photograph of Saskatoon at night. You can imagine my response. I had moved to a place where my point of origin, the place I called home, had the cultural status of a punchline. This article traces, through my own experience, some strands of what Rob Shields describes as the social spatialization of place,[1] in an attempt to move beyond the transparency of geography to recognize the prairies as socially constituted space, and to examine how the prairies come to mean, and what those mean-ings are.

My initial impulse for this article was to write about the negative images of the prairies that continually surface in popular culture. This popular prairie is a strange and paradoxical place, at once a weird, gothic landscape populated by alienated and malevolent rednecks (as in popular representa-tions of Alberta), and also a warm, decent place inhabited by honest, hard-working folks with good community values (as in the pictures of church socials that often grace the pages of *Canadian Living* magazine). The popu-lar prairie is primarily defined by its landscape, which, like its population, is seen as extreme.[2] Frequently, landscape and people appear in a kind of cause-and-effect relation: the prairie environment is seen to breed a certain type of person, whether it is the inherent goodness of the folks seen in CBC's series *Jake and the Kid*, or the inherent eccentricity of the characters in the movie *Fargo*, to use an American example. I thought of writing about the insistence in popular culture on placing the prairies in the past, positioning them resolutely in a discourse of dust storms, deserts, and Bennett buggies. But by focussing on *what is done to* the prairie, on extra-regional definitions of the place that function to construct the prairie as nostalgic, declining, and dependent, I realized that I would be replicating that notion of regional passivity. People in the prairie provinces are not victims: instead, they actively define themselves, working out of complicated mythologies of their own, developing narratives of identity to fill various individual or cultural needs. The inadequacy of the victim mentality and the need to consider regions relationally rather than in isolation was brought home to me on one visit to Saskatoon, where I was introduced as being "from Ontario." My new acquaintance smiled broadly, extended a hand, and said, "Don't worry … we'll try not to hate you." My poor-me perspective deflated.

The Ideal Rural Past

My first winter in Ontario was cold. I was on campus early each morning, and as my colleagues from Ontario arrived, I noticed a pattern. Each person entered the room, mentioned the weather, and then turned to me and said, "Of course, it wouldn't feel cold to *you*." I complained about it to my friends back home, citing it as yet another example of Eastern ignorance. (In Saskatchewan, Ontario is the East.) But then I went home for Christmas … and when I came back, I was doing it too. You call this cold? Why, in Saskatchewan it's so cold *that we plug in our cars*!

I mention my complicity with what I had formerly characterized as Eastern ignorance as a way to lead into a discussion on prairie identity as it is produced within the region. I use the word *produced* because one of the chief characteristics of prairie identity as it manifests itself in popular culture is its ability to be very consciously produced.[3] This production can be motivated by a mixture of many desires: to differentiate oneself from a generalized Canadian or global culture, to affirm one's place in a particular group, or to tie into particular market forces, among other possibilities. None of these possibilities is inherently good or bad. But I want to examine the implications of a particular kind of prairie identity, typified in two books by Dave Bouchard, *Prairie Born* and *If you're not from the prairie….*[4] The two books are similar: *If you're not from the prairie…* is described on the sleeve as "a nostalgic pilgrimage to a place that symbolizes a unique lifestyle," and *Prairie Born* is described as "a book that will stir warm memories for all those 'prairie born,' no matter where they find themselves." Bouchard's verse is complemented in each book by paintings of prairie scenes, with children playing hockey, waiting for the school bus, or picking stones in a field. These books are deliberately nostalgic, seeking to evoke warm feelings for a place of safety, childhood, and home. These may be children's books,[5] but I've seen *If you're not from the prairie...* on coffee tables and under Christmas trees from coast to coast. I went to a wedding at which the groom's family, from Regina, presented the bride's family, from Cape Breton Island, with a copy of the book, to further understanding between the two. My mother sent me a T-shirt printed with lines from the book, to keep me company in Ontario. As of the summer of 1999, the books carry stickers reading "over 100,000 sold."

As the title *If you're not from the prairie...* implies, this book is about identity, and the implications of the kind of prairie identity it posits should not be accepted uncritically. Bouchard's text draws on the idea of community, but in that community are embedded particular kinds of exclusion that are very far from idyllic. The book's title signals a dichotomy: there are those who are from the prairie, and then there are those who are not. There is no connection between the two groups: "If you're not from the prairie," Bouchard writes, "You don't know me. You just can't know ME."[6] The prairie dweller's essential self, emphasized by Bouchard's capitalization, remains inaccessible to an extra-regional audience. The text of *Prairie Born* turns on a series of contrasts, in which the narrator first addresses the experience of his imagined reader (who, interestingly enough, is not from the prairie), and then contrasts that with a description of his own, different experience. An example is his description of autumn:

> Go back for a minute, remember your fall
> Leaves changing colours, you raked and you hauled,
> I too know this season, but for me it's much more
> And the earth knows my secret's not found on her floor.[7]

Bouchard thus creates a prairie community by insisting on its alienation from other places: the "secret" of the prairie can only be understood by those who have direct experience of the place. This is a kind of retrospective community, based on a childhood identification with a landscape of origin. Regional commonality is forged by excluding others.

The reason for this distinct prairie community is, according to Bouchard, the environment, as the impact of the landscape and the weather forges a common prairie ethos. This environmental determinism is explicit:

> If you're not from the prairie, you can't know my soul,
> You don't know our blizzards, you've not fought our cold.

> You can't know my mind, nor ever my heart,
> Unless deep within you, there's somehow a part …
> A part of these things that I've said that I know,
> The wind, sky and earth, the storms and the snow.
> Best say you have—and then we'll be one,
> For we will have shared that same blazing sun.[8]

Identity is grounded in landscape, where the experience of "shar[ing] that same blazing sun" creates a particular kind of person. My own response to the weather-based comments of my Ontario colleagues comes from the same logic: emphasizing the extremity of the conditions of a Saskatchewan winter marked me as a member of a particular community (here, one signified as "not-Ontario") and posited a kind of superiority based on endurance.[9] In other words, landscape and weather made me different. However, this difference was to a certain extent fictional: I was cold in both provinces.

Basing an identity on an ostensibly neutral landscape may seem innocuous, but it does have a few unpleasant effects. As W.H. New points out in *Land Sliding*, landscape and power are inextricably linked in Canada.[10] Roberto Dainotto has argued convincingly that much regional theorization is based on a frequently unstated desire for purity and authenticity, in an attempt to reach back to a supposedly simpler, happier time.[11] This simple vision requires exclusivity: to posit a strong, cohesive prairie identity, all complexity must be suppressed. The boundaries of identity cannot, in this essentializing model, be permeable. We see this kind of rigid simplicity in the nostalgic idyll Bouchard creates. In describing only one kind of prairie experience, Bouchard evokes a sense of nostalgia for a prairie that never really existed. In his books, the person who is from the prairies is exclusively rural and exclusively white. The young boy in the ball cap seen in the first of Henry Ripplinger's paintings, *Time Out*, grows up to become the narrator's stand-in on page 25, the weathered farmer in the ball cap standing in his newly harvested field. *If you're not from the prairie…* takes a very particular kind of prairie experience and generalizes it to become *the* prairie experience, an assertion that denies a "prairie" identity to those whose experiences are outside this model: people who grew up in a prairie city, for example, or on a reserve. No people of Aboriginal ancestry appear anywhere in these books, an omission that, given the demographics of the prairie provinces today, points to the inadequacy of the title *Prairie Born*. And because these books are deliberately nostalgic in tone, they also do not recognize the increasingly complicated immigration patterns and racial diversity in the region. In fact, these books work against a recognition of the multiracial composition of the prairie provinces by erasing what multiracial contact historically occurred: the prairies are represented as only White space. Prairie identity is thus frozen at a particular historical moment, walled off from other regions, unable to evolve to reflect the hybrid identities of prairie dwellers today.[12] Such arrested ideas of identity are, as Dainotto writes, "menacing and childish."[13]

But just because I can analyze and criticize this nostalgic, rural identity as inadequate does not mean that it has no importance. Saskatchewan, for example, is a shrinking province: many of its young people move elsewhere to look for work, and much of its older population moves elsewhere to retire. And they take books like Bouchard's with them as cultural souvenirs, even though the culture reflected in the pages may have very little to do with their own lived prairie experience. The books are appealing because their narratives have the familiarity of fairy tales, wrapping up with a happily-ever-after ending. It is precisely the seductive quality of these books that makes me uncomfortable with their claim to represent accurately an ideal, real world. Ursula Kelly writes that "cultural nostalgia is not only weakening, it is also blinding."[14] In situating prairie identity *only* in the past, *only* in an idealized rural landscape that may not ever have existed, these books deny regional identity a future. The prairie becomes a place that once existed, and now is only a warm memory. Its decline can thus be figured as inevitable: if the region is a lost Eden, already vanishing in the imagination, then the economic and cultural deprivations it suffers can be easily naturalized. "Why do our regions seem forever to be passing away?" asks Jim Wayne Miller. "Why are we always surprised to discover they are still there?"[15] The answer, I think, is not just that general Canadian culture constructs the prairies as a region in decline, but that in a search for identity, those of us from the prairies are invited to cling to an artificial, land-based nostalgia that locates us and our place firmly in the past.

The Romantic Landscape

The evocation of an idealized rural past is one way in which people from the prairie provinces might choose to identify themselves with place. Another dissimilar, but not entirely unrelated, popular model they might follow involves mystification of the landscape as seen in Courtney Milne's very popular collection of photographs, *Prairie Dreams*,[16] and Sharon Butala's bestselling memoir, *The Perfection of the Morning*.[17] The popular interest in these books can be related to a general cultural interest in environmental issues combined with a search for New Age spirituality, and is partly motivated by the same sort of nostalgia that impels readers to purchase *If you're not from the prairie*.... The back jacket of Milne's collection advertises that it "captur[es] the prairie region in all its wonder and diversity." But there are no photographs of the urban prairie in this book: in fact, virtually all images of houses or buildings are of structures that are abandoned or decaying. Similarly, the extracts of poetry and prose that accompany the photographs either celebrate the beauty and/or harshness of the prairie environment, or describe farming experiences. The images are beautiful: the landscape is stunningly photographed. But again we see the celebration of a particular kind of prairie experience, the evocation of a particular kind of history, to the exclusion of others. There are no people in these photographs, perhaps because to display the real people who live on the land would shatter the illusion of an unpopulated, starkly beautiful wilderness.

A similar lack of community appears in *The Perfection of the Morning*. This memoir narrates Butala's rejection of what she describes as an unhealthy, unhappy, academic urban existence in favour of a more meaningful life on a ranch in southern Saskatchewan, and chronicles the ways in which she attempts to come to terms with the landscape and with herself. Using a mixture of ecofeminism, Jungian psychology, and New Age and Native spirituality, she navigates through a sense of alienation and loneliness, finally achieving a kind of unity with the place. One of the reasons that Butala's book has been so popular, I think, is that it fulfills a kind of escape fantasy for a largely urban audience, being a narrative that suggests that, given the right circumstances, one can leave a cold, unhealthy city for a fulfilling life in the "wilderness." This romantic idea of the recuperative wilderness is not new, of course; its lineage can be traced back through Thoreau and Emerson to the early Romantics.[18] What I find interesting is that Butala never acknowledges this lineage. Instead, her Romantic explorations of self and landscape are presented as the accidental experiences of a naïve narrator, untutored and unschooled. She appears as, in Randall Roorda's term, a "nature savant."[19] Given the premise of her memoir—that the urban is bad and the rural is good—she could hardly present herself otherwise: to appear at all intellectual would be, in her terms, to be somehow inauthentic, not a real prairie person at all. As she writes in "The Reality of the Flesh," "There are those novelists who, when the impulse to write comes upon them, turn to look out the window, or go outside for a long walk across the prairie, or drive out to Fort Walsh, or go to have a talk with an old man; and there are those novelists who go to a literary café, to their bookshelves, to their memories of the great works of other novelists, and to long, learned conversations with scholars whose ideas are built and honed. I am one of the former and I view the latter with respect and not a little envy mixed with a dash of perplexity."[20]

In this description, the "real life" writer has privileged access to prairie landscape, history, and people, while the "literary" writer, insulated from prairie reality, works from a generalized and imported literary culture. The ideas of the true prairie writer are not "built and honed": rather, they come directly from the environment, unmediated by any theoretical agenda or aesthetic theory. The prairie person exists in nature, without thought.

My objections to Butala's ingenuous presentation become clearer when one examines how she represents the farmers and ranchers she encounters in her new life. These neighbours rarely speak: they exist only in place, naturally *there*, in an entirely unreflecting way. They are true naturals, in the sense of being one with nature and also in the now outdated meaning of "simple." The textualized Butala, on the other hand, is far more complex, and must wrestle, sometimes almost literally, with the spirit of place, trying again and again to make it accept her. All this wrestling is accomplished without acknowledging that intellectual inquiry is, in fact, what she is undertaking, that she is not an untaught child of nature writing things down just as they happen, but is rather a skilled author deliberately shaping the materials at hand into a life narrative. There is a kind of dishonesty here that I find disturbing. Rather than finding a new and empowering memoir of prairie experience, I locate in this narrative the same tired paradigms at which most prairie dwellers chafe: the notions that the only true prairie person is a rancher or a farmer, that no real prairie person has any sort of intellectual curiosity, and that "prairie" is an ossified definition with strict and impermeable boundaries. In her self-construction as the naïve artist, the authentic prairie writer, Butala cheapens both the lives of the prairie dwellers she records and her own literary achievement.[21]

The Value of the Definition

I have said that prairie dwellers are not victims, that they actively work to define themselves. But while definitions of the prairies that come from within the region may respond to, incorporate, and challenge externally imposed images, these self-definitions often lack the cultural currency of the more popular, pan-Canadian ones. An example of this inequality can be seen in the response to the discovery of a *Tyrannosaurus Rex* skeleton in Eastend, Saskatchewan, in 1994. A front-page article in the *Globe and Mail* about the find suggested that the dinosaur had died of boredom; clearly, small-town Saskatchewan was a place far removed from the hip, urban culture represented by southern Ontario.[22] In response to this article, a radio station in Saskatoon sponsored a contest to suggest possible causes of a dinosaur's death in Toronto. The winning response posited that a Toronto dinosaur would have succumbed to solar confusion—in other words, that it would have died from the belief that the sun shone out of its own posterior.

There are several interesting if distasteful things going on in that radio contestant's suggestion, but I want to use it to point to the idea of audience. The *Globe and Mail* is a national newspaper. A Saskatoon radio station, on the other hand, has only a small listening radius and a limited audience. The kind of political and cultural protest encapsulated in the contestant's suggestion will have little impact and will almost exclusively reach an audience of the already converted. The same is true, I suggest, for anthologies like the ironically named *The Middle of Nowhere*, a collection of historical and contemporary non-fiction writings about aspects of Saskatchewan.[23] The anthology's subtitle is "Rediscovering Saskatchewan," but the fact that it was published by a small, "regional" press (Saskatoon's Fifth House) means that it will be accessible primarily to an audience already familiar with the place. A book like Butala's *The Perfection of the Morning* may achieve bestseller status, but I suggest that its popularity lies in the fact that it can easily be appropriated to a dominant culture through its reinforcement of prevailing stereotypes.

People from the prairies are often angered by the stories others tell about us, but it is time to examine the stories we tell about ourselves. Claiming a prairie identity means taking a good long look at the place we call home and recognizing it in all its complexity. In her essay "Can You Tell the Truth in a Small Town?" Kathleen Norris eloquently describes how nostalgic visions of the prairie make us believe in a past that never was and prepare us for a future that will never be.[24] There is nothing wrong with looking to the past for strength and community: the danger lies in choosing to believe in a false and simple past. Acknowledging our complicity in constructing nostalgic and exclusive representations of the prairies also means that we acknowledge our power to change those representations. The result, one hopes, will be images of the prairie in popular culture that are as complicated, messy, and vibrant as prairie culture itself.

Endnotes

1. Rob Shields, *Places on the Margin: Alternative Geographies of Modernity* (London and New York: Routledge, 1991).

2. For more elaboration on the effects of the belief that the prairie environment is particularly extreme, see my article "'The nearest approach to a desert': Implications of Environmental Determinism in the Criticism of Prairie Writing," *Prairie Forum* 23 (1998): 171–82.

3. For a look at similar issues in the context of the Maritime provinces, see R.M. Vaughan, "Lobster Is King: Infantilizing Maritime Culture," *Semiotext(e)* 6, no. 2 (1994): 169-72.

4. Dave Bouchard, text, and Henry Ripplinger, illustrations, *If you're not from the prairie*…(Vancouver: Raincoast, 1994); Dave Bouchard, text, and Peter Shostak, illustrations, *Prairie Born* (Victoria, BC, and Custer, WA: Orca, 1997).

5. Of the two books, only *Prairie Born* is catalogued as "juvenile poetry."

6. Bouchard and Ripplinger, *If you're not*, 22.

7. Bouchard and Shostak, *Prairie Born*, np. The absence of leaf-producing trees in this passage invalidates an urban prairie childhood: I can testify from personal experience that kids growing up in a prairie city rake a lot of leaves.

8. Bouchard and Ripplinger, *If you're not*, 28.

9. Endurance in the face of extreme suffering is one of the most common hallmarks of prairie self-definition and is related to the importance of the homesteading moment in the regional imagination. This kind of prairie identity is deeply paradoxical, where unity with place is based on the idea of battling it—if you have "fought our cold," "our blizzards," and "our blazing sun," then you can claim prairie citizenship. The privileging or aestheticization of suffering is also related to the dominance of prairie realist texts as "prairie" texts, and is perhaps responsible for the logic-defying loyalty of fans of the Canadian Football League's Saskatchewan Roughriders.

10. W.H. New, *Land Sliding: Imagining Space, Presence, and Power in Canadian Writing* (Toronto: University of Toronto Press, 1997).

11. Roberto Maria Dainotto, "'All the Regions Do Smilingly Revolt': The Literature of Place and Region," *Critical Inquiry* 22 (1996): 486-505.

12. It is possible to write a book for children that represents prairie culture as diverse and evolving, as shown by *A Prairie Alphabet*, written by Jo Bannatyne-Cuget and illustrated by Yvette Moore (Montreal: Tundra, 1992). This ABC book contains representations of Aboriginal and Hutterite families, for example, and the changing family farm is shown in the contemporary machinery featured in several illustrations. The book also shows the centrality of women's work, depicting women in both traditional and non-traditional roles and showing them as equal partners in the family, thus working against standard constructions of prairie space as an exclusively male domain. For a discussion of male and female spaces on the prairies, see Robert Kroetsch, "The Fear of Women in Prairie Fiction: An Erotics of Space," in *The Lovely Treachery of Words* (Toronto: Oxford University Press, 1989), 73-83. For one reply to Kroetsch, see Aritha van Herk, "Women Writers and the Prairie: Spies in an Indifferent Landscape," in *A Frozen Tongue* (Sydney, Australia: Dangeroo Press, 1992), 139-51.

13. Dainotto, "All the Regions," 505.

14. Ursula Kelly, *Marketing Place: Cultural Politics, Regionalism, and Reading* (Halifax: Fernwood, 1993), 79.

15. Jim Wayne Miller, "Anytime the Ground Is Uneven: The Outlook for Regional Studies and What to Look Out For," in *Geography and Literature: A Meeting of the*

Disciplines, ed. William Mallory and Paul Simpson-Housley (Syracuse: Syracuse University Press, 1987), 3.

16. Courtney Milne, *Prairie Dreams* (Grandora, SK: Earth Vision, 1989).

17. Sharon Butala, *The Perfection of the Morning: An Apprenticeship in Nature* (Toronto: HarperCollins, 1994).

18. Randall Roorda, *Dramas of Solitude: Narratives of Retreat in American Nature Writing* (Albany: State University of New York Press, 1998).

19. Ibid., 199.

20. Sharon Butala, "The Reality of the Flesh," in *Writing Saskatchewan: 20 Critical Essays*, ed. Kenneth G. Probert (Regina: Canadian Plains Research Centre/University of Regina, 1989), 98.

21. I would further argue that this simplification is one reason for the popularity of *The Perfection of the Morning*: urban audiences can have their cake and eat it too, at once fulfilling an escape fantasy and also having their own urban superiority affirmed. The desire of urbanites for a wilderness escape can clearly be seen at any shopping mall, where sport utility vehicles crowd the parking lot while their owners rush to Eddie Bauer stores.

22. See an account of this incident in Roger Gibbins and Sonia Arrison, *Western Visions: Perspectives on the West in Canada* (Peterborough, ON: Broadview, 1995), 37.

23. Dennis Gruending, ed., *The Middle of Nowhere* (Saskatoon: Fifth House, 1996).

24. Kathleen Norris, "Can You Tell the Truth in a Small Town?" in *Dakota: A Spiritual Geography* (Boston and New York: Houghton Mifflin, 1993), 79-88.

An Interdisciplinary Approach to the Role of Climate in the History of the Prairies

Gerald T. Davidson

WHEN WE THINK about the Prairies, one of the first defining features that comes to mind is aridity. The Prairies always impressed new arrivals by their scarcity of trees, which has been, throughout human history, a primary mark of aridity. Yet when we attempt to define the Prairies in terms of their lack of moisture, we run immediately into problems. All parts of the Prairies are not equally dry. And we are learning that the general climate has been changing dramatically, even in recent years.

In part because the environmental definitions of the Prairies shift with time, and because perceptions of the Prairies are subject to cultural biases, Gerald Friesen[1] has suggested that environmental models no longer provide a meaningful framework for defining the Canadian Prairies (or the northern Great Plains). This is in clear contrast to the work of Walter P. Webb,[2] who suggested some sixty years ago that aridity is the primary determining factor for the human societies on the Great Plains. Webb, however, was writing mainly about the southern region of the US Great Plains, and much of his analysis of the environment must be modified for the northern regions. So it is appropriate that we re-examine the environmental models, particularly climatic models, to find where they fit in the current definition of the northern Prairies.

Webb's definition of the Great Plains is formulated in terms of their general aridity. But aridity has little influence on many human activities, such as the development of cities and mechanized transportation systems. Both human societies and ecological communities have found ways to adapt to the average climate. As the Prairies become more urbanized, aridity becomes less and less relevant. So, too, with the cold winters. While people on the Northern Plains joke about cold winters, by and large they have made the necessary adaptations. But there is one climatic and ecological event that leaves an imprint on both urban and agricultural societies: drought. Sustained droughts push the agricultural and ecological systems over the edge and cause profound displacements of people and ecological groups. I suggest here that one factor that has not been fully appreciated is the susceptibility of the Northern Plains to cyclical prolonged droughts, lasting many years. (While the terms Great Plains, Northern Plains, and Prairies are often used interchangeably, I prefer to use the notion of the *Great Plains* as defining a special ecological region, and the *Prairies* as a geographical, historical, and social construct.)

If historians, ecologists, and climate researchers are to find effective ways to deal with drought, we must formulate new approaches to the occurrence of temporal cycles. While cycles have not always been fashionable in historical research, they form an essential part of the methodology of ecological and climatic research. We must find common methods for dealing with natural phenomena that repeat at fairly regular intervals. The Prairies do not exist in a static environment, with deviations that might be explained by simple chance or probability. The cyclic climate variations may be as important as the general aridity. The interior regions of North America have experienced significant long-duration climate changes in recent centuries, and those changes may have had intricate consequences for the history of the region.

The problems in dealing with climate change are exacerbated by the brevity of the historical data. I offer below a discussion of the types of data encountered in studies of historical climates, the implications of tree-ring data to droughts on the Prairies, and some of the scientific and historical evidence for prolonged droughts in the nineteenth century.

Climatic Effects on History

Of the events that shaped European Americans' perception of the Great Plains environment, two especially stand out. The first was the journey of Zebulon Pike, in 1810, of which he noted that the central Great Plains "in time … may become as celebrated as the sandy desert of Africa." Again, in the late 1850s, another explorer, John Palliser, visited the Canadian portion of the Great Plains. Palliser's reports, too, expressed doubts that the area immediately north of the US-Canada border, in what is now Saskatchewan and Alberta, could ever support agriculture.[3] The regions the explorers saw have become rich farming lands. That not all early visitors to the Prairies saw an arid wasteland is evident in the journals of Lewis and Clark, who were impressed by the apparent fertility of the land. On his return voyage down the Missouri, Merriwether Lewis recorded many overcast, rainy days, accompanied by rivers running full in late July and early August.

How were perceptions of the Prairies so dramatically transformed between the time of Palliser's explorations and the onset of extensive settlement after 1865? The reports of Pike and of Stephen Long, who followed a route slightly south of Pike's from 1819 to 1820, which led to the designation of the "Great American Desert," are often mentioned in terms that suggest the early explorers were fools, or at least ignorant of the nature of true deserts. A partial vindication of Pike and Long comes from analyses of climate variations evidenced by tree rings, showing that the Great Plains experienced nearly a decade of dry years, centred on about 1810.[4] A few years earlier, Lewis and Clark had passed along the upper Missouri River during a brief hydrological optimum period. The drought on the southern Great Plains (which were the focus of Pike's and Long's explorations) was perhaps more severe than on the Northern Plains, and comparable to the droughts of the 1930s. The drought was not confined to the Plains; at the same time the Southwest Deserts were experiencing a long period of aridity more intense than anything noted in the twentieth century.[5]

The Northern Railroad Survey of 1853-1854, led by Isaac Stevens[6] across the northern United States, must also be mentioned, because it preceded the Palliser expedition by only a few years. The motives and objectives of that expedition were different from Palliser's, so the aridity was not stressed in official reports. It may be significant, however, that Stevens took special care to note whenever the river bottoms had sufficient water for railroad operations and timber for firewood. It was also noted that some of the rivers and streams on the Plains dried up in the summer and fall. The drawings of John Mix Stanley, who accompanied the expedition as photographer and artist, indicate the presence of trees, though they were perhaps not as dense as they are today. Though the report is not specific about lack of moisture, it is generally consistent with Palliser's report. A critical re-reading of the Stevens and Palliser reports might shed much light on the interplay of European-American value systems in forming attitudes toward the Prairies.

Whatever the basis for the widespread view of the Prairies as a region unsuited for agriculture, settlement on the northern US and Canadian Prairies was delayed for many decades. Immigrants hurried across the Great Plains with little thought of staying. Thousands passed through on their ways to Oregon, California, and the Rocky Mountains, but left only a scattering of settlements that sprang up along the way to serve the needs of travellers.

Issues of climatic effects on history have proven elusive because they involve data from several distinct disciplines, whose methods and objectives are not always compatible. On the scientific side, we have masses of supposedly quantitative data, which can be interpolated over time and space because the instruments and techniques of measurement are assumed to be well understood. Historical data, conversely, have been regarded as subject to great uncertainties because of language differences, missing records, and so forth. This view is greatly over-simplified, but, nonetheless, both bodies of data must be structured in such a way that their applicability to historical problems is well understood. When the data are properly categorized and calibrated, we will have a foundation for understanding climate and history.

I find it useful to categorize the types of data as *primary*, *secondary*, and *tertiary*. Primary data are quantitative measurements derived from instrumental records. For example, temperature and precipitation can be measured directly with relatively primitive instruments. If we know what instruments were used in the past, we can calibrate such data so that the records spanning hundreds of years are equivalent to what might have been measured using present-day instruments.

Secondary data are those that involve an additional calibration step, so that one variable can be derived from measurements of another. The vague designation "proxy data" has been commonly used for both secondary and tertiary data; there is, however, a profound operational distinction between the two. Secondary data are those for which a quantifiable calibration model exists, within a broad theoretical framework. Calibration in this case generally invokes a theoretical model of the response to climate parameters, and the existence of base points for which there exist the pertinent primary data. Thus, data on the spacings of tree rings can be used to infer climate parameters such as precipitation and temperature of the past.

Secondary data are generally quantitative, though their applicability may be limited by the imprecision of the data and the inadequacies of the models. Such data are not limited to instrumental data and laboratory measurements. For example, measures of global or regional climate change can be inferred from the growth or recession of mountain glaciers.[7] Though old drawings and photographs give only a rough idea of the exact extent of the glaciers, comparisons of maps and pictures over many years yield an approximate index of climate variability. In this example there exists a quantifiable but imprecise model that can be applied to calibrate data of an historical nature.

Primary and secondary data are those data that fit within the current scientific and historical paradigms of climate change.

Tertiary data are those for which there is as yet no quantifiable calibration model; moreover, their place in the paradigm of climate change is inadequately understood. These are the data that pose the greatest difficulties of interpretation, since they could be used to infer either climate changes, or the impact of climate on history. The use of such data has occasionally caused controversy because it is not always clear what problem is being addressed. An illuminating example is the monumental work of LaDurie,[8] who used chronicles of wine harvests, advances and retreats of forests and glaciers, and other such data to reconstruct the climate in Europe over hundreds of years. Some such data could be elevated to the status of secondary data, given a model based on appropriate calibration points in the past, but the work of LaDurie has not been fully accepted, either by scientists or historians.

Many kinds of scientific data have been invoked in the study of climate. Primary data are usually inadequate beyond the past hundred years. Only secondary data permit the reconstruction of climate hundreds to thousands of years in the past. Among these are: growth patterns and isotopic composition of tree rings; the composition of sediments deposited in lakes and on coastal plains; evidence of the retreat of mountain glaciers; isotopic composition and thickness of layers in ice cores from continental and mountain glaciers; and growth of corals and long-lived marine organisms.

The list is ordered roughly in order of decreasing application to the Prairies. The data from these sources are generally consistent and well correlated with historical evidence.[9] Tree rings are especially useful in analyzing periods of drought, when there is inadequate moisture reaching woody plants during the growing season.

Tertiary data regarding indirect influences, such as the difficulty of transportation and communications through the snow-blocked mountain passes, should not be overlooked in studies of the Great Plains.[10] These could have been very important to the first contacts between European Americans and Native Americans, and to the patterns of settlement by European Americans before 1900.

The overwhelming climatic event of the past several hundred years was the Little Ice Age, a cool period that began about 1550 and lasted until the

mid-nineteenth century.[11] The Little Ice Age was coincident with a period
of unusual solar activity, called the "Maunder Minimum," when there was
a pronounced deficiency of sunspots on the sun.[12] The role of the sun in
determining climate at periods of hundreds of years is not understood, but
it may be related to changes in the electromagnetic processes that drive the
circulation of the sun's outer layers. Electromagnetic fields and charged
particles produced at the sun can dramatically influence the earth's iono-
sphere and upper atmosphere; auroral displays are one manifestation of this
influence. The Little Ice Age may have been related to a cyclic phenomenon with a mean period of several hundred years.

Cycles of droughts appeared throughout the Little Ice Age and have
continued up to the present time. Their occurrence appears sporadic or
irregular because of the complexity of the atmospheric and oceanic circulation system. Nonetheless, present understanding of the mechanisms of
climate change, reinforced by the physical models, leads us to believe that
some long-period phenomena may exhibit regular cycles.

Prolonged droughts occur when there is insufficient moisture several years
in succession. These show up clearly in measurements of the widths of tree
rings. Figure 1 shows temperature and precipitation records for the Northern Great Plains, redrawn from the analysis of tree rings by Fritts and Shao.[13]
Shaded bars have been added to the figures to indicate the periods of drought;
the degree of shading indicates roughly the severity of the drought. The
temperature has been plotted as a dashed line, to indicate the degree of
correlation with the precipitation. Generally, when the years become drier
they also become warmer, which exacerbates the effect of drought on plants.
At first sight the record appears to suggest that droughts occur in cycles,
perhaps lasting tens of years. A standard technique for analyzing such data is
spectral analysis, which yields an auto-correlation function or power spectrum. The peaks in the power spectrum correspond to periodic components of the data. When several-hundred-year runs of data are analyzed, the
Great Plains precipitation records are found to exhibit evidence of a cycle
of thirty-three to thirty-seven years; there is also evidence for a weaker
cycle at nineteen to twenty years. The precipitation records for the southwest deserts also show cycles with periods near thirty-three years, but they
are not as pronounced as the cycles on the Plains.

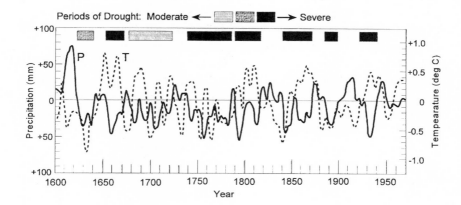

Figure 1: Reconstructed temperature and precipitation for the northern Great Plains, extracted from the work of Fritts and Shao

Several periodic or nearly periodic natural phenomena have been identified that might influence the climate and weather over intervals ranging from years to hundreds of years. The eleven-year sunspot cycle is very regular, and evidence has been accumulating in recent years that it may be linked to climate, but the physical cause-and-effect mechanism remains unknown. (That a thirty-three-year drought cycle comprises three sunspot cycles is almost certainly a coincidence; there is no known or hypothetical mechanism that could result in such a triple period.) The direct influence of the sunspot cycle is probably weak. Of more significance are cycles that affect the circulation patterns of the Pacific and Atlantic oceans. The El Niño Southern Oscillation (ENSO) results from a change in the circulation of the equatorial Pacific Ocean, with periods of about four to seven years.[14] The ENSO events are recognized mainly by shifts in the wind and precipitation patterns along the western coasts of North and South America. A less well-known but equally important circulation cycle is the North Atlantic Oscillation (NAO), which results from changes in the oceanic circulation near Greenland. The NAO has a period similar to the ENSO, and mainly affects northern Europe. Either of these could have produced a weak signal in the data shown above, but such a supposition cannot yet be verified.

It has been suggested by H.H. Lamb that variations in the inclination of the moon's orbit could influence the circulation of the northern oceans,

thereby weakly driving the atmospheric circulation.[15] This happens because the moon's orbit wobbles; the line of nodes where the orbital plane
crosses the ecliptic rotates with a period of 18.6 years. Approximately every
18.6 years the greatest tidal ranges are reached in the northernmost ocean
basins as the declination of the moon reaches a maximum near the time of
the equinoxes. Doubling that period leads to a thirty-seven-year variation,
consistent with the drought cycles on the Great Plains; the difference between thirty-seven years and the derived period of thirty-three minus seven
years is within the uncertainty of the data analysis. It is not clear, however,
why the cycles are strongest at the double period. This may be because the
resonance is sharpest when 37 tropical years = 13,514.0 days coincides
with 38 eclipse years = 13,518.8 days. Further support comes from reports
of 34.8-year cycles reported for European weather,[16] and 36-year cycles in
China.[17]

The idea of a lunar tidal influence on droughts on the Great Plains is
consistent with the reported presence of an anomalous high-pressure zone
that formed in the North Pacific from 1841 to 1860. Such a high-pressure
region can block the flow of humid air from the ocean, so the summer
weather on the Northern Plains would be dominated by dry continental
air. The Southern Plains generally receive moist air from the Gulf of
Mexico,[18] so this mechanism is less effective there. Indeed, one might de-
duce that the Southern Plains, being closer to maritime air flows and more
strongly influenced by the relatively short El Niño cycle, are not so suscep-
tible to long-lasting droughts.

At the end of the Little Ice Age there was a long moisture-deficient
period from 1840 to the mid-1860s. The evidence from the Palliser reports
and other historical evidence indicate there was indeed a long, deep drought
on the Northern Plains.

Were the severe droughts of the nineteenth century a final climatic spasm
marking the end of the Little Ice Age? In the twentieth century the cycles
have become less distinct and the intervals between severe droughts may
have increased. Over recent decades the alternating cycles of moist and dry
years have been replaced by a gradual warming trend, which has been
referred to as "global warming."[19] Well-founded predictions of the climate
trends through the twenty-first century, based on changes in the atmosphere caused by man-made pollutants, indicate that the warming trend
will continue to the point where it affects human activities. The implications of global warming are so momentous that we must examine the
records of past climate fluctuations to obtain insights about how agricultural production, forestry, and eco-systems might be affected.

Interpreting the Historical Record

Despite a widespread awareness of short-term climate variations, the decade-long climatic deterioration at the time of Pike's exploration was overlooked or ignored. The profound deterioration on the Great Plains, lasting from about 1840 to 1865, has gone largely unnoticed in historical commentaries. Palliser went west to the Canadian Prairies during the deepest years of that drought. The recovery and improvement in the 1870s, on the other hand, was acknowledged because it coincided with the prevailing mythology. At that time we began to hear such notions as "rain follows the plough." That idea, which formed the basis for an entire system of agriculture, was justified by seemingly reasonable theories that turning up the sod prevented the escape of moisture from the soil.[20] The settlers were disillusioned by new, briefer droughts in the 1890s, but that did not prevent further waves of homesteading in the early twentieth century. The return of droughts in the 1920s and 1930s finally killed the US homesteading era and most of the dry-farming fads, but even then there was nothing like a return to the prolonged drought conditions of seventy-five years earlier. The prevailing trend throughout the twentieth century has been toward a moister, warmer climate on the Northern Plains.

Generally, the effects of long-term climate change on human cultures and institutions have gone unrecognized because of masking by the much stronger short-term variability. Apart from the work of LaDurie and the *annaliste* school of France, historians of the West and the Prairies have not yet devised a methodology that could be effectively used to integrate historical and climatological studies over periods of tens of years or more.

The historical record of climate changes on the Prairies is frustratingly incomplete. We have none of the extensive records of grain and grape harvests collected by LaDurie. Even those Native Americans who practised agriculture on the Prairies did not keep almanacs or year-to-year chronicles. Among the potentially useful data are:

1. Oral traditions of Native Americans, noting particularly crop failures, famines, migrations to seek improved conditions, and influxes of other peoples.

2. Reports of agents responsible for managing and securing the well-being of Native American tribes.

3. Oral traditions and other reports of scarcity or plenitude of game. The populations and movements of bison, deer, smaller mammals, and birds

are only indirect indicators of climate, but widespread drought could cause them to shift their ranges.

4. Archaeological evidence of living conditions, revealing, for instance, the types of foods consumed by late prehistoric people.

5. Archaeological evidence of abandonment of settlements.

6. Archaeological evidence of mortality patterns among relatively sedentary peoples. Collecting this kind of data has become more difficult because of concerns for the sensitivities of Native peoples, but data exist from many studies in the past.

7. Records of river levels by travellers and explorers. Especially useful would be the logs of boats ascending and descending the great rivers.

8. Reports detailing railroad operations might also be useful because they present a day-to-day record for a broad slice across the country.

9. Stories of difficulties traversing mountain regions during the winter.

10. Descriptions of vegetation by explorers.

11. Old illustrations—particularly paintings, sketches, and photographs—showing vegetation along the rivers and streams. Trees grow so slowly on the Great Plains that the effects of prolonged drought could be evident twenty or more years afterwards.

12. Records of agricultural productivity after the 1860s.

These mostly fall in the category of tertiary data. Developing a suitable methodology is beyond the scope of this essay. I will, however, present several examples, mainly related to the retardation of vegetation, to show that the mid-nineteenth-century drought may have had important effects lasting down to the end of the century.

Settlement and the development of agriculture throughout human history have been strongly conditioned by the lack of moisture whenever agriculture reaches its marginal limits.[21] The interpretation of the influences of climate on history requires that we first understand fully the implications of the scientific data pertaining to drought and agricultural productivity. Such data usually only indicate trends in a single variable. We do not have, as yet, a single climate indicator that would fold together annual averaged temperature, annual moisture available for growth of vegetation, length of the growing season, and severity of winters. We must, therefore, pick our way very carefully though the mass of data that have been collected.

We must also be wary of assuming a strict correlation between drought and elevated temperature. The popular perception of drought as occurring in very hot years may not always be valid. The distribution of moisture depends upon regional and global atmospheric circulation patterns.[22] On the Prairies there appears to be an inverse correlation of yearly average temperatures and precipitation, in which hot years are correlated with dry years (see Figure 1). We must also be careful to understand that an elevation of the annual average temperature does not necessarily mean hotter summers.

Among the many variables that must be considered is the atmospheric circulation during the winter. Rapid or premature melting of winter snows could reduce the amount of moisture available in the soil. This is an especially important concern on the northern Great Plains, where chinook or foehn winds are often regional in extent.[23] In other regions of more complex terrain, foehn winds are mostly local phenomena, affecting only a band several kilometres wide at the leeward foot of a mountain range. On the Northern Plains between latitudes of forty-seven degrees and fifty-three degrees, these warm winter winds frequently extend as far as western Saskatchewan, several hundred kilometres east of the Rocky Mountains.

The implications of future global warming to the Prairies of North America are especially problematical. It should not be assumed that a warming trend will result in diminished annual moisture. Since the expected warming trend is caused by agents never seen before, its effects could be quite different from warm episodes and droughts of the past. It is possible that the first signs of global warming in some regions, where the circulation is dominated by adjacent mountain ranges, would be enhanced precipitation, which, if it occurs mainly during the winter, might result in local cooling.

When we turn to written reports of the European American travellers and settlers, we are often presented with sporadic, detailed reports interrupted by long, blank, intervening years. The reports of explorers are intriguing, but they are compromised by the limited duration of the time the explorers stayed. Would Pike, Long, and Palliser have altered their judgements if they had remained long enough to see the resumption of adequate rainfall? For purposes of climate assessment, the reports of farmers, military garrisons, Indian agents, and more-or-less permanent residents are probably more useful. In the annual reports of the US Commissioner of Indian Affairs we find many tantalizing reports by individual agents across the Prairies. For instance, Thomas Fitzpatrick noted in 1851 that a trip from St. Louis to the Arkansas River was agreeable "with the exception of a very unusual scarcity of water, a deprivation which is often attended with disastrous consequences in the wilds of the West."[24] Several years later conditions were apparently much improved, and it was reported that the Arikaras and Mandans had expressed "a wish that no more corn should be brought them; ... they raised enough for their own use and a large quantity to sell ...."[25] But at the same time, the Indian agents were also reporting a rapid decline of the bison herds, long before the intensive slaughter of the 1870s.

It is not known whether John Palliser was influenced by assessments of the value of the "Great American Desert." Palliser spent several seasons exploring the Prairies, accompanied by experienced scientists and natural- ists. The words of their reports read very much like those of Pike, several decades earlier: "Sterile, or with scanty pasturage. ... Sage and cactus abound, and the whole of the scanty vegetation bespeaks of a scanty climate," or "The true arid district ... acquires even very early in the season a dry parched look."[26] Palliser's descriptions of the vegetation and climate in what is now southern Saskatchewan are quite detailed, and accurately describe arid regions that today lie far to the south in the basins of Wyoming. They are quite inappropriate for present-day Saskatchewan.

The especially severe climatic fluctuations of the early 1860s are marked by events in the US Indian agents' reports. In 1861, which may have been the deepest year of drought on the Northern Plains, waters on the Mis- souri River were so low that ships had difficulty making the trip up to Fort Benton. After the dry year of 1861, the year of 1862 was notable for high waters and spring floods on the Northern Great Plains. In one trip up the Missouri, very high waters were noted as late as the 2nd of June.[27] The moisture, when it did appear in the early 1860s, came at the wrong time, or fell in torrents. About that time we begin to hear about the sad fortunes of the demonstration farm established by the government for the Blackfoot Indians near the Sun River. In 1862 the crops were almost totally destroyed by the floods. At harvest time, the agent reports drily that "the Indians were not impressed by the experiment."[28]

In 1863 the severe drought returned. There must have been very little precipitation during the winter. In that year the upper Missouri was ex- tremely low, even in June. The water was so low that the annuity boat bringing supplies to the Blackfoot Indians was unable to ascend beyond Fort Union.[29] By July the water was even lower, and still falling.[30] If a boat designed for the shallow waters of the Missouri was unable to ascend be- yond Fort Union, about 500 miles below the source, many of the smaller streams feeding the upper Missouri must have been entirely depleted by the end of the summer. The next year, in 1864, the annuity boat was again delayed by extremely low water; this time it was grounded about 150 miles below its destination at Fort Benton.[31] We don't hear much about the demonstration farm on the Sun River, but the agent must not have had much grounds for pride. We do hear that the crops were destroyed in 1864 (or 1865) by rains in May. Again in 1866 we hear that the crops at the demonstration farm failed; this time the excuse was that the fields were "poorly maintained." By 1870 we begin to hear encouraging news that the agency garden was successful, but the next year the crops were damaged by early frost.[32] Apparently, moist conditions had returned, but the temperatures had also fallen.

Old illustrations of recognizable places on the Prairies and adjacent regions show a striking scarcity of vegetation.[33] This has often been noted, and documented recently by K. Johnson, who retraced the route of the Haydn expedition across Wyoming, comparing the photographs of William Henry Jackson with the present vegetation.[34] Other striking examples can be found in the "Rephotographic Survey" work of Mark Klett, et al.[35] Of course, places that now support towns and cities have benefitted from trees planted by the inhabitants, but the changes in vegetation are readily apparent even where humans have not planted or encouraged trees. In both the Prairies and the mountainous regions, the profound change in the vegetation may be largely due to suppression of fires; but we must ask whether a significant part of the changes in vegetation is due to the recovery from the severe droughts of the early and mid-nineteenth century.

Trees are important indicators of climate because of their long lifespans. Trees have an amazing ability to spread and cover the land whenever conditions permit, surviving the occasional unfavourable year with retarded growth rather than perishing. In the fertile, glacially enriched soil of the Northern Plains, there is nothing lacking, except moisture, that would hinder the growth of trees. As late as 6000 to 8000 years ago, several thousand years after the great continental glaciers receded, the entire region was covered by vast forests, extending far southward into the Dakotas and Nebraska.[36] The surrounding forests on the Prairies were eradicated by droughts lasting hundreds of years, much more severe than anything we know today.

Prolonged drought has profound effects on the composition of wooded areas. While droughts may have little effect on mature trees, a lack of moisture in the growing season makes it nearly impossible for young trees to become established. Some years later there is a deficiency of young, semimature trees, and a near-normal number of old and dying trees. Fires, on the other hand, would eliminate the older trees and dead wood, and perhaps encourage new growth. Drought accompanied by fires would leave an extremely attenuated land cover.

There is an abundance of pictorial evidence of former vegetation patterns on the Great Plains, beginning as early as the 1830s. To find evidence useful for reconstructing former climates, we must look to sparsely inhabited places, parks or reserves, and isolated forests of little timber value. For example, the upper Missouri River, from Fort Peck Lake to the town of Fort Benton, is even today scarcely touched by humans. We have an excellent series of illustrations of this region, made by Karl Bodmer in 1833 and 1834. Bodmer's skill was so acute that his paintings of landscape, wildlife, and people can be accepted as historical documents. He made an important pair of paintings from a spot just north of the site of present-day Fort Benton, looking northeastward to the Bearpaw Mountains and southeastward to the Highwood Mountains. In the foreground is the Missouri River, flowing along a course not much different from the course it follows today. The paintings were apparently made in the summer, when the trees could be expected to be full of leaves. Even today there isn't much to betray human presence except a single farm. The trees along the river are definitely thicker and more lush today.

Later in the nineteenth century, photography made it possible to document the West precisely, without the need for drafting skills. Photography travelled westward with explorers, railroad builders, and settlers. The emphasis throughout the 1850s and 1860s was on the scenic grandeur of the mountain West, so we have many photographs of forested places, but few of the Prairies.

One Prairie locale caught the attention of several pioneer photographers: the place where Custer and his soldiers were annihilated near the Little Bighorn River in Montana. At the site of the battle we have an excellent documentary record of the changes in a miniature piece of the Prairies from 1877 to the present. The Little Bighorn River is a small stream, generally no more than about ten to twenty metres broad; but it supports rather abundant vegetation. The early photographs show the river clearly, bordered by rather thin cottonwood trees and brush. A series of photographs was made shortly after the battle, in the spring of 1879, by S.J. Morrow, who accompanied a military expedition charged with cleaning up the battlefield. The river today still runs freely along its valley, unobstructed by dams, but it is everywhere obscured by the trees and brush along its banks. The composition of the woods in the earlier photographs, with sparse growth of mature trees and a deficiency of vigorous young growth, suggests the effects of drought. Other factors might have influenced the growth of vegetation, such as trampling of brush by bison, changes in browsing habits of animals, effects of fires, increased runoff of fertilizer from farms, and the Indians' harvesting of firewood in the earlier days. None of those could explain why trees are everywhere more abundant today. It may also be significant that the river is at the edge of a park area, the Little Bighorn National Battlefield and Cemetery, so this location is perhaps more pristine than many others.

The photographs of the Little Bighorn Battlefield were made long after the severe droughts of the third quarter of the nineteenth century, but trees grow so slowly on the Great Plains that they would still show the effects of prolonged drought for twenty to forty years afterward. The scarcity of trees in photographs taken on the Prairies before 1900 could well be due to the droughts of the mid-nineteenth century.

Fires would have been especially effective during periods of prolonged drought. Whether the depleted composition of the riparian vegetation was due to drought-induced suppression of new growth, or to fires encouraged by drought, is an important issue for further research. One could argue, however, that if fires were the dominant controlling mechanism, they would have left only a few mature trees, rather than an impoverished mix that seems to include trees of nearly all ages except the most recent. It is more likely that the vegetation on the Northern Plains was controlled by both mechanisms. Mountain regions and their surroundings would have been cleared mainly by fires, leaving landscapes bare of both shrubs and mature trees.

The observations of Palliser may be significant to the issue of fires on the Great Plains. Palliser reported a "zone of ancient forest cleared by fire" between the northern forests and the arid plains.[37] Apparently the signs of fire were highly evident during the late 1850s, suggesting that widespread fires had consumed the region since the droughts began in 1840. Part of that zone today embraces the regions around Saskatoon, which are now so humid that, in absence of suppression, widespread fires would be usually quite implausible.

Many kinds of historical records from the Northern Great Plains and Canadian Prairies provide evidence of climatic stress and long-term changes consistent with the scientific reconstructions of past climates. The data are tantalizingly incomplete, perhaps in part because archivists and custodians of collections have not always been aware of the implications of many items. Visual materials, particularly photographs, are often collected for the light they shed on customs or on narrowly limited historical events. Unless it has significant sociological or scenic value, the occasional photograph showing an uninhabited place may be neglected. The examples presented here mainly demonstrate the direct effects of long-term climate change. The implications to the course of history are more elusive. There is a pressing need for a new framework and methodology for dealing with climate change in an historical context; this need exists on both a global scale and a regional scale. The approach must be interdisciplinary and should result in mutual reinforcement of traditional scientific studies, historical studies, social studies, and economic studies. In our region there is an acute need for a new approach, aimed particularly at the study of places where large parts of the historical record are absent.

Several specific problems can be raised regarding the role of climate change on the Prairies. We may ask: What was the role of climate change in the decline and displacement of Native American peoples and the bison? Were European Americans' perceptions of the Prairies, and the Prairies' suitability for agriculture, determined by true and accurate information about the climate? How thoroughly did European Americans take account of climatic variability when they began to settle on the Prairies? What role did the twentieth-century warming trend play in the present economic and social decline of the Prairies?

This last question bears directly on a problem that has occupied many social and historical commentators,[38] and has profound implications to the prospect of global warming. This is an issue that pertains to arid regions everywhere in the twentieth century. Even Fernand Braudel, in his massive study of the social and economic structure of France, comments on the decline of arid and semi-arid regions there.[39] The combined study of history and climate is vital to the survival of present-day economic activities on the Prairies, in the face of an impending episode of global warming, beginning in the second half of the twentieth century.

Endnotes

1. Gerald Friesen, *River Road, Essays on Manitoba and Prairie History* (Winnipeg: University of Manitoba Press, 1996), 164ff.

2. Walter P. Webb, *The Great Plains* (Lincoln, NE: University of Nebraska Press, 1931), 17-33.

3. J.M. Palliser, *The Publications of the Champlain Society—The Papers of the Palliser Expedition 1857-1860,* ed. I.M. Spry (Toronto: Champlain Society, 1968).

4. H.C. Fritts, *Reconstructing Large-Scale Climatic Patterns from Tree-Ring Data* (Tucson, AZ: University of Arizona Press, 1991).

5. For another interpretation of this issue, see M.P. Lawson and C.W. Stockton, "Desert Myth and Climatic Reality," *Annals of the Association of American Geographers* 7, no. 1 (1981): 521-35.

6. I.I. Stevens, *Narrative and Final Report of Explorations for a Route for a Pacific Railroad near the Forty-Seventh and Forty-Ninth Parallels of North Latitude from St. Paul to Puget Sound* (Washington, DC: War Department), 1855.

7. For some representative examples see J.M. Grove, *The Little Ice Age* (London: Methuen, 1988).

8. E.L.R. LaDurie, *Times of Feast, Times of Famine, A History of Climate Since the Year 1000,* trans. from the French *Histoire de Climat Depuis l'an Mil* (New York: Farrar, Strauss, and Giroux, 1971).

9. Ibid.

10. For an interesting account of how winter snows affected the development of a small mountainous region of Colorado, see D.A. Smith, "A Country of Stupendous Mountains: Opening the Colorado San Juans, 1870-1910," in *The Mountainous West, Explorations in Historical Geography*, ed. W. Wyckoff and L.M. Dilsaver (Lincoln, NE: University of Nebraska Press, 1995), 92-113.

11. H.H. Lamb, *Climate, History and the Modern World* (London, UK: Methuen, 1982).

12. J.A. Eddy, "Climate and the Role of the Sun," in *Climate and History, Studies in Interdisciplinary History* (Princeton, NJ: Princeton University Press, 1981), 146–67.

13. H.C. Fritts and X.M. Shao, "Mapping Climate using Tree-Rings from Western North America," in *Climate Since A.D. 1500*, ed. R.S. Bradley and P.D. Jones (revised, London, UK: Routledge, 1995), 269-94.

14. W.H. Quinn and V.T. Neal, "The Historical Record of El Niño Events," in *Climate Since A.D. 1500*, ed. R.S. Bradley and P.D. Jones (revised, London, UK: Routledge, 1995), 623-48.

15. H.H. Lamb, *Climate, Present, Past and Future*, vol. 1, *Fundamentals and Climate Now* (London, UK: Methuen, 1972).

16. E. Brückner, *Klimaschwankung seit 1700, nebst Bemerkungen über die Klimaschwanjungen der Diluvialzeit* (Vienna: Hôlzel, 1890).

17. Wang, Shao-Wu, and Zhao Zong-Ci, "Droughts and Floods in China, 1470-1979," in *Climate and History, Studies in Past Climates and Their Impact on Man*, ed. T.M.L. Wigley, M.J. Ingram, and G. Farmer (New York: Cambridge University Press, 1989), 271–88.

18. Lamb, *Climate, Present, Past and Future,* 86.

19. See particularly the collection of articles in *Climate Change, The IPCC Scientific Assessment,* ed. J.T. Houghton, G.J. Jenkins, and J.J. Ephraums (New York: Cambridge University Press, 1990); and *Climate Change 1992, The Supplementary Report to The IPCC Scientific Assessment,* ed. J.T. Houghton, B.A. Callander, and S.K. Varney (New York: Cambridge University Press, 1992).

20. D. Bark, "History of American Droughts," in *North American Droughts, AAAS Selected Symposium 15,* ed. N.J. Rosenberg (Boulder, CO: Westview Press, 1978), 9-23.

21. M.L. Parry, "Climate Change and the Agricultural Frontier: A Research Strategy," in *Climate and History, Studies in Past Climates and Their Impact on Man* (1989), 319-38.

22. H.E. Wright Jr., J.E. Kutzbach, T. Webb III, W.F. Ruddiman, F.A. Street-Perrott, and P.J. Bartlein, eds., *Global Climates Since the Last Glacial Maximum* (Minneapolis, MN: University of Minnesota Press, 1993).

23. D. Riley and L. Spolton, *World Weather and Climate* (New York: Cambridge University Press, 1974), see especially 90-95.

24. T. Fitzpatrick, Indian Agent, Reports to Congress, Washington City, 24 November 1851.

25. A.J. Vaughn, Indian Agent, Reports to Congress, Fort Pierre, 19 October 1854.

26. J.M. Palliser, *Papers of the Palliser Expedition,* 18.

27. P.J. DeSmet, Acting Superintendent of Indian Affairs, Reports to Congress, Yankton, Dakota Territory, 8 October 1862.

28. H.W. Reid, Blackfoot Agent, Reports to Congress, 1862.

29. W.P. Dolen, Dakota Superintendent, Reports to Congress, 23 September 1863.

30. Reid, Blackfoot Agent, 1863.

31. Dolen, Reports to Congress, 1864.

32. J. Armitage, Blackfoot Agent, Reports to Congress, 1871.

33. M. Klett, E. Manchester, J. Verburg, G. Bushaw, R. Dingus, and P. Berger, *Second View, The Rephotographic Survey Project* (Albuquerque, NM: University of New Mexico Press, 1984).

34. K.L. Johnson, *Rangeland through Time: A Photographic Study of Vegetation Change in Wyoming 1870-1986,* Wyoming Agricultural Exp. Station, Misc. Pub. 50, Laramie, WY, 1987.

35. M. Klett et al., *Second View,* 62–63.

36. E.C. Pielou, *After the Ice Age: The Return of Life to Glaciated North America* (Chicago: University of Chicago Press, 1991).

37. Palliser, *Papers of the Palliser Expedition.*

38. For an interesting perspective on this issue, see J.C. Stabler and M.R. Olfert, *Restructuring Rural Saskatchewan, The Challenge of the 1990s* (Regina: Canadian Plains Research Centre/University of Regina, 1992).

39. F. Braudel, *The Identity of France,* trans. from the *French L'Identité de la France* (New York: HarperCollins 1986), see especially 674-79.

Indelible Grasslands: Place, Memory, and the "Life Review"

Molly P. Rozum

AAGOT RAAEN'S NORWEGIAN PARENTS migrated to Dakota Territory in 1874, a period when migrants often compared wild big bluestem grasses tousled by wind to the waves they crossed on their transatlantic voyage. Yet, when assigned by a university professor to write a sonnet about the ocean, the land-locked Aagot, who had never seen one, did not think of tall, wild, waving prairie grasses. Instead, she remembered commercial fields and "imagined [an ocean] must be something like the endless stretches of wheat fields in North Dakota."[1] Aagot and other children of the late-nineteenth-century immigrant populations of the Prairie provinces of Canada and the northern Great Plains of the United States differed significantly from their pioneer parents in their geographic perspectives. Migration to the grasslands west and conquest of contested lands would not be central experiences of their adult lives. Instead they—to borrow historian Elliott West's phrase—"grew up with the country" and held their home-places on North America's grasslands as the first landscapes with which to compare all others. Northern grasslands environments "helped shape and define reality itself" for those who matured physically and emotionally in an active engagement with local prairie and plains ecologies: river tree-stands, grain acreages, and forage grasslands.[2]

Relying on the powerful autobiographies of two women, Aagot Raaen and Annora Brown, this essay turns on the relationship of remembered landscapes to the creation of personal and regional "sense of place."[3] Raaen and Brown lived on opposite edges of North America's northern grasslands, in eastern North Dakota and southern Alberta, respectively, but they shared an environmental experience filtered by what historians have called the second great capitalist transformation of the rural countryside. The "endless stretches of wheat fields" Aagot remembered as a turn-of-the-century student were only one sign of this transformation. In the first half of the twentieth century, various US and Canadian governmental policies promoted "industrial goals" in rural life: mechanization, farm consolidation, consumer consumption, and commodity (over)production. Such goals spread slowly across the countryside, simultaneously altering the landscape and abetting rural depopulation.[4]

Life histories set in the context of this gradual, industrial reconfiguration of the northern grasslands began to emerge at mid-twentieth century as the children of late-nineteenth-century immigrants to the region passed into old age. Brown's and Raaen's autobiographies are particularly engaging products of what psychiatrists have called the Life Review process,[5] when aged persons revisit past events through reminiscence, storytelling, and reflection, and suddenly achieve heightened levels of consciousness. As eighty-year-old Annora Brown explained, "For many years I had carefully wrapped my memories in moth balls and had tucked them down into the innermost recesses of my being. Forgotten!" When she began to recall her past, however, "for days it was like living with a poltergeist. Fragmentary memories buzzed about angrily. Occasionally one arrived complete ... but before I could even smile another memory would come hurtling at me with such force as to bring tears to my eyes, leaving me bruised and beaten." She could look back at this stage in life and observe how memories "lay dormant" and get "swollen all out of proportion" at one point, then settle back again to be interpreted differently when one is once again "in a less anxious frame of mind" (*Sketches* 10). Folklorist Patrick Mullen suggests that reviewing life in old age is an act of "maintenance of identity" through the creation of a selective, thematic projection of self.[6]

Life Reviews often reveal microenvironments of intense personal experience impressed in childhood and remembered, formed, and reformed over a lifetime. The review of life, then, also constitutes an act of the creation of place. Scholars have given considerable attention in recent years to both the role of memory in the creation of social and individual meaning[7] and the concept of "region" in history, especially western history.[8] Yet scholars have not explored the contribution of the physical milieu, both to the shaping of "experience"[9] over a lifetime and to the construction of memory. This essay explores how the textures, surfaces, physical properties, the flow and growth of seasons characteristic in a land area as it was constituted at a particular historical moment, inform remembered regional "experience."[10] Environmental attributes *all* affect or "encode" any experience of place. But environment is not a deterministic force or a separate, static, unresponsive, impervious entity. Remembered regional "experience" is as much created *by* individuals as they move through everyday cultural spaces, organized by cultural lifeways, senses recording, interacting all the time. Moreover, not all local landscapes are carried forward; only those landscapes that become bound to identity through the process of re-remembering, again and again, survive over time.

When southern Alberta-born Annora Brown, the child of a Mounted Police officer and a schoolteacher from England, climbed up to her "favourite perch ... on top of the house, near the chimney," she undoubtedly could not remember how she *first* viewed the surrounding prairie. The pervasiveness of such sights during her life, however, would merge to become core to her remembrances.[11] Writing of this choice rooftop spot in the 1970s, long after the establishment and decline of towns such as Fort Macleod, Brown recalled how she "could see the whole world around me." The views she remembered were like panoramic pictures shot over a day, throughout the seasons: "the Porcupine Hills changing in colour and mood with every shift of cloud and sun"; "a fringe of blue mountains reached out in a semicircle"; "the massive, square-topped bulk of Chief Mountain, ... seemed to rise sharply from the prairie"; and "Belly Buttes ... turning blue and pink in the setting sun." Between these two landmarks "a winding trail" had led, back then, to Fort Benton, Montana. "To the east was row upon row of prairie trails worn deeply. ... To the north the tops of the trees in the river bottom; beyond the trees was distance and more distance" (*Sketches* 40).

The vast sky, as it looked from Dakota Territory near the north-flowing Red River, also captivated the Raaen sisters. These young women disliked being closed inside and wished always to see the sky overhead. Entitling the first chapter of her autobiography "The Blizzard," for example, Aagot Raaen used the storm to introduce her and her siblings' collective fascination with the outdoors, especially the sky. She and her two sisters fight and push each other to be in front of "the only window in the log cabin" to see little birds frantically flock in search of safety from the impending storm. Aagot recalled how, when they built a playhouse outdoors, her little sister begged her to leave the house roofless, substituting the "leaf-covered branches" rising far above into the sky as the roof, because "through them we can sometimes see the stars or a bit of red sunset." "The outdoors never said 'Don't,'" Aagot's sister believed. How much the sky permeated their thinking emerges even in housecleaning. As a part of the usual round, the sisters refurbished their flour-sack bed-tick with fresh hay. Aagot recalled how on the way back indoors with the newly stuffed mattress, they "balanced it on their heads and steadied it with their hands," imaginatively "playing that they were carrying the sky into their house and upstairs" (*Grass* 3, 24, 64, 45).

Sky vastness, viewscapes, or Brown's "blue distance" (*Sketches* 31) infused with seasonal kaleidoscope colours, combined with the particular language of memoir writing, lend a pronounced visual aura to these memories as texts. To write is to draw scenes, to frame stories, and to build a setting. Aagot Raaen wrote how "One by one, indelible pictures, stamped on my very being, crowded out everything else until I began to put them in writing." Through memory, she explained how she "lived again dramatic scenes and events of the old neighborhood" (*Grass* xxxi). She also wrote her personal history in the third person, suggesting a photograph-like distance between subject and object, life and memory. Similarly, to construct her narrative, Annora Brown positioned herself "floating" above, looking through an "'inward eye' of memory" as if "looking down on a different planet" (*Sketches* 55, 194, 223). These techniques and phraseology reinforce the apparent dominance of the optic or visual sense in memory and recall.[12]

More than still-life images, however, were impressed upon their childhood and developing minds. The "distance and more distance" Annora Brown viewed from her perch *moved* "often miragelike ... never static," interacting with her retinas, producing scenes both real and illusory. She *felt* the everblue hot summer atmosphere as it "weighted" on her skin. The homemade mattresses that Aagot Raaen and her sisters imagined as the sky *smelled* "sweet" when stuffed with new-mown hay (*Sketches* 40–41; *Grass* 66, 187). Environmental "experience," rather than simply a remembered photographic view, is multi-sensual, relying on *all* the senses: sight, to be sure, but also touch, taste, hearing, and smell. Senses, affected by personal biochemistry and culture, record and filter atmospheric information as it bounces off the land and through space, as it runs into and through objects, until that environmental information finally reaches an interpreting, sensually perceiving individual. The pictures of memory, in short, are alive with the motion of sensual experience. Although smelling, hearing, tasting, and feeling or touching cannot be pictured like views that organize the raw substance of optic sensations, autobiographers reveal that such environmental information is assembled by the other senses in the process of absorbing specific, historic environments. Indeed, the mind and body remember and record this information.

At eighty, Brown described how she could "still recall my sensations as a child." The southern Albertan summer "air was alive" with "haze" and the "ripple [of] heat waves." Her favourite locality, the town's pile of glacial rocks, was hot; her bared feet *touched* hot rocks (*Sketches* 41). Aagot Raaen and her sisters came of age awash in a North Dakotan environmental experience, digging "toes into the cool moist earth," sinking "hot, tired feet . . . into the good earth, so soft" (*Grass*, 135, 136). These young women played *with*, not merely *on*, the ground. Brown recalled one time when she dug down through the geologic strata with her hands and a shovel, from "soft earth" through to "glacial gravel with rocks worn round and smooth" until she ended up with a "twenty-foot-length trench, two feet deep at one end and six feet deep at the other" (*Sketches* 48). Aagot and her sisters "scoop[ed] out an opening in the hillside" and dug "light clay" from the "steep bluffs" along the river, then shaped it, and baked it in the sun (*Grass* 46-47). As active, playful children, Annora Brown and Aagot Raaen not only recorded photograph-like views; they *created* environmental experiences that they would later recall.

Annora Brown's hands felt petals, blades of grass—coarse, fine, and seed-laden—sticky stems, and the pricks of pointy leaves. Wandering the prairie with bare feet, she hunted "shooting stars [with reddish violet reflexed petals], sleep heads, [and] buffalo beans." She watched in May for the "dainty hood's phlox that formed mats of white blossoms against mosslike foliage." The "scent of wild roses and [silver-yellow] wolf willow boiled up" out of the river bottoms into the upland prairies. June air filled up with the "scent of wheat" and the "smell of melting snow," while the "fat furry buds of prairie anemone" (crocus flowers) dotted the new-growth short grasses. Annora's feet ran over miles of "prairie wool" short grass and through scattered "sandy dust pits" (*Sketches* 41, 6, 31, 135, 172). The Raaen children also rejoiced as the budding of pasque flowers and buttercups indicated warm weather. Amidst the melting snow of spring, the girls ran barefoot all day and "ate what nature had to offer—young shoots of grapevines, fresh sorrel from the ground, tender budding basswood leaves, the bark of young branches on the chokecherry bushes," and a variety of nuts too. "I must have some sour grass!" Aagot shouted from the pages of her memoir as she recalled the sharp taste. She and her siblings sipped "sweet drips from the box elders" out of tree-bark cups or "drank deep" of the spring through "a hollow reed" used as a straw. They gathered "moss, green hazelnuts, leaves, roots, [and] bark" to use as colouring in homemade dyes for homespun clothes. While Aagot picked berries, the air softly resounded with the "swish" of the sickle and the odour of "new-mown" grasses that wafted up, first from the meadow, then from the prairie (*Grass* 26, 180, 141, 11, 66).

Each new season brought new sensuous experiences. Raaen remembered how winter months could be "so cold that the snow felt like sand underfoot." She recalled how "snow water did not taste good" (*Grass* 54, 6). Blizzards of winter "whistled and banged against the windows" of Brown's family home, while the grasses outside and the house itself "wailed" to their force. She recalled distinctly how, as she ventured out-of-doors during a blizzard, the winds threw "spirals of icy particles" against her, blinding her. The "freezing wind" burned her (*Sketches* 25–26). Similarly, the Raaen girls heard and felt blizzards blow in: the wind "howled," "screeched," "screamed," and "whistled" while the cabin "shook" (*Grass* 5, 8, 58–59). Aagot described the "drowsy numbness" of the body beginning to freeze, how the "stinging cold . . . bit her face," and the white of her temporarily inert "frost-bitten limbs." But she also recalled how she often "walked in a fairy world" from her family home to a country school when "millions of diamonds sparkled on the snow and on the frost covered trees." When "her hands grew numb" on these calm but frigid days, she "had to stop and beat her arms around her shoulders." Nevertheless, only on fiercely cold days would the atmospheric ice crystals transform into beautiful, luminous "sundogs in the sky." "Miles and miles" of countryside passed by the Raaen sisters and their neighbourhood friends on "moonlight nights" from the viewpoint of a bobsled, the air alive, echoing with their "singing" as sound freely moved through unblocked snow-packed spaces, resonating with them as they flew (*Grass* 57, 193–94, 54, 163). On peaceful winter days, Brown remembered how she "nibbled the pith of a rosehip" found here and there in the snow. Warm chinook winds, flowing along the foothills of the Rocky Mountains, melted snow, but also "pushed" Annora along or "bent" her body over, her head "nearly to the ground." As she slowly made her way walking during these times, the clouds arched in "blackness" above a "green-blue sky" (*Sketches* 45, 30–31).

As she wrote and remembered, Brown claimed to "listen" to the sounds of her southern Alberta locality "echoing down the long corridors of memory." The acoustic properties of the prairie made the life of it sound like "some great orchestra." She heard again the summer sounds of fuzzy-textured "transparent" grasshopper wings "scraping" and bees "buzzing," while the tone of the meadowlark's call was "clear" and the curlew's cry "plaintive." The "rustling" of dry winter grasses spoke to the "calls" of meadowlark, horned larks, and sparrows tucked down between clumped blades of grass; these birds harmonized with prairie ponds lapping in the "whir of wings" of geese, ducks, and swans that "honked, chattered, and whistled" (*Sketches* 39, 186, 41). The young Raaen women sat inside a bluff-side dugout, letting local birds "come and go at will," "chattering, questioning, hopping all over them, eating out of their hands and laps." Aagot's sister even learned "bird dialect" and often called in catbird, owl, whippoorwill, robin, and wren until the birds approached close to the family's log house for all to admire (*Grass* 29).

The ecological composition of different localities provided multiple sensual experiences within a given season or climatic situation. In what Brown called the "tree world" of the fertile, flat river bottoms below the prairie, poplar, willow, balm of Gilead, and black birch thickets provided a unique environmental texture. It was in the river tree-stand, Annora recalled, that she learned the scent of "hot sun on green leaves" and the sounds of "toads in the reeds," "water bugs" scurrying, and "water striders" skating. She tasted "mouth puckering but edible" chokecherries, Saskatoon berries, and "vermilion" bull berries, which she knew were ripe for picking when the "bitter smell of frosted leaves" filled the air. "Holding a basket of freshly picked berries . . . is a satisfying sensation. . . . One feels the joy of cupping yet untasted richness," she recalled, as if she could touch the tangles of bush, a plump berry, and the very same basket at the moment of her remembering (*Sketches* 43–45, 74).

While Annora Brown highlighted the taste, smells, and sounds of the berry-bushed terrain, Aagot Raaen described the tactile version of this pervasive "berrying" grasslands experience, showing differences between the prairie and river bottoms, not just in terms of the diverse fruit of regional ecology, but in terms of the vegetation's effects on the human body. She recalled that by the time they picked gooseberries during July, "the skin was thick on the heels and soles of their feet" from work and play out-of-doors. But as gooseberry picking began, the "small sharp needles" on the bushes "stung and scratched" their bodies. Toothed, stinging hairy leaves of "nettles burned their bare legs." In turn, the hardened skin of Aagot and her siblings' limbs—a result of berry picking—served them well as they, in bared feet, hand-raked the ripe-smelling grasses of the meadow into haycocks. When they moved to haying beyond the grazed meadowlands, however, the "sharp grass and stubble" of the unbroken prairie began to "hurt their arms and legs" anew. But Aagot recalled how haying on the prairie brought compensating pleasures, at least "at first," because "the birds and insects of the prairie were different from those in the woods." Away from the shade of the river stands, however, by the time a midday sun shone "well up in the heavens," the family all longed for protection in the "shade of a haycock." Here they "stretched" out on a pad of matted grasses (*Grass* 20–21, 68, 72, 70). "Scratched" bodies and thickened skin from haying,

berrying, and playing, all lingered on the body as reminders of these environments. The skin reacted to such pressures, building up a rough texture
in response to the land, the work, and active play. Feet grew large, spreading
wider until most regular shoes would not fit, Aagot pointed out. Like the
visual, auditory, olfactory, and tactile nature of their memories, the thick,
wide soles of prairie-formed feet would be with northern grasslands children for a lifetime (*Grass* 136, 138).

The response of the body and mind to landscapes provides historicity to
sense of place or regional identity. Through childhood ventures out into
the multiple microenvironments of the grasslands, Aagot Raaen and Annora
Brown *created* their prairie experiences from the sound, feel, sight, and smell
of the prairie ecosystem. Memories of sensuous experience, moreover, not
only varied as Aagot and Annora moved from one ecological locale to
another; "experiences" flowed out of an historically changing ecology. The
prime of Annora Brown's and Aagot Raaen's lives occurred in a time of
gradual consolidation of the rural enterprise system from bases of 160-acre
homesteads to larger farms and ranches, with fewer farmers and ranchers,
and with ever-increasing acreage of the northern grasslands commercially
utilized. Consolidation continued dramatically through the farm depression of the 1920s, the regional drought and dust storms and the world
economic depression of the 1930s, and the mobilization for war in the
1940s. The ecology of North America's northern grasslands shifted from
one of big bluestem, little bluestem, Indian grass, western wheatgrass,
threadleaf sedge, blue grama and buffalo grasses, among other wild, native
grasses, to mainly the ecology of commercially produced wheat, oats, barley, corn, and alfalfa and other forage grasses. As little girls, Aagot and Annora
experienced much of the native unploughed grasslands. Ploughed or grazed
meadows merely dotted the larger grasslands environment of their knowledge. By the time they were elderly adults, however, the grasslands were
well on their way in transformation to a landscape predominantly shaped
by industrializing farm and ranch agriculture. By mid-twentieth century,
the dots interrupting the dominant regional ecology became remnants of
native prairie and plains, even sometimes scantily clad or grassless patches,
rather than the small-acre, oxen-ploughed fields scattered about the environmental context of their girlhood. This moment of capitalist transformation of North America's grasslands becomes clear in closer analyses of two
examples of sites widely experienced during the era of Annora's and Aagot's
childhoods, one of especial memory to each of them.

Annora, her sisters, and other town children played at the edge-of-the-town "Stone Pile," where rocks grew into "a heap on the prairie" as people cleared the land around Fort Macleod. Brown recalled, "my life was spent with rocks. Rocks to throw … to break … for building playhouses … for games—smooth … rough … coloured.… I loved them.… They talked to me in their own language." Her child's imagination mixed the stones, birds, rodents, clumped prairie grass, and "bigger" and "brighter" blue violets, sunflowers, and "long plumed red avens" (known as "prairie smoke" or "old-man's whiskers") into what Annora called, some seventy years later, a "magic playground." Annora herself stood *still* on sun-hot rocks in her remembered account. This seems an unlikely stance for the girl she was then, whom she also records running, turning over stones, checking ground birds' nests, picking flowers, jumping from one hot rock to another. Flowers were, of course, "bigger" and "brighter" in her favourite place simply because she was smaller and also because memory has the capacity to embellish. But they were vivid too because the snow in rock-shaded crevices melted more slowly and provided water much longer there than to those flowers out in the distant grasses. The optimism Brown found in this experience is the child's hope that her very presence could make her favourite prairie flora secure and fixed. But, as Brown acknowledged from her adult narrator's perspective, the stone pile no longer existed at all; it had "long given way to homes and gardens" (*Sketches* 41, 12-13).[13]

The very "piled rocks" that frame Brown's discussion of profound environmental experience nevertheless represent evidence of the capitalist transformation of the era in which she lived. The pile acknowledged, metaphorically, in its creation and growth with the expanding town of Fort Macleod, the displacement of one ecosystem by the economic development of the grasslands ecology towards commercial crops. Even the balcony that provided the little-girl Annora her oft-remembered sky views, a "feature added when the house was enlarged" during the 1910s, symbolized the general prosperity and economic expansion of turn-of-the-century times. Spurts of frenetic building, and the more gradual and ultimately longer-lasting ecological impact of such economic development, transformed the lay of the land. The turn-of-the-century homestead rush and expansion of commercial agriculture increasingly reconfigured an older landscape of corporate-ranch grazelands, which had before reconfigured former Cree and Blackfoot grasslands.[14] As Brown phrased it, "The prairie was shut away," adding in emphasis, "We no longer looked out on a rocky waste and a prairie that stretched to the horizon" (*Sketches* 52). Economic development of town and hinterland alike consigned the girlhood views and the rock pile she prized to memory. From a temporal distance of some sixty years, she could see over historical time, the slides imprinted in her memory, click-flashing through an internal projector, moving closer to the present:"with every house that was built, with every field that was ploughed, the flat expanse of grass was broken"(*Sketches* 40-41).[15]

What the rock pile on the edge of town was to Annora Brown's memory of place, the Goose River wood-stand was to Aagot Raaen's. She recalled that on "weekdays during the summer months when [we] ... were not working ... [we] always played in the woods." Aagot focussed particularly on a remembered riverside "play homestead" created out of the woods of oaks, ash, elms, thornapple bushes, buffalo brush, and willow thickets. Using "dry stumps" prised loose and "dry branches," she and her sisters built the walls of a house by filling in the spaces between four large, leafy trees that grew in a near-square. Small, "fallen and dried out" trees, bark from other trees, and bits and pieces of scrubby brush, buffalo berries, and raspberries became household furnishings and food. From the nearby prairie, the children dragged back sun-bleached "buffalo bones of many shapes and sizes," which became oxen, cows, calves, sheep, lambs, and chickens inhabiting a "dugout" stable the girls hollowed out themselves. The children played farm, complete with three sets of "tree-people" neighbours (seen in the "queer growths," mottled shapes of dead, dry branches), and re-enacted the conversations, community squabbles, rituals of births, deaths, marriages, and the farm routines they witnessed daily (*Grass* 13, 21, 23-24, 177, 40-41, 45-47).[16]

As the Raaen children's parents turned the drought-prone grasslands into commercial pasture and wheat fields, the children turned the remnants of the last wild buffalo into domesticated farm animals, and the brittle, dry, sepia-grey trees into a "home." Imitating through body and behaviour, the Raaen children unconsciously learned the reason for their migration to the prairie. The girls cleared their home-place environment of buffalo bones (a necessary task for preparing commercial agricultural land). With their father, they ploughed and harvested the wild, native prairie grasses for hay. Incorporated into grasslands historical ecology, their own footpaths penetrated the earth. Such ruins overlaid and lay next to topographical traces of Lakota cultures marking the land. One ecosystem replaced another; the Lakota landscapes of buffalo, grass, and sheltering tree-stands were transformed as the Lakota themselves transformed in response to the reservation experience. Similarly, Annora Brown would recall the "buffalo jumps," "circles of rocks," and "clumps of undecayed buffalo hair" in the "rich earth," all reminders of the historical life and land claims of displaced

Blackfoot and Cree, whom she met often in her daily rounds of life (*Sketches* 141–42). [17] With the arrival of new immigrants, like the Raaen and Brown families, and the play of children, such as Aagot and Annora, the nineteenth-century ecological balance of the grasslands, an environmental response to Native American lifeways, began a period of refashioning or transformation in response to the advent of twentieth-century intensive commercial agriculture.

The material linkage between the Raaens' family "log home" and the children's "play house" underscores the historic moment of this transforming grasslands "experience." Both the adult "real" home and the child's "play" house were made from the river-bottom tree-stands. The elemental flora that the Raaen sisters played with in their "imaginary" house did, in fact, become the daily furniture, utensils, and substantial food in the family's "real world" log home. Raaen's father constructed much of the family's furniture and carved many household utensils—spoons, bowls, and brooms—out of the woods near their home. Both Annora Brown and Aagot Raaen processed the berries they picked into daily fare such as sugar, sauce, syrup, and preserves that would provide variety and nutrients essential for "our winter's supply of fruit" or even "to sell for the bare necessities of life" (*Sketches* 43; *Grass* 21, 178). Sleeping indoors on and surrounded by the aroma of products gleaned from the land, and living inside and outside surrounded by essentially the same environmental materials, as did the Raaen sisters, all mirrored a general melding of ideas and feelings about "inside" and "outside" materials. Only degrees in states of refinement existed between unfettered and crafted "nature." The mix of gleaning, crafting, and industrializing of the land and its products constitutes the historic moment of turn-of-the-century, modern, rural transformation in which the Raaen and Brown families lived. The particular mixes of material life they processed, moreover, infused that "experience" with a regional flavour.

Berry bushes and forbs such as crocuses, buttercups, and avens, even unbroken grasslands, lingered, in reduced and degraded forms, within the grasslands region, as these women wrote and remembered some fifty years later. But the experience of such elements of local ecology as routine, with such high levels of the corporeal, sensuous self in intimate *touch,* changed, gradually, in response to the industrializing environment. New ideas and awareness concerning safety and comfort and items of new, mass manufacture met to change both regional ecologies and the multi-sensual "experiences" of the remnant old, the transformed new grasslands landscapes. "Homespun" clothing, clipped, carded, and knitted from the Raaens' stock of sheep, "chafed and made tender sore spots," "raw spots wherever it touched bare skin." Even the thought of manufactured calico, to be purchased in years ahead, "delighted" Aagot's sister (*Grass* 27, 31–33). Aagot's daily work and play involved exposed, bared feet. If one wore shoes "in the field," those shoes would "wear out" too soon, she attempted to explain to her possibly surprised readers (*Grass* 136, 138). Even though children can still run barefoot on the grass and through wheat fields of the region, the levels of exposure and the land's textures both have changed. So too, then, were the markers of such experience on the body different in degree and kind by the latter twentieth century. So too was the sensuous information altered in output, input, and interpretation. By the time of their writing, both Raaen and Brown also noted how the abundance of berry-heavy bushes no longer remained. Brown explained how "People [in cars] . . . broke the shrubs and trampled the undergrowth . . . bulldozers did the rest. Weeds sprang up where the turf was broken" (*Sketches* 44; *Grass* 178). Walking in blizzards and bobsledding across the land created an entirely different experience of environment than that associated with riding in modern automobiles that eventually even included modern heaters. And while the variety of berries they picked remained as regional treats, they no longer served the same historic, nutritive role they once served. Change conceptualized in this way is always twice-reflexive. That is, new cultural filters changed both the sensuous experience of the landscape and the shape of the land, the makeup of the vegetation, and in turn changed the sensuous experience of the landscape. Although Aagot and Annora could not view the ever-changing landscapes of their childhood in the mid-twentieth-century present with the same imagination, nor even through the same eyes of their childhood pasts, they nevertheless *felt* and carried on their bodies, in their minds, suffusing their very beings, memories of historic multi-sensual experience of grasslands localities.

Geographic sensual experience, impressed in childhood, remembered, and submitted to comparison and variation with later-life encounters, would become entangled with strings of memory. But how do place and memory work together over time? As she wrote, Aagot Raaen experienced an incidence of remembering an act of remembering that provides a clue to this process. This simple story of recall corresponds to what Annora Brown referred to as unanalyzed "impressions" from childhood lying "dormant," available to be used for a continuum of elastic meanings (*Sketches* 47, 56–57). As Aagot stood staring at a course list one day at Normal School in the late 1890s, a scene from her childhood in the early 1880s came to her. She described her moment of flush recalling in the third person, writing, "Pictures etched into her memory long ago came to life. She heard herself once more making up stories about the stars to satisfy [her sister] Kjersti. Far [her father] had helped them locate the Big Dipper, the North Star, and the Pleiades. She saw herself again lying flat on her back on top of the haystack looking up at the sky." The experience of remembering her simple girlhood wonderings led her, as a student, to take an astronomy course to learn more about "the heavens" she had thought about so often (*Grass* 209). Annora Brown's autobiography reveals a similar layering, or chance reinforcement of selected memories. Working in art school under Arthur Lismer, a member of the famed Canadian Group of Seven nature painters, she recalled that Lismer often teased her. "You Westerners," he said, would miss "a fifty dollar bill lying at your feet," adding, "You would be too busy looking at the distance." "All that met our eyes was distance," she recalled again the original moment of self-recognition, remembering how, back then, she remembered girlhood events that found truth in Lismer's observation (*Sketches* 154-55). Remembering reinforced these already "etched" pictures in the mind, transferring them and their meaning to an adult context. Further, the more scientific understandings of the sky Raaen learned, and the perspective Brown gained as a trained artist, supplemented the imaginative "experiences" of girlhood and added another layer of meaning—without destroying the old—that would be carried forward to the time some fifty years later, when Aagot and Annora finally committed them to Life Review and formal autobiography.

Aagot's memoir revealed that she re-remembered the scenes of the Goose River locality many times as she began her teaching career at the turn of the century. During one of her first significant stays away from home, she worked for a term at the Oak Grove High School for Girls just outside Fargo. At Oak Grove she felt comforted by the "forest of natural trees—oaks, elms, ash, box elders, [and] familiar bushes" against the Red River; they had been her "friends as far back as she could remember." Encountering another river wood-stand with similar ecology provided an opportunity for remembering the familiar environment of comfort, an anthropomorphism similar to the twisted tree-limb people she invented in her childhood. While working on her BA degree at the University of Wisconsin, she often "stole up on the campus [after midnight], threw herself on the cool grass, listened to the wash, wash, wash of Lake Mendota and looked at the stars overhead till she was calmed and rested." Many years later, in the 1920s, she recalled how, as an adult, "She was suddenly possessed with a wild desire to run away into the woods." Ending her autobiography, she wondered, significantly, at the "reflections of bare elm trees on leaf-covered ground," asking, "'Will I be able to take this cherished picture with me into eternity?'"[18]

During the 1920s, Annora Brown reinforced and reformulated her girl-hood attachments to the local landscapes, or, as she once called it, "my dry prairie." She returned to "the outskirts of town to sit on the prairie" where she could sink her "spirit deep into the earth and the distance." Brown re-experienced the place by sleeping on the "open prairie ... under the stars" during sketch outings. She ate meals made from "everything ... edible— the early shoots of cow parsnip, the springtime shoots of bracken, the roots of balsmorhiza.... Berries ... mushrooms, puff balls, and shaggy manes were a delight." In the 1930s, while spending many hours "crawling about on hands and knees, wiping up the layers of dust that had gathered on floor and table" of her home, she also "took myself out onto the prairie when the wind was blowing or about to blow." "As I stood on the peaceful, sunlit prairie," she recalled, "I would see, bearing down on me from the north, a sky-high cloud of reddish-black dust." A west wind "wild and gusting" was still, as in her childhood, "almost impossible to stand against." Chinook "gales" roared out of the west and "tore along the surface of the earth." The disappointments and bleakness of the 1930s, as a result of her melding of past and present views, lay amidst "a country so beautiful." The "great sweep of the plain" surrounding one "dispirited," "sinking," abandoned house could still be "opalescent in the evening light" with "alternate [sun] rays, bounc-ing off some large surface of water or grass." Brown transferred these expe-riences to paintings, "impressions of a corner of the world," focussing on, for example, "a spring flower ... in its relationship with the earth, the grass, the gophers, the melting snow" (Sketches 43, 119-20, 130, 132-33, 57, 139, 219-20). She painted, moreover, in the same bedroom sheltered by the roof on which she had once perched to experience the view.

The alignment towards "industrial goals" over the first half of the twentieth century changed the northern grasslands landscape. In the post-World War II years, a further contraction that rural historians have labelled the "great disjuncture" occurred as modern agribusiness increasingly became the norm.[19] In some real sense, then, Annora Brown and Aagot Raaen did in-deed "look ... down on a different planet" when they remembered the landscapes of their youths. Many of the localities they knew so well had either disappeared, or the spatial organization of communities had been reconfigured once again. In waning years of life, many residents realized, with Annora, "that the country we loved was changing before our very eyes." Though she was on that land for most of the period, Brown asked of Alberta's short grasslands, "Where had you gone when I was not looking?" The changes had been so complete that sometimes it was "difficult to believe that memory is not playing tricks" (*Sketches* 182-83, 69). As a "gray-haired woman," Aagot Raaen described how she returned to the "very hills and woods" of her family homestead, "searching for the spring underneath the bluff, looking for the place where the footbridge used to be, lingering along the footpaths among the trees, gazing with tear-dimmed eyes at the gnarled gooseberry bushes."[20] The earth remained, but the landscape that Aagot Raaen and Annora Brown experienced, and the way of life they structured in and out of its textures, was overlaid by a new, if still rural, grasslands landscape. Their sensuous experiences of the turn-of-the-century northern grasslands era, however, remained with them, recorded in mind and body, and remain available to all as inscriptions on the pages of Life Review autobiographies.

Endnotes

1. Aagot Raaen, *Grass of the Earth* (St. Paul: Minnesota Historical Society Press, 1994 [1950]), 233. Subsequent quotations from this book will be given within parentheses in the text.

2. Elliott West, *Growing Up with the Country* (Albuquerque: University of New Mexico Press, 1989), 45. West makes his argument for the context of the entire Trans-Mississippi US West, while this article utilizes his argument in reference to a binational northern grasslands sub-region of the North American West.

3. Raaen, *Grass*; and Annora Brown, *Sketches from Life* (Edmonton, Alberta: Hurtig Publishers, 1981). Subsequent quotations from *Sketches* will be given within parentheses in the text. Although life reviewers use memory as their key tool, they often reach for personal documents from the period. See also Mss 177, Aagot Raaen Papers, and Mss 8, Aagot Raaen Collection, both at the North Dakota Institute for Regional Studies, Fargo; and No. 83-116, Annora Brown Collection at the BARD facilities of the University of Alberta Archives, Edmonton.

4. Mary Neth, *Preserving the Family Farm* (Baltimore: Johns Hopkins University Press, 1995), 5; Hal S. Barron, *Mixed Harvest* (Chapel Hill: University of North Carolina Press, 1997); and Gerald Friesen, *The Canadian Prairies: A History* (Toronto: University of Toronto Press, 1987).

5. Psychiatrist Robert Butler was the first to write of the "Life Review" as a coherent process in the elderly. See his "The Life Review: An Interpretation of Reminiscence in the Aged," *Psychiatry* 26 (1963):65-76. The classic study is Barbara Myerhoff, *Number Our Days* (New York: E.P. Dutton, 1978); see also her essay collection,

Remembered Lives (Ann Arbor: University of Michigan Press, 1992); and Clyde A. Milner, II, "The View from Wisdom: Four Layers of History," in *Under an Open Sky*, ed. William Cronon et al. (New York: W.W. Norton, 1992).

6. Patrick B. Mullen, *Listening to Old Voices* (Urbana: University of Illinois Press, 1992), 18.

7. The classic work is Maurice Halbwachs, *The Collective Memory* (New York: Harper & Row, 1980 [1950]). Recent works include: Jacqueline Dowd Hall, "'You Must Remember This': Autobiography as Social Critique," *Journal of American History* 85 (September 1998): 439-65; Michael S. Roth, *The Ironist's Cage* (New York: Columbia University Press, 1995); Michael Kammen, *Mystic Chords of Memory* (New York: Alfred A. Knopf, 1991); Paul Connerton, *How Societies Remember* (New York: University of Cambridge Press, 1989); James Fentress and Chris Wichkham, *Social Memory* (Oxford, UK: Blackwell, 1992).

8. For recent analyses of "region" in western history see Patricia Nelson Limerick, *The Legacy of Conquest* (New York: W.W. Norton, 1987); Edward L. Ayers, Patricia Nelson Limerick, Stephen Nissenbaum, and Peter S. Onuf, *All Over the Map* (Baltimore: Johns Hopkins University Press, 1996); Patricia Nelson Limerick, Clyde A. Milner, II, and Charles E. Rankin, eds., *Trails* (Lawrence: University Press of Kansas, 1991); and Catherine Cavanaugh and Jeremy Mouat, eds., *Making Western Canada* (Toronto: Garamond Press, 1996).

9. Joan W. Scott, "The Evidence of Experience," *Critical Inquiry* 17 (Summer 1991): 773-97. Scott argues that "It is not individuals who have experience, but subjects who are constituted through experience" and due to the "productive quality of discourse," we should view "the emergence of a new identity as a discursive event" (779, 796-97). Cultural geographer Yi-Fu Tuan also notes the "constructed" nature of "experience," explaining it as "a cover-all term for the various modes through which a person knows and constructs a reality." For Tuan "experience" means "acting on the given and creating out of the given." "Human feeling is not a succession of discrete sensations; rather memory and anticipation are able to wield sensory impacts into a shifting stream of experience. . . . It is a selective and creative process in which environmental stimuli are organized into flowing structures." See Tuan, *Space and Place* (Minneapolis: University of Minnesota Press, 1977), 8-10.

10. This essay suggests, after Paul Rodoway, that "the senses are not merely passive receptors of particular kinds of environmental stimuli but are actively involved in the structuring of that information." In this view, environment "participates with us in constituting a world." That is, environments have "structure" (a "complex of surfaces, edges, textures, and movements") and that structure is the "source of information, not merely raw data." See Rodoway, *Sensuous Geographies* (London: Routledge, 1994), 4-10; Tuan, *Space and Place*, and *Topophilia* (New Jersey: Prentice-Hall, 1974); and John Eyles, *Senses of Place* (Warrington, Cheshire, England: Silverbook Press, 1985).

11. Connerton, *How Societies Remember*.

12. Yi-Fu Tuan argues that "the organization of human space is uniquely dependent on sight. Other senses expand and enrich visual space" (*Space and Place*, 16). Other geographers, Rodoway cited here, have suggested, however, that since the earliest cultural geographers built upon a "visual foundation," due to the field's early reliance on the concept of "landscape," all geographic explorations are "conditioned" by this "visualism" or "the tendency to reduce all sensuous experience to visual terms,"

Sensuous Geographies, 115–17. See also Helen Lefkowitz Horowitz, ed., *Landscape in Sight* (New Haven: Yale University Press, 1997); Estelle Jussim, "The Eternal Moment," in her *The Eternal Moment* (New York: Aperture Foundation, 1989); Jussim and Elizabeth Lindquist-Cock, *Landscape as Photograph* (New Haven: Yale University Press, 1985); and the classic, William M. Ivins, Jr., *Prints and Visual Communication* (Cambridge: MIT Press, 1969 [1953]).

13. See also Lauren Brown, *Grasslands* (New York: Alfred A. Knopf, 1985); and T.M. Barkley, ed., *Flora of the Great Plains* (Lawrence: University Press of Kansas, 1986).

14. For large corporate ranching and the Canadian system of leasing range lands, see David H. Breen, *The Canadian Prairie West and the Ranching Frontier, 1874-1924* (Toronto: University of Toronto Press, 1983). For the cultural origins and diffusion of ranching systems, including the open-range system of the United States, see Terry G. Jordan, *North American Cattle-Ranching Frontiers* (Albuquerque: University of New Mexico Press, 1993). For Canada's twentieth-century homestead boom, see Paul Voisey, *Vulcan* (Toronto: University of Toronto Press, 1988).

15. Brown refers to "the screen of my memory," *Sketches*, 148.

16. This playhouse was built circa 1880.

17. Simon Schama, *Landscape and Memory* (New York: Alfred A. Knopf, 1995), 17.

18. Aagot Raaen, *Measure of My Days* (Fargo: North Dakota Institute for Regional Studies, 1953), 41, 53, 112-13, 273 and 322.

19. John L. Shover, *First Majority—Last Minority* (De Kalb: Northern University of Illinois Press, 1976).

20. Raaen, *Measure*, 178.

Novels that Named a City: Fictional Pretexts of Flin Flon

Birk Sproxton

THE MANITOBA MINING TOWN of Flin Flon stands as an anomaly among "prairie" communities. Though Flin Flon belongs to Manitoba, in conventional parlance a Prairie province, the town perches on the rocks of the Canadian Shield, a good many miles north from the landscape commonly denominated as prairie. Yet to reach the city by road, for example, will require most people to travel through prairie, and then back to prairie. Flin Flon dangles there at the end of the line, in a world of rocks and lakes, a world dramatically different from the prairies, yet intimately attached to the prairies by highway and waterway. A road trip to Flin Flon from the South highlights what prairieness might be by declaring what it is not; a trip by waterway would make the point even more forcefully. Though the city is located within the system of the great prairie river, the Saskatchewan, Flin Flon is not prairie; whatever prairie might be, it cannot be Flin Flon.

Flin Flon is anomalous in other ways. Many readers will know that the name "Flin Flon" comes from the nickname of one Josiah Flintabbatey Flonatin, hero of a 1905 science fiction adventure called *The Sunless City*, a novel recently reprinted with a fiery red cardboard cover, the book kept alive by the persistence of the city now sunning itself on the rocks of the Shield.[1] A city named after the nickname of a fictional character is in itself a curiosity. What makes the story curiouser and curiouser is that the Flin Flon mine was the topic of a second novel, now mostly forgotten, Douglas Durkin's *The Lobstick Trail: A Romance of Northern Canada,*[2] published in 1921, some seven years before Flin Flon was joined to the South by a railway, and nearly ten years before the mine went into production.

The city was therefore preceded by two novels. The city had a story before it was a city. In the story of this city, which I will argue is at once both prairie and not prairie, we have a neat variation on Robert Kroetsch's notion that we don't exist until someone tells our story.[3] By an amazing narrative twist, Flin Flon was born before it existed, its story twice-told before the place came to be.

These novels stand as fictional pre-texts for the town. *The Sunless City* donates the name (Flin Flon), the character (Josiah), and the clutch of uto-pian fantasies about wealth that every successful mine to some degree en-acts. *The Lobstick Trail* fictionalizes the town history and impresses its story into the existing literary maps of Manitoba and Canada. The "Northern Canada" of the subtitle in fact is the area between The Pas and what is now Flin Flon. The Flin Flon story, in its shifts and paradoxes and multiple ver-sions, emblematizes the problem of defining prairie. The name does not match the place, for no name can quite measure up, either to the idea or to the reality—but the name persists.

With its boundaries only recently (in 1912) extended north to the 60th parallel of latitude, and east to Hudson Bay, Manitoba in 1920 was eager to exploit its new "northernness," and Durkin writes out of that new sensibil-ity, as he does in the other novels of what I call his New Manitoba trilogy.[4] In *The Lobstick Trail,* Durkin takes a contemporary story, the development of the Flin Flon mine, and constructs a moral fable out of that material. He shows the machinery (and chicanery) of industrial capital, the interplay of metropolis and hinterland, and celebrates a vibrant world where canoes and dog teams remain an integral part of everyday life.

In writing of the North, Durkin re-defines Manitoba and calls into question her usual nomination as a Prairie province. Though the word *prairie* does not appear in the novel, Durkin nonetheless carefully assigns recognizable geographical and social coordinates to his fictional world. These show his effort to encompass within the ambit of Manitoba, and northern Canada, the new mining world of the western Shield.

In this essay I analyze *The Lobstick Trail* in the contexts of *The Sunless City* and the gradually realized city of flesh and blood, copper and gold. In my reading of these discourses, the character "Flin Flon," by a kind of metonymic trick, slips out of the novel he was born in to become the name of a place without a name. No place (ou-topia) becomes the good place (eu-topia). Flin Flon travels from mind-site to mine-site; Flin goes from noun to ground and town, all the while en route to fame and fortune, to re-nown. Ulti-mately, Flin Flon becomes an enduring paradox, a prairie mining town, a character and noun planted within that shape-shifting and disputed site denominated *prairie*.

1.

Begin with a tattered paperback called *The Sunless City*. In 1914 Tom
Creighton and his fellow prospectors find the book on a portage near the
Churchill River, face down, let's say, in a blueberry patch. One of the men
picks up the novel and begins to read. Incredibly, the novel is about a
character named Josiah Flintabbatey Flonatin who plunges in a man-made
fish down to the bottom of a bottomless lake where he finds an under-
ground city, "where gold was so plentiful that it was literally a base metal—
truly the Mecca sought by all prospectors."[5] In this city, the people have
tails, and the women are in charge. Undaunted, the prospectors pass the
book around. Unfortunately, the concluding pages of the novel have been
torn out, and the prospectors hunker down for the winter, without knowing what happens to Flin. Then, in the next summer, they hit upon a rich
showing of ore in a hollow near a small lake.[6] At this point Tom Creighton
supposedly remarks, "'That must be the hole where old Flin Flon came up
and shook his gold dust laden whiskers, so what do you say if we call the
discovery Flin Flon.'" The other prospectors agree and though some people later object to the name "as sounding too much like flim flam," the
name stuck.[7]

Flin's story of rags-to-riches clearly appealed to the prospectors. They
were not bothered by the novelist's making Flin the target of his satire.
Described as "a gentleman conspicuous for two things—the smallness of
his stature and the largeness of his perception" (*The Sunless City* 2), Flin
Flon is the son of a line of grocers with their roots in Bologna. "When
nature constructed [Flin]," our narrator says, "she must have suddenly run
out of materials, because she commenced a head that would have done
credit to a giant in stature as well as intellect. But getting as far as the neck
the old dame found apparently she had made a mistake, so finished him off
hurriedly. From the neck downwards he was strangely disproportioned and
very scanty" (4). Flin Flonners, later, saw humour in the character, if not
satire, and in the early 1960s they contacted cartoonist Al Capp of "Li'l
Abner" fame, who made a sketch of the intrepid adventurer. Subsequently,
"Flinty," as Flin Flonners call him, became a larger-than-life sculpture, and
now, with one hand raised to his brow and spectacles perched on his potato
nose, Flinty gazes smilingly over the mammilated rocks of the Canadian
Shield and welcomes visitors to his town. Flinty gives the town character.

2.

In 1920 Douglas Durkin writes *The Lobstick Trail* out of the Flin Flon story.
By the outbreak of the First World War, mining had begun in the Northern

Manitoba Mining District, notably at Mandy Mine, three miles from what would become Flin Flon. Mandy herself was a mine so rich that her owners could profitably ship raw ore 100 miles by barge, horse-drawn wagon, and sternwheeler to the railhead at The Pas, there to be transported another 1800 miles to the smelters at Trail, British Columbia. Eyes turned northward in Manitoba, as they did in Ontario and Quebec. The excitement of northward expansion informs the novel.[8]

As Durkin's subtitle—"A Romance of Northern Canada"—indicates, he writes from the South and to the South, where his audience is located. Accordingly, he incorporates within his narrative an explanation of "lobsticks," and he sets his hero out on various escapades through the romantic North. Lobsticks function as a chronotopic image of this world.[9] To have lobsticks and trails, you must have boreal forest and sparsely charted wilderness. Durkin allows his hero, Kirk Brander, to offer a definition of lobstick to the southern mining entrepreneur, Marion Curtis. They are out on the trail, under the northern lights, when Marion notices an unusual tree.

> Sharply outlined against the sky one tall spruce tree lifted its head clear above the others and stood out like a sentinel on duty. She could not help noticing that the branches in the middle of the tree had been cut off for a distance of ten or twelve feet leaving only a large tufted head and a thick base of branches near the ground. In the space that had been thus cleared of limbs two long branches like the arms of some gaunt spectre stretched out in opposite directions from the tree trunk, their ends weighted down with the soft snow that clung to them. (112-13)

Kirk explains to Marion that these lobsticks function as guideposts. "'That arm there,' he said, pointing to the branch on the northern side of the tree, 'shows the direction we are taking across the lake to our friend Dags. When we get there we'll find another stick—and others along the way marking short-cuts and portages and old trails that are the only lines of communication in this part of the world'" (113). While they sit by the campfire to drink their hot tea, Kirk carries on his discourse. He tells her "more of the romance of the lobstick, how it had been used by the Indians as a means of marking the spot where a hunter had killed a very large moose, or where one man had buried another who was his friend, or where a young brave had made love to a maiden" (113). This elaborate definition shows Durkin's determination to ground his romance in the discursive practices of the northern world.

In addition to such extended definitions, Durkin's strategies for bringing the North "home" to his southern readers include (1) his use of familiar place names, (2) repeated description of the area's waterways, (3) occasional use of local expressions, and (4) robust declarations about the prospects of the future. By these often overlapping strategies, Durkin situates his unnamed and not yet extant town within the expanding prairie world to the south.

Familiar Names. Durkin presents his narrative as a contest over ownership of a very promising but unproven mine. He blends two stories, a mining story and a love story; both are embedded among other, larger, continental and Eurocentric narratives. As Durkin moves back and forth between micro-narrative and macro-narrative, he has his characters or his narrator deliver exposition as necessary.

At the micro-level, our hero Kirk Brander drives his dog team from the north country into The Pas with a load of furs he will sell before he returns to the East. In the East he had become "a regular booze artist" (32) but five years in the North have made him into "a man" (3). He expects to leave town immediately after the dog derby. Part of his mission in The Pas, therefore, is to say good-bye to the friends he has made in the past five years.

He seeks out his comrades in their favourite Chinese café and then stands up to speak. Warmed by a second glass of water, his drink of choice, Kirk offers a salute to his (male) comrades. He also announces a nationalistic vision of the future, an announcement that both betrays his deep attachment to the North and prefigures his subsequent fate:

> "For two hundred and fifty years Canadians have been puddling along on the southern rim of a country as rich as any country in the world and have handed the rest of it over to a company of moneyed Englishmen who never saw Canada and don't give a tinker's damn if they ever do or not. But we've got to pull in our belts.... God Almighty's going to give Canada the next hundred years to make good in, an' she's got to make good by herself or forget about it and let someone else handle the deal. We've got enough fish in the lakes north of the Saskatchewan to feed the rest of the world week-days and Fridays." (20-21)

In this view of the world, Canada's history begins with the Hudson Bay Charter, and the future is hers to seize. Kirk goes on, in his fashion, about salmon in Hudson Bay, and water power, and timber and stone and minerals. Ultimately, the future will depend upon the inner resources of Canadians, Kirk asserts as he tugs his belt, "'It's a question of whether we're packing the kind of stuff here ... that'll handle the deal'" (21).

In this enthusiastic outburst, we hear echoes of Durkin's contemporaries: Laurier and the Group of Seven, Jack London, and especially Ralph Connor, he of the muscular morality. Clearly, Durkin touches on popular currents of thought in his time. Good hearts, good humour, and young muscles, he seems to assume, will win the future. (In this novel, Durkin takes us back into a time before the Great War and the sea change it brought. He fixes his vision on the future and how to make it happen; in *The Magpie* he deals with the aftermath of the war.)

Durkin draws relatively simple historical and geographical coordinates, at least in Brander's speech, but the economic forces in the novel are much more complex. The Pas, described as "a northern Manitoba frontier town," is the local centre of civilization (3). The capitalists who contend for the northern mine, the unscrupulous Warren Paxton and the beautiful widow Marion Curtis, travel to The Pas from Winnipeg on a train called "The Tamarack." In making one of his contenders a woman, Durkin continues a pattern he introduced in *The Heart of Cherry McBain* (1919) and elaborated in *The Magpie* (1923). His female characters, including Marion Curtis, tend to show determination, competence, and intelligence, qualities necessary for achieving the new world that Durkin envisions.

Two stubborn old men who hold the rights to the mine site complicate things for Curtis and Paxton. One is John Allen, an "eccentric old Englishman," who in an interesting reversal has reached this northern site "by way of the Saskatchewan from the west" (46). He first builds a beautiful log cabin near an enchanting waterfall, and then he travels to Saskatoon and returns with his daughter Jule and "a half dozen large freight canoes loaded with furnishings and supplies" (124). At his new place Allen takes up gardening, much to the dismay of Paxton, who finds the old man more interested in talking about cabbages than in selling his property.

The second old man is John McKay, "a retired servant of Hudson's Bay Company" (37), a double to John Allen in that he too has a beautiful daughter—her name is Ruth. McKay's connection with the Bay suggests a link with the past; Allen's determination to build a garden, to domesticate the bush garden, as it were, seems somehow more forward-looking. Ironically, Allen meets his death by drowning under suspicious circumstances, and near the end of the novel, Ruth McKay too drowns, this time in the waterfall that was so important to her friend Jule.

Water Country. Durkin maps his country by reference to the waterways. Crucial to the novel is the Saskatchewan River; it marks the line, generally speaking, between south and north. The railhead at The Pas is on the Saskatchewan; priests and RCMP officers are located further west on the

Saskatchewan at Cumberland House. Some fifty miles north is Sturgeon Landing, a place to land and unload or re-load your cargo. Sturgeon Landing is the head of steamboat navigation (historically speaking, the site where the ore from Mandy Mine would be transferred to sternwheeler en route to the railhead). North of Sturgeon Landing lies the Shield country, where the waterways are marked by rapids and waterfalls.

Durkin stresses the difficulties posed by the physical terrain. The ore body held by Allen and McKay is huge but the ore is low-grade. These low values, combined with the difficulty of transport, demand that a local smelter be built. Such a mining and smelting complex will also require a rail line from The Pas and a source of electrical power. These economic demands intensify and give scale to the central conflict between Curtis and Paxton. "Between the Burntwood system of waterways sloping towards the north and the Saskatchewan system draining towards the South there lay, at one point, only a narrow strip of dry ground, scarcely more than a mile in width. To the north of the portage lay Cranberry Lake and to the south Lake Athapapuskow; the railway would have to follow the narrow height of land between them" (150). (The rail line does in fact follow this route. The height of land is actually an old shoreline of Glacial Lake Agassiz and is now the site of Cranberry Portage. The town is built on the sandy shores of the ancient lake within a mile of the rocky outcrops of the Precambrian Shield.) To enhance his drama, Durkin assigns ownership of this narrow strip of land to the bullying capitalist, Warren.

Localisms. In dwelling on waterways, Durkin employs local language and idioms. When challenged about his intentions to leave the north country, Kirk says his going out is "surer than jackfish for malamutes" (19). Many northern fishers regard the jackfish as food for the dogs. Jacks, or northern pike, often referred to snakes or slimy jacks or slough sharks, live in weedy waters and prey on other fish; they will also attack and eat ducks and small waterfowl. Sport fishers prize jacks for the fierce fight they offer, but their bony structure and dubious diet makes them less prized as an eating fish. Hence, they make good food for malamutes.

Another local expression appears in Kirk's hymn to the North, when he salutes "the men who live north of fifty-three" (18). Today people from The Pas and district wear shirts saying "North of 53" (and people from Flin Flon, "North of 54"). These inscriptions invite translation, for they are what Foucault calls "the little tactics of the habitat"[10] by which people place themselves in the world.

To wear a shirt saying "North of 53" speaks of a local pride, generalized and comfortable and far-reaching. The shirts also may suggest an identification between the wearer and the lifestyle of trappers and prospectors who wander the northern bush. We know exactly where we are, the phrase seems to say, and it sure as hell is not South. Not South of 54, but North of 53, as if the latitude were a dividing line between a chartered and domesticated southern life and an unfettered and nomadic northern life. "North of 53" in the Durkin novel encompasses The Pas and Sturgeon Landing and the traplines and mining camps of the district around what became Flin Flon. A land big enough to encourage the bullshit artist and all kinds of wacky rumours and fantasies. A land big enough to provoke emotional outbursts from Kirk Brander. The people who live "North of 53" (or "North of 60") presume to tell you that you're in a new space where things are done differently from how they are done in less northerly places.

This manner of mapping by latitude both resembles and differs from Robert Kroetsch's in *Seed Catalogue*, where, in the opening segment, the poet gives his address (at least) twice, an Alberta address incised with precision:

the home place: N.E. 17-42-16-W4th Meridian.
the home place: 11/2 miles west of Heisler, Alberta,
on the correction line road
and three miles south.[11]

For all their differences, both methods of location tell of our western space, how we wrestle with bigness and how we put ourselves on the map. The abstract imaginary lines, meridians and latitudes, mark our place.

In Durkin's novel, South serves as "topographical paradigm," a paradigm that remains relatively stable because the bulk of western Canada's population, including the novelist's reading audience, lives in the South.[12] But the habitual paradigm is being challenged. Tomson Highway's 1998 novel, *Kiss of the Fur Queen*, offers a new way of mapping. Born and raised in Manitoba just south of the 60th parallel, Highway sees the world from the North. In a wonderfully poetic passage, Highway describes how his character flies south on the wings of his music:

Jeremiah's sixteenth notes played on. For six years, they played without pause. Sprouting wings, they lifted off Kamamagoos Island that autumn, honked farewell to Eemanapiteepitat twenty miles to the north, then soared in semi-perfect V-formation over the billowing waves of Mistik Lake, past the village of Wuchusk Oochisk, over the craggy rocks where the Mistik River joins the Churchill River, past Patima Bay, Chigeema Narrows, Flin Flon, and—following the route Abraham Okimasis [Jeremiah's father] had raced back in February 1951—through Cranberry Portage to Oopaskooyak, where they touched down to slake their thirst on the memory of the Fur Queen's kiss. After a detour of some years at the Birch Lake Indian Residential School twenty miles west of Oopaskooyak, the music curved south until it levelled onto the great Canadian plain and landed, just so, in the city of Winnipeg, Manitoba, eight hundred miles south of Eemanapiteepitat, in the pink salon of another woman in white fur.[13]

Where Durkin uses Winnipeg as a starting point for his mining entrepreneurs, Highway considers Winnipeg a destination (or stopping point). Highway sees Canada through northern eyes; however far Highway's characters range from Eemanapiteepitat, however far south those musical birds might fly, he implies, they will return to that northern Manitoba place. What Durkin calls The Pas, Highway calls Oopaskooyak, the Cree name for this centuries-old community. For Durkin, The Pas serves as entry to the North; for Highway, Oopaskooyak and the residential school serve as entry to the South. In his naming Highway asserts historical precedence, and reminds readers of our habitual South-oriented and Eurocentric biases.

Like Highway and Kroetsch, Durkin too wrestles with questions of scale. Though he gives local details in a relatively precise fashion, Durkin develops his theme of bigness by placing his mining drama within a continental economy: "There was undoubtedly a newly awakened interest in the limitless possibilities of this great north country. Men of means and the big interests both in Canada and in the United States were turning their eyes in the direction of this, probably the last unexploited mineral district on the continent" (*The Lobstick Trail* 42). In this way Durkin moves between the macro- and micro-dimensions of his fictional world, and in so moving he enlarges the fictional map of the province. The lookers, the big interests, by which he means capitalists, may live in the South, but they will find their opportunities in northern Canada.

Future Prospects. Two kissing scenes will illustrate how Durkin develops his intertwined plots of mining and love. First, on the way north by dog team to the mine site, Kirk and Marion Curtis find themselves alone under the aurora borealis. Marion says to Kirk, "'If you weren't such a boy I believe I could make something really big out of you. I'd like to hold the destiny of a real man in my hands. By George—I'd make a man out of him'" (119). After a delay suitable for a man of his moral fibre, Kirk pulls Marion to him to press upon her lips a kiss. This occurs in full parka. End of scene. They rush northward to the mining claims.

Eventually neither Paxton nor Marion Curtis gets the mine. They are outsiders, and the land and mine, and by extension the future, at least in Durkin's vision, must lie in the hands of those who love the North. Paxton is removed from contention by Marion's threats to reveal his hand in the untimely death of old John Allen. (Allen dies of injuries suffered travelling north of Sturgeon Landing on the treacherous Rat River.) In playing this card, Marion also removes herself from contention for the love of Kirk Brander. The mine passes into the hands of Jule Allen, who has grown to womanhood in this northern place. And of course she has fallen in love with our hero, who finally realizes that he can't leave the North.

The novel closes with a second kissing scene, more than 100 pages after the first. Upon receiving a communication from Marion Curtis in Winnipeg, Kirk bubbles over with glee. She has sent him good news.

> "[The mine is] going to be even bigger than I dreamed," [Kirk] said with full boyish enthusiasm. "We'll have to bring power here, enough power to work one of the biggest mines on this continent. We may have to go all the way to the Burntwood [River]. . . . We'll have to put in a cofferdam and drain half the lake to work the ore-body properly. It'll take a year or more for the government to build the railway in from The Pas—but that's settled. And we'll have a town of our own, Jule, with five thousand people. Jove, girl, there's a man-sized job right here that'll take a whole lifetime" (331).

Kirk then takes Jule in his arms, kisses her and repeats, "A man-sized job!" When Jule asks what the woman's job might be, he replies, "Making a man—man's size" (331).

In this ending, Durkin reverts to masculinist and capitalist fantasies of unending expansion.[14] He lived in momentous times, and the Canadian North was seen to be very much part of the nation's future. But in a way that Durkin could not have known, his hero's dreams came true.

3.

The Flin Flon mine, though never named such in Durkin's novel, becomes a metonym for northern Canada, the last and vast unsullied great good place. Durkin identifies the future of the country with the purity and riches of the Shield, as his contemporaries, the Group of Seven and their literary cohorts F.R. Scott and A.J.M. Smith, were also doing in central Canada. Yet Durkin writes his North independently of them, and indeed Durkin never refers explicitly to the Shield, but speaks instead of the country where "lakes abound." He figures this country as an outpost of prairie, well beyond the borders of prairie, in fact, but nonetheless bound to the prairie place. To situate his mine, Durkin uses coordinates familiar to his audience: the cities of Saskatoon and Winnipeg, the town of The Pas, the Saskatch-ewan River. When he ventures into what would be for his readers un-known territory, he makes specific and largely accurate references to places and events. To develop the mine at Flin Flon, a cofferdam was built and a lake was drained. Hydroelectric power was brought in, not from the Burntwood to the east, but from the Churchill River to the west, a distance of about seventy-five miles. The mining and smelting operation did indeed become huge; according to a 1938 *Fortune* magazine article, Flin Flon was the biggest development in the mining world in the last fifteen years. [15]

The article's title and subhead are telling: "Flintabbatey Flonatin, Esq. . . . or the tale of Hudson Bay Mining, and its $27,500,000 investment in Mani-toba's bush. Moral: success comes to those used to it, in this case the Whitneys." [16] With an investment of these millions, the C.V. Whitney inter-ests of New York found success where others had failed. A rail link was built in 1929 and the mine came into production in 1931. The town even-tually grew much larger than the 5000 people Durkin foresaw: in the early 1960s the population was over 10,000. As these details confirm, though Durkin styled his book a "romance," he was also writing a story that was unfolding around him. The lobstick trail, he saw, was soon to be surmounted, if not replaced, by the great steel lines of the railroad.

In constructing this vision of Canada's North, Durkin invites a re-consideration of our naming habits and the unexamined notions they carry with them. His unnamed outpost, his imagined town—the name Flin Flon whispers throughout his text—that imagined real place signals a prairie province's desire for the future. Yet the site lies in a non-prairie world, one so different that Durkin must resort to extended explanations, perhaps to the detriment of the novel's narrative interest. What I want to stress, though, is the richness of Durkin's vision. He shows Manitoba to be both South and North, bushland and prairie, mining camp and city. His vision gains substance when *The Lobstick Trail* is read alongside his next novel, for in *The Magpie*, Durkin's hero takes a job at the Winnipeg Grain Exchange and decks himself out in "a suit of business grey instead of the toggery of ro-mance." [17] Like Highway's Eeemanapiteepitat and Oopaskooyak, Durkin's The Pas and his (unnamed) Flin Flon are not prairie places and yet they lie within the ambit of prairie. [18] By force of habit and tradition, we name and misname this vast place "prairie," condensing into one name a plurality of stories. The two Flin Flon novels, *The Sunless City* (which I treat elsewhere) [19] and Durkin's *The Lobstick Trail,* pretexts for a real place, paradoxically be-long in the "prairie" archive. [20]

Endnotes

1. J.E. Preston-Muddock, *The Sunless City* (London: F.V. White & C. Ltd., 1905). Subsequent quotations from this book will be given wihin parentheses in the text. The cover of the photographic reprint includes a cartoon of Flintabbatey Flonatin beside his man-made submarine. An iron sculpture of Flin Flon's submarine, modelled on the drawing, now stands beside Ross Lake on Manitoba Highway 10. The town has grown around Ross Lake; Flin Flon Lake has long been drained and lies within the boundary of Hudson Bay Mining and Smelting Company property (if a lake that is not a lake can be said to lie).

2. Douglas Durkin, *The Lobstick Trail: A Romance of Northern Canada* (Toronto: The Musson Book Company, 1921). Subsequent quotations from this book will be given within parentheses in the text.

3. "Robert Kroetsch in Conversation with Margaret Laurence," in *Trace: Prairie Writers on Writing*, ed. Birk Sproxton (Winnipeg: Turnstone Press, 1986), 30.

4. The last of these novels, *The Magpie* (Toronto: The Musson Book Company, 1923), dramatizes the Winnipeg of the General Strike, and the first, *The Heart of Cherry McBain* (Toronto: The Musson Book Company, 1919), tells of the arrival of the railway into the Swan River Valley in the 1880s.

5. Tom Creighton, "How Flin Flon Got its Name," *Northern Lights* [a Hudson Bay Mining & Smelting Company employee magazine] 1, no. 5 (July 1942): 32.

6. How they came upon this place is a matter of dispute. Geological survey records indicate that David Collins, a trapper in the region, took Creighton to the site. In the article above, which may not have been written by Creighton at all, there is no mention of David Collins. See Irene Hewitt, "What's Yours Is Mine. Creighton vs Collins. Who Really Found Flin Flon?" *The Winnipeg Tribune Magazine* (May 24, 1980): 8-10. In *Headframe:* (Winnipeg: Turnstone Press, 1985) I offer a version of the discovery story in the segment called "Document Section," 67-95; see especially the prose poems on pages 80 and 75.

7. For a history of the discovery and development of the mine, see Valerie Hedman, Loretta Yauck, Joyce Henderson, *Flin Flon* (Flin Flon: Flin Flon Historical Society, 1974).

8. This excitement lasted throughout the 1920s. As late as October 1929, on the eve of the Great Crash, Canadians looked to the North for great things. In an article for *The Canadian* called "How Far North Is North?" Toronto writer John Duke shows this enthusiasm. Interestingly, he too speaks of the town that isn't yet a town. "Northern Manitoba . . . is a rather interesting blend of frontier life and civilization. Take Flin Flon for instance. There isn't any town there yet but there are 2,000 men and probably 30 or 40 women living in log cabins and bunk houses. It looks very rough and uncouth to the city-bred person. But in the hospital at Flin Flon they boast better x-ray equipment than will be found in the city of Winnipeg. In the machine shop they have the largest lathe in western Canada. The Chinese restaurant stocked my favourite cigar" (7). The article, complete with photographs of the Flin Flon construction site ("the lake in the background will be drained in order that the ore may be dug out" [6]), may be found on pages 6-7 and pages 36-37.

9. The word *chronotope* was used by Einstein to signify "time-space." See M.M. Bahktin, *The Dialogic Imagination* (Austin: University of Texas Press, 1981). Another reading might argue that lobsticks function as icons, in the sense of the lobstick being a "broad cultural symbol." See Ian Adam, "Iconicity, Space and the Place of Sharon Butala's 'The Prize,'" *Studies in Canadian Literature* 23, no.1 (1998): 178-89.

10. Michel Foucault, *Power/Knowledge: Selected Interviews and other Writings, 1972-1977* (New York: Pantheon, 1980), 149.

11. Robert Kroetsch, *Seed Catalogue* (Winnipeg: Turnstone Press, 1977), 13. For a lively discussion of the "home place" see Deborah Keahey, *Making it Home: Place in Canadian Prairie Literature* (Winnipeg: University of Manitoba Press, 1998), 3-12. See also pp. 126-43 for Keahey's analysis of home in Kroetsch's *Completed Field Notes* (Toronto: McClelland and Stewart, 1989).

12. Adam, "Iconicity," 180.

13. Tomson Highway, *Kiss of the Fur Queen* (Toronto: Doubleday Canada. 1998), 96.

14. John Duke quotes Captain Harvey Weber, "transport king of the north" (6), to say, "Yes, sir, there's gold and silver and copper and waterfalls and big trees all the way between here and the Arctic circle. . . . So long as there are men with enough real 'go' to them who want to get out and to see things no one else has ever seen and to find mines that no one else has ever dreamed about there will be real development in this country" (6-7). In this passage Weber sounds very like Durkin's Kirk Brander.

15. *Fortune* (June 1938): 53-60, 116, 118, 120, 122. See also page 26.

16. Ibid., 53.

17. Durkin, *The Magpie*, 6.

18. John Duke concludes his 1929 essay with a comment on the sliding signifier "North": "There isn't any permanency to the location of the Farthest North. What is the north country to-day will dissolve into the community of older Canada to-morrow and then there will be a new Farthest North—for a few years" (37). This process of dissolution into the older Canada seems to be an ongoing phenomenon. I am arguing that the "prairie" creeps northward in spite of all the signs that say this north is not prairie. By writing in his trilogy about what is not prairie, Durkin has a good deal to tell us about what prairie signified in his time.

19. In *Headframe:* I offer a digested and condensed version of the novel in the segment called "A Likely Story" (99-109).

20. In this essay I have followed the basic strategy that Durkin uses: I explain the North by referring to the more familiar (such as Robert Kroetsch). One could also read *The Lobstick Trail* under the rubric of encounters with the Canadian Shield, for there is a long foreground to Durkin's novel, including, for example, narratives by Alexander Henry, Robert Hood, John Franklin among prominent explorers, and by J.B. Tyrrell, among prominent Canadian surveyors and prospectors. I am currently writing a North-oriented reading of the West, under the working title of "Shield Notes."

The Prairies as Cosmopolitan Space: Recent 'Prairie' Poetry

Jason Wiens

> Vernacular intellectuals define a literary culture in conscious opposition to something larger; they choose to write in a language that does not travel—and that they know does not travel—as easily as the well-traveled language of the cosmopolitan order.…That this 'local' in turn typically comes to be constructed as dominant and dominating for smaller cultural spaces is a further step in the cosmopolitan-vernacular transformation and unthinkable without it.[1]

THE TASK OF "DEFINING THE PRAIRIES" necessarily involves at some point an engagement with a received definitive paradigm. While prior articulations of prairie poetics demonstrate that this paradigm remains a contested field, we can, I think, discern a number of entrenched characteristics that various sites of institutional power—specifically, the academy, and regional literary presses and publications—have established. To this extent, the mandate of this collection is tautological. Yet this insistence upon definition is *itself* a defining characteristic of a prairie poetic, at least as it has been articulated by its major poet-theorists over the past two decades—another tautology of sorts. I am thinking here specifically of Robert Kroetsch's essay "The Moment of the Discovery of America Continues,"[2] where the persistent demand "how do you write in a new country?" becomes a sort of refrain, its repetition establishing at once a point of departure and return, in which the question can never be fully answered but must, nonetheless, continue to be asked. I also have in mind Dennis Cooley's call for a "different aesthetic" that would allow us to "write poetry out of the Prairie,"[3] a call he himself has tried to answer by championing (and producing) a regionally specific vernacular poetics. Kroetsch's and Cooley's arguments are, broadly speaking, extensions of William Carlos Williams's doubled emphasis on the local and the new as emancipatory strategies for the twentieth-century North American writer, a debt they both directly acknowledge.[4] In this formulation, poetry, for all three writers, operates both proactively and reactively—deploying the new as an articulation of local difference in a region-building (and ultimately nation-building) project that might offer some defence against a homogenizing global culture, the aesthetic standards of which are determined in distant metropolitan centres.

I will provide here a critique, an assessment, and, inevitably, a contribution to that same project. Since much of my argument addresses a binary opposition between a geographic "outside" and "inside" implicit in a regional construction, my choice of texts reflects this opposition. I want to offer a brief critical overview of this received paradigm of prairie poetics, re-reading the region as an internally differentiated, cosmopolitan site. I will argue, through an explication of a recent text by a poet whose lived relation to the prairies is problematic, that a prairie poetic has now become sufficiently established that its various codes, strategies, and markings may be recognized, appropriated, and re-deployed by such a poet in the production of a text that, for all intents and purposes, could be (mis)recognized as a "prairie poem." Having demonstrated just how defined this poetic has become, I will then turn to a contemporary text, written on and in the prairies, in order to examine how such a text might force a re-definition, or at least an expansion, of what might be termed "prairie poetry."

The most persistent discursive frame conditioning the production, reception, and definitional criteria of prairie poetry in Canada remains an approach that reads the landscape as almost proprioceptively impinging on the writer's consciousness and her subsequent textual production. From Henry Kreisel's 1968 assertion that "all discussion of the literature produced in the Canadian west must of necessity begin with the impact of the landscape upon the mind"[5] to Laurie Ricou's famous thesis that prairie writers demonstrate "an awareness of the surrounding emptiness,"[6] this landscape has as dramatically inflected critical thought about the poetry as it has the poetry itself. If it is true, as Ricou has further claimed, that prairie writers give "unusual prominence to landscape," the same claim could also be made of prairie critics, a situation that would appear to support Frank Davey's observation that "strong regionalisms develop narratives and figures that imply the geographic inevitability of the cultural manifestations that partly constitute the region."[7] While a number of critiques could be and have been directed at this critical emphasis on various grounds—that it de-privileges domestic space, elides the geographic diversity of the three provinces, ignores the region's increasingly and overwhelmingly urban character, and posits a facile and deterministic understanding of the relationship of geographic place to art—I do not wish to develop further such critiques here. In fact, one could argue that a consideration or celebration of landscape might in some cases aid the poetry in developing a cultural site-specificity, which is, to me, one of its most crucial functions at the present time. A recognition that, as Herb Wyile puts it, "these ostensibly definitive tropes, themes, or images emerge through the process of critical selection, interpretation, and emphasis,"[8] does not render such tropes, themes, or images any less useful or valid. Yet I do think there is room for critical framing and theorizing on prairie poetics to be expanded or shifted to account for what I will term here the increasingly cosmopolitan character of the place.

I deploy the term *cosmopolitan* in the sense that Paul Rabinow has defined it, as "an ethos of macro-interdependencies, with an acute consciousness (often forced upon people) of the inescapabilities and particularities of places, characters, historical trajectories, and fates."[9] Rabinow further points out that "we have done rather poorly in interpreting this condition," preferring "to reify local identities or construct universal ones." For the purposes of this paper I would like to substitute "global" for "universal" in Rabinow's formulation, as my argument is primarily concerned with a local relationship to a global condition—both in terms of how that relationship has heretofore been negotiated, and how we might currently re-negotiate it. This negotiation seems particularly tricky in the context of Canada; the country's perpetual struggle with forging a coherent national identity—which we might consider, following Kroetsch, a "modernist" project[10]—has only been exacerbated in recent decades by the growth and increasing cultural and political influence of non-European diasporic communities. Yet if we can no longer pretend to occupy a fully reified "local," the putative existence of authentic "locals" *elsewhere* underwrites this "postmodern" global dynamic that has challenged the modernist nation-building project.

One of the dangers of a so-called cosmopolitan perspective may be its apparent refusal of local specificities, collapsing global cultural diversity into a homogeneous urban mass in which subjects from Tokyo to Toronto negotiate differing relations to a uniform, hyper-commodified cultural field. Yet my use of the term here is specifically aimed at avoiding such a position. By figuring the prairies as a "cosmopolitan" space, I hope on the one hand to account for its predominantly urban character and increasingly diversified economic base, and the social and cultural transformations it

continues to undergo as national and global migration patterns shift, but
also to describe how the "prairies" might be imagined and situated on a
global grid: as a distinct cultural entity among a global assembly of similarly,
though to differing degrees, diverse entities—what Bruce Robbins would
term one of the world's "discrepant cosmopolitanisms."[11] I recognize that
the term is a loaded one; on top of the images of the privileged "citizen of
the world" possessing "independent means, high-tech tastes, and globe-
trotting mobility,"[12] the notions of pluralistic diversity evoked by the term
are problematic. The first sense in which I am using the term runs the risk,
as noted above, of collapsing prairie cosmopolitanism into a paradoxically
homogeneous global culture; the second, of reducing the prairies and the
cultural specificities that define it to one of many "objects of apprecia-
tion for the passing connoisseur." It is this second problematic that I
wish to address in a consideration of Adeena Karasick's "Prairis/cite
Maintenance."[13]

Karasick's biography follows a relatively common Canadian migratory
trope in recent decades: although born in Winnipeg, she grew up in Vancouver and has subsequently pursued post-secondary education in Montreal and Toronto. To this extent, the relation of "Prairis/cite Maintenance"
to the "prairis" it cites is troubled: the text could be read as expatriate,
migratory, or travel writing, but probably not a local or "indigenous" production. I mention these biographical details not in an attempt to fetishize
the author, nor to question Karasick's authority to represent a specific geographic local, but to emphasize the fluidity of certain received poetic conventions across and between differing localities.

"Prairis/cite Maintenance" appears marked by a number of what I consider prairie conventions, not only in its referential index of "currents,"
"alkali slough," and "wheatfields and flaxseed," but more significantly through
its formal strategies. Isolated fragments of text, forging distant connections
across an overwhelmingly empty space, establish a textual homology between the page and the prairie landscape:

> an' I thot I was a prairie writer
>
> 'cause I heard
> the call of the wild geese
>
> and the red grain
>
> risin' outside of

chokecherries
caught in—

& confided like

/ *a prayer.*

When I appear as a prairie writer
    a prairadox

writing the West out of—

prairie grasses

(a grasseous mass)

[de nada]

Aqua Nada[14]

These lines, with the Olsonian phonetic spelling of "thot" and the apostrophes that serve to fragment the words and convey the elision of "properly" articulated endings and beginnings, render the "speech-based" or vernacular poetic that Cooley has aligned specifically with prairie poetry.[15] Where "Prairis/cite Maintenance" appears most "prairie," though, is in its cross-textual engagement with Kroetsch's *Seed Catalogue*,[16] one of the most widely read and, to my mind, important of prairie long poems. Typographical play with italics, boldface, and slashes, an integration of popular cultural texts from children's nursury rhymes ("Prairie, Prairie / Quite contrary / How does yr / Garden grow?") to popular music (Creedence Clearwater Revival's "Proud Mary"), and direct references to "binder twine," gardens, and "grid coordinates" are some of the strategies that directly echo (or cite) Kroetsch's text. *Seed Catalogue*'s concerns with developing a new literature in a new place, writing "de nada," out of the absence of, for Kroetsch, "clay and wattles," for Karasick, "the musk of [] / successive / silences," appear to be continued here. "Prairis/cite Maintenance" thus appears to demonstrate, first, Kroetsch's synecdochical relationship to prairie poetry as such; and, second, the extent to which the strategies that "define" this poetry are immediately discernable, recognizable, and ripe for citation.

It is important to remember that "Prairis/cite Maintenance" comprised a section of Karasick's 1996 book *Genrecide,* which, according to the publisher's blurb on the back cover, "explores the intersection of multiple cultures, codes, idioms and constructs that impact on the social construction of female identity." In a sort of critical preface to "Prairis/cite Maintenance," Karasick further situates her text within a feminist challenge to inherited prairie representations:

> Throughout Canadian Literature, the "prairies" have been constructed as a traceless space, marked by ellipsis, elusiveness and ambiguity. Synecdochically, they have come to represent female identity. "Prairis/cite Maintenance" questions this radical misrepresentation, as well as a textual-political history which has harnessed the 'prairies' into a geographic s/cite with a stable, coherent, identifiable locus. Occupying a hyper-marginalized space, where otherness and alterity are re-translated through geography and language, the "prairies" are re-viewed as a multiperspectival praxis of discovery; a libidinal, "geograpoetic" graphematrix or a parasitical echonomy where place feeds off place and is replaised in hyperspatial interplays.[17]

Given this critical/poetic contextualization, Karasick's text demands we approach it as a politicized, critical rewriting of a received prairie poetic. In this reading, lines such as "writing the prairies / out of" or "writing the West out of—" gesture not towards a sort of archaeological recovery of found materials out of which to write, but to write an inherited discourse away, "out," as in Kroetsch's priest who "had named / our world / out of existence." Yet paradoxically, the strategy Karasick employs in performing such an erasure involves a "paratactic sacrifice" toward a "toponymy of accumulation"[18]: a layered hyper-referentiality of a specific discourse toward the discovery, indeed toward the establishment of a "praxis of discovery" (to extend the tautology I describe above), of yet another "new" poetic. Although "Prairis/cite Maintenance" maintains this cross-textual dialogue with *Seed Catalogue* throughout, there is a diachronic development in the poem towards the more linguistically investigative, etymological writing characteristic of *Genrecide* as a whole:

ridin' deep into
this prairie aporia

(prairie
    / arable

  or parable)

in repair:

    p(a)rairy
    prière
    patairy

as power pries
on par or para / as par for []
parries

        (et)ceteras p(r)a(i)rabis[19]

We might thus view Karasick's text as critically inhabiting Kroetsch's poetic in *Seed Catalogue*—which Karasick appears to equate unproblematically with a prairie poetic—in a polemically transformative strategy. What I find most striking about Karasick's critical/poetic project of "re-viewing" the prairies as this "multiperspectival praxis of discovery; a libidinal, 'geograpoetic' graphematrix," is that her text inhabits a regional writing that apparently provides ready-made strategies for this project. Despite the text's polemical and in fact antagonistic stance in appropriating a prairie poetic, and a rather narrowly defined one at that, in order to transform it into one more able to accommodate difference, in this instance more specifically gender difference, Karasick's text reinscribes that poetic and seems to affirm Wolfgang Klooss's position that prairie regionalism in Canada, "if conceived primarily in *artistic* and *linguistic* terms, must ... be understood as a *(de-)constructive form of poetics*, pronouncing difference and otherness."[20]

Let me be clear: I agree with Karasick that a prairie poetic, as it has heretofore been articulated, has demonstrated a certain blindness with respect to gender difference, and I would further argue that any nation-building project is complicit with patriarchal systems of domination.[21] My point in addressing Karasick's text, however, is not to determine whether a prairie poetic might be heterogeneous, accommodating of difference, and politically enabling, but rather to demonstrate how readily discernible its discursive markings have become. What I read through "Prairis/cite Maintenance" is a strange trajectory in which discursive constructions of the prairies are initially accused of a "radical misrepresentation" and of harnessing the region into a geographic site with "a stable, identifiable locus," followed by a text that paradoxically and parasitically inhabits a Kroetschian "prairie poetic" in order to deconstruct this misrepresentation, and which, through this paradox, ends up reifying this inherited poetic. Within the larger context of *Genrecide*, "Prairis/cite Maintenance" is placed alongside other texts that demonstrate an affinity to a number of other discernibly distinct poetics: so-called "Language Writing," mixed-media text, concrete poetry, and polylingual writing, to name a few, all spliced with critical commentary demonstrating the pervasive influence of contemporary theory, as the names Derrida, Cixous, Bhabha, and Kristeva suggest. In a text that demonstrates a certain cosmopolitan awareness of diverse aesthetic and intellectual currents (and I use the word with the double entendre fully intended), the situation of a prairie poetic in relation to these currents testifies both to the maturity of that poetic as well as to the interest it holds "outside" the prairies. This is not, of course, to suggest that prairie poetry requires such external validation to prove its cultural significance; rather, to return to an earlier point, and at the risk of repetition, "prairie poetry" has become, if Karasick's text is any indication, a recognizably "discrete field of literary practice"[22] within a global cultural network.

While this would appear to be an overwhelmingly positive situation, suggesting a regional poetry that is vibrant and distinctive, we could as easily recognize it as alerting us to the risks of cultural ossification and commodification, both from without and within. If local and regional commodification "is one of the most widespread techniques for cultural competition and survival in the new late-capitalist global economy,"[23] such commodification also brings with it the unfortunate consequence of papering over the complexities of local histories, politics, and differences, of actually endangering what Frank Davey sees as a positive force of regional affirmation: its enabling of "contextually local evaluations of practices and products."[24] It is for this reason that Davey—who appears to maintain a persistent antagonism towards regionalisms in his critical work— argues for a transformation of critical focus from region to "regionalities," as cosmopolitan sites more open to "internal differentiation by other ideologies,"[25] including those based on gender, class, and ethnicity. Indeed, for Davey this shift from region to regionality enables a more specific historicization and contextualization of the latter without rejecting the potential offered by regionalities "to act as strategic political and cultural sites for democratic resistances to global assumptions."

While the feminist critique of "Prairis/cite Maintenance" explicitly attempts to differentiate internally a received, prairie, regional ideology, we can also discern challenges to this ideology emerging in recent writing on the prairies that situates itself less overtly within a regional paradigm. *I do not know this story*, a performance piece by tjsnow of the Nakoda Sioux First Nation, seems to me a "regional" text in the more politically enabling sense Davey describes, insofar as it encourages this "contextual local evaluation" of social practices. The text was both performed and published in collaboration with a number of other artists and writers from Calgary (with one participant from the UK), with tjsnow's reading of the text situated in a sort of disjunctive dialogue with songs, saxophone improvisation, and occasional articulations of poetry or personal narratives by the other participants. The published chapbook[26] (which assigns authorship of *I do not know this story* to tjsnow) attempts to inscribe this polyphony through an often overlapping, multi-fonted text that at times functions to echo and thus buttress the main text, and at others, places it under erasure.

Like "Prairis/cite Maintenance," *I do not know this story* situates itself critically within the immediate context of the published page by providing an "afterword." But this afterword is not only critical but social, dedicating the text "to the memory of pamela george, her struggle, and the struggles of women who must live through her story" and thus explicitly directing its critique of systemic racism at a specific historical event: the killing of Pamela George by two white males in Regina in April 1995.[27] The epigraph, as well as the text's referential index of "Regina," "Winnipeg," "Calgary," "weyburn," coulees," "moose jaw," and "main and albert and smaller lanes to roadie bars separating the prairie wind," situates the text within a specifically prairie context. Moreover, we might say that *I do not know this story*, similarly to "Prairis/cite Maintenance," critically inhabits a number of received discourses—not the least of which are those of Canadian nationalism, including "O Canada" and excerpts from the *Charter of Rights and Freedoms*. In fact, most of the songs performing within/against the text are associated with specific locales and nationalisms: the South African national anthem or southern spirituals, for instance. Throughout the text's network of signs, I could identify a number of equivalencies between this poem and the received prairie poetic I've discussed above, including this heteroglossic (one might say documentative) incorporation of competing discourses, the focus on the pub as communal site ("those women talked sometimes all night about the bars they been at") and the homology it establishes between the land and its human occupants:

> The road came
> long ago, but after the rail-
> road, pulling up the roots and
> laying down ones more per-
> manent. And it wasn't so
> lonely then, when they
> brought in the foreigners to
> work the land and leave the
> metal spike embedded deep
> along the land. Still had scar
> tissue. The women were
> shaking their heads in agree-
> ment, knowing this was true,
> they agreed that the scar still
> cut deep.[28]

We could also note an equivalence between this text and, say, Cooley's project in *The Vernacular Muse* of finding a space and form for the articulation of marginalized voice. As tjsnow writes in the afterword: "in this story we realized that to reintroduce the stories of women, to reintroduce the voices that are often left unheard, introduces something very powerful.... We have tried to restore culture to the text that allows us to access the voices that matter, the voices that become matter, intensely."

But the point at which the concerns of *I do not know this story* and that of a received prairie poetic most clearly overlap is in both projects' concerns with orality ("the last i heard this story in passing fused to the firefly and starburst chattel of women talking around the fire"; "that back when he would speak about those things"; "those women talked"). Even the most cursory of glances at the critical work done on First Nations writing in Canada on the one hand, and prairie poetries on the other, demonstrates this confluence,[29] and I do not have room here to delve into the nuances of these arguments. In fact, at this point I must admit some discomfort in how I am situating and addressing *I do not know this story,* partly because it engages with and emerges from a differing literary tradition and must be critically situated as such, but more immediately because my juxtaposition

of the text with a prairie paradigm is a piercing reminder of the embarrass-
ment of this particular region-building project as it has been articulated.
Despite the anti-European stance that has informed this project, it remains
fully complicit with a Eurocentric, colonialist attitude to this space, a space
that was and remains by no means "empty" or absent of history. The question never was, after all, "how do you write in a new country?" It was, and
remains, the much less heroic but not less crucial "how do you write in a
European language in a context removed geographically from Europe?"
And, of course, in its relentless critique of contemporary nation-state for-
mations and particular Canadian national mythoi (such as the railroad), *I do
not know this story* directs an attack at the ideological substrata and teleology
of the prairie regionalist project.

On the other hand, *I do not know this story* is a text that in fact *demands*
attention to a regional context. The Pamela George story, although occu-
pying the national media stage,[30] certainly received the most discursive
attention throughout the prairie provinces; and while the story is one that
speaks to the conditions of First Nations peoples across Canada, indeed
across the Americas, the historical and cultural specificities of those First
Nations who occupy what I am terming the prairies are central both to the
George case and to this poem. In this sense, this text and its contextually
local evaluations would enjoy the most discursive power when circulated
within this particular regionality. Situated within a regionalist paradigm of
prairie poetics, *I do not know this story* offers a transformative voice, weakening some of the ideological underpinnings of that paradigm, while demonstrating and deploying its more politically enabling tactics. Addressing the
concerns of those worldwide still struggling with the consequences of
European imperialism, the text seems to me cosmopolitan in the doubled
sense of that word: specifically and contextually local (without falling into
the trap of cultural commodification), but at the same time demonstrating,
like Karasick's text, a familiarity with transnational poetic communities
and strategies.

In a recent essay Herb Wyile claims that "regionalism is not a discrete
field of literary practice, but the nexus of a series of debates, contestations,
critical prescriptions, and a territorialization of literary practice."[31] I would
argue that critical work on prairie poetry still needs more consciously to
move away from attempting to establish a discrete field of literary practice
and toward embracing the conflicts and transformations of Wyile's nexus. I
am not, of course, claiming that discussions of prairie poetry have been
characterized in the past decades by a cozy, back-patting consensus; rather,
I think if we examine historically how prairie poetry has been framed,

constructed, and championed in academic discourse, we *can* discern consensus on certain crucial points, and it is precisely towards troubling such
consensus that I think our critical energies need to be directed. Such a
criticism would allow for difference both between and within regionalities;
the consequences of this for a prairie regionalism would be a move toward
more fluid and ambiguous "boundaries," which would allow for and encourage transregional—and national—aesthetic and political affiliations, and
a continued poetic focus on local histories and polities through an informed, though antagonistic, relation to an inherited poetic tradition. If
the Canadian prairies have truly become a "cosmopolitan space"—in terms
of both its competing internal constituencies as well as its external relations
to other, perhaps more glamorous, "cosmopolities"—then critical framing
of the poetry must take such relations into account.

Endnotes

1. Sheldon Pollock, "The Cosmopolitan Vernacular," *The Journal of Asian Studies* 57, no. 1
   (February 1998): 8.

2. Robert Kroetsch, *The Lovely Treachery of Words* (Toronto: Oxford University Press,
   1989), 1–20.

3. Dennis Cooley and Robert Enright, "Uncovering Our Dream World: An Interview
   with Robert Kroetsch," in *RePlacing*, ed. Dennis Cooley (Downsview: ECW Press,
   1980), 27.

4. In "The Moment of the Discovery of America Continues," Kroetsch cites Williams
   as claiming the acquisition of a local pride enables us to create a new culture by
   "lifting an environment to expression" (Kroetsch, *Lovely Treachery*, 6). Cooley, in his
   introduction to *RePlacing* (a 1980 collection of statements, interviews, and essays on
   prairie poetics) acknowledges that, with respect to poets deploying new forms so as to
   authentically articulate their own voices, "ultimately, that release derives from William
   Carlos Williams" (Cooley, *RePlacing*, 17).

5. Henry Kreisel, "The Prairie: A State of Mind," in *Trace: Prairie Writers on Writing*, ed.
   Birk Sproxton (Winnipeg: Turnstone Press, 1986), 6.

6. Laurie Ricou, *Vertical Man / Horizontal World* (Vancouver: University of British
   Columbia Press, 1973), ix.

7. Frank Davey, "Toward the Ends of Regionalism," in *A Sense of Place: Re-Evaluating
   Regionalism in Canadian and American Writing*, ed. Christian Riegel and Herb Wyile,
   vol. 9, *Textual Studies in Canada* 9 (Spring 1997): 4.

8. Herb Wyile, "Regionalism, Postcolonialism, and (Canadian) Writing: A Comparative
   Approach for Postnational Times," *ECW* 63 (Spring 1998): 145.

9. Paul Rabinow, "Representations Are Social Facts: Modernity and Post-Modernity in Anthropology," in *Writing Culture*, ed. James Clifford and George E. Marcus (Berkeley: University of California Press, 1986), 258.

10. See "Disunity as Unity: A Canadian Strategy" in Kroetsch, *Lovely Treachery*. Although in this essay Kroetsch claims Canada as a "postmodern country" because of the obsolescence (or absence) of national meta-narratives, I for one suspect the modernist project of nation-building remains alive and well in Canada.

11. Bruce Robbins, "Comparative Cosmopolitanism," *Social Text* 10, no. 2-3 (1992): 181.

12. Ibid., 171.

13. Although an excerpt from "Prairis/cite Maintenance" was included in the special "Jewish-Canadian Writing" issue of *Prairie Fire* 17, no. 3 (November 1996), it was published in its entirety in her collection *Genrecide* (Vancouver: Talonbooks, 1996).

14. Karasick, *Genrecide*, 76-77.

15. See Cooley, *The Vernacular Muse* (Winnipeg: Turnstone Press, 1987), especially "Placing the Vernacular: The Eye and Ear in Saskatchewan Poetry" and "The Vernacular Muse in Prairie Poetry."

16. Robert Kroetsch, *Seed Catalogue* (Winnipeg: Turnstone Press, 1986).

17. Karasick, *Genrecide*, 73.

18. Ibid.

19. Karasick, *Genrecide*, 80.

20. Wolfgang Klooss, "Multiculturalism, Regionalism and the Search for a Poetics of Disparity in Contemporary Canadian Writing," in *Anglistentag 1991 Düsseldorf*, ed. Wilhelm G. Busse (Tübingen: Niemeyer, 1992), 357.

21. These criticisms have already been well made; indeed, the strongest and most productive challenges to Cooley's and Kroetsch's arguments have been made from feminist positions. See, for instance, Pamela Banting, *Body Inc.: A Theory of Translation Poetics* (Winnipeg: Turnstone Press, 1995); Di Brandt, "Questions I Asked Dennis Cooley about the Vernacular Muse," *Prairie Fire* 9, no. 3 (Autumn 1988): 94-96; and Susan Rudy Dorscht, *Women, Reading, Kroetsch: Telling the Difference* (Waterloo: Wilfrid Laurier University Press, 1991).

22. Wyile, "Regionalism," 152.

23. Davey, "Toward the Ends of Regionalism," 14.

24. Ibid., 15.

25. Ibid., 16.

26. tjsnow, *I do not know this story* (Calgary: House Press, 1998). House Press, a micropress dedicated to experimental and unusual forms of poetry and prose, was established by Calgary artist, writer and publisher derek beaulieu in 1997. The press, which has published over 100 chapbooks by writers from Canada and around the globe, would also be an example of an emerging prairie cosmopolitanism, particularly in Calgary.

27. The judge in the case instructed the jury to remember that George was "indeed a prostitute" when they considered whether she consented to the sexual assault, consent being a determining factor as to whether the men were guilty of first-degree murder. The men, Steven Kummerfield and Alexander Ternowetsky, were eventually each

convicted of manslaughter and sentenced to six and a half years in prison, a sentence which many view with outrage as too lenient.

28. tjsnow, *I do not know.* The text is unpaginated, and subsequent citations are n.p.

29. The work on orality and First Nations writing I have in mind includes, but is by no means limited to, Peter Dickinson, "'Orality in Literacy': Listening to Indigenous Writing," *Canadian Journal of Native Studies* 14, no. 2 (1994): 319-40; Susan Gingell, "When X Equals Zero: The Politics of Voice in First Peoples Poetry by Women," *English Studies in Canada* 24, no. 4 (December 1998): 447-66; and Penny Petrone, *Native Literature in Canada: From the Oral Tradition to the Present* (Toronto: Oxford University Press, 1990). Petrone makes the interesting point that "each linguistic group [among the First Nations] has its own particular set [of oral narratives] that accords with its own regional ecologies" (10), another confluence that might be worth pursuing.

30. For an ongoing collection of media clippings related to the George case, see http:www.walnet.org/csis/news/regina_96/pam_george.html.

31. Wyile, "Regionalism," 152.

Western Frontiers and Evolving Gender Identity in Aritha van Herk's *The Tent Peg*

J'nan Morse Sellery

BY COLONIZING GENDER, sexuality, and male language, Aritha van Herk re-defines the western Canadian frontiers through a discourse about men's and women's expectations and identities in some "pretty overwhelming locales."[1] That rocky mountainous belt with its adjacent prairies snaking its way from Canada to the United States is consistently labelled male. In considering the impressive vastness of the prairie landscape, Henry Kreisel, George Bowering, Eli Mandel, Rudy Wiebe, and Robert Kroetsch acknowledge its impact upon the male writer's mind.[2] Simplified, when Canadian writers invent western frontiers, they think in human terms. The land actually affects human endeavours, for western "locales" shape men's and women's sexual relationships and gender attitudes. Consistent with the ruggedness of the Rockies, the wind, and the vastness of the prairies, male writers fashion stories of location that emphasize male prowess. Taking on the physical elements and the social conditions of western Canada as it is developed and homesteaded, male writers use "an architectural structure" to create "giant fiction," which Rudy Wiebe insists "breaks into the space of the reader's mind with the space of the western landscape and the people in it."[3] "In novels set on the Canadian prairie," George Bowering explains, "place is a determinant, sometimes even a character."[4]

In these gender-defining and sexual Westerns, written mostly by men, readers learn that the macho male hero is always "a full-grown adult male" who is more interested in "bonding" with other men than in establishing a relationship with women.[5] In any Western, because of the actual threats to life and limb, the male goal is to achieve "manhood," which is the only value worth "dying for."[6] Male self-preservation, then, sets up the hero's bravado role to "squint" and "swagger," to control the elements, animals, and women. Given these male parameters, it is no wonder that van Herk remarks, "Try being a writer there. Try being a woman."[7]

In 1979 in "The Fear of Women in Prairie Fiction: An Erotics of Space," Kroetsch asks, "How do you make love in a new country?"[8] Man's desire for, or, perhaps, even the love of, woman becomes troubling when the options are, to use Kroetsch's prairie metaphors: man's travel by "horse" and woman's stasis in the "house"("Fear" 76). Kroetsch writes, "To be *on* a horse is to move: motion into distance. To be *in* a house is to be fixed: a centering unto stasis. Horse is masculine. House is feminine. Horse: house. Masculine: feminine. On:in. Motion:stasis. A woman isn't supposed to move. Pleasure: duty. The most obvious resolution of the dialectic, however temporary, is in the horse-house" ("Fear" 76). Thus, man's lonely travel across the bald prairies by horse results in woman's remaining stuck in the house. Referring to Sheila Watson's *The Double Hook*, Kroetsch notes that both men and women suffer from the separation and the connection. "The problem is how to live: here: now. Individuals, alone, living together. Together, living alone."[9] That "living together" and "living alone" is what Kroetsch and van Herk parodically deconstruct in their essays and fiction.

Kroetsch's argument is that one way to deal with the binaries of male/ female or horse/house is to recognize that behind that male bluster resides sexual anxiety. Why do men fear the actual power of nature, animals, and women? The tension in the western novel is the conflict between man's love of woman and his fear of her "as the figure who contains the space" in the house, and "who speaks the silence"("Fear" 76). So, western fictions continually reinvent "men's fear of losing their mastery, and hence their identity."[10] The problems include the gender differences of sex and voice, of "living together" in a small space, and of women and men "living alone," of being unable to cross the distance of that large and undeveloped physical and psychological space. So, "How do you establish any sort of *close* relationship in a landscape, in a physical situation whose primary characteristic is *distance*?" ("Fear" 74).

In "The Fear of Women," Kroetsch elucidates a parallel discourse about two prairie novels.[11] First he makes clear that sheer physical distance acts as a metaphor for the inordinate conflicts inherent in men's and women's ability to relate. The second and more revealing discourse is about how and why writers write to and for each other in their western Canadian essays and novels. Kroetsch asks and van Herk relates how writers create an "erotics of space" so that "book and world have intercourse" ("Fear" 74). Writing from the West, Kroetsch and van Herk acknowledge the macho cowboy genres, but deconstruct those binaries of man/horse and woman/house by moving readers into a love of the "book" and their gendered and conflicted "world." Canadian Western writers create that "erotics of space" so that the gendered worlds included in their books speak to each other's books. Of a different gender and a generation later than Kroetsch, van Herk recognizes the power of their origins near the Battle River, and relies in her discourse with Kroetsch, like Margaret Laurence in *The Diviners*, upon the natural power of the river flowing both ways. While theirs is an inside discourse of games and disguises played out in their essays and novels, the result is the erotic intercourse of books and western Canadian landscapes.

In "Women Writers and the Prairie: Spies in an Indifferent Landscape," van Herk responds to Kroetsch's discourse about the "erotics of space." Acknowledging the traditional Western as "male," "masculine," "manly," "virile," and bowing to male writers—"Grove, Mitchell, Ross, Wiebe, Kroetsch"—she asserts that the landscape "has been masculinized in art, descriptive passages of a land instinctively female perceived by a jaundiced male eye."[12] Recognizing the male argument that nature is "instinctively female," van Herk remonstrates that despite their horses, men are sexually afraid to "enter the landscape," that they can only "look and describe," asking "Where? Where, in this landscape constrained by male vantage, does the woman writer of the prairies enter?" Responding to "The Fear of Women," she acknowledges that "the construct is a marvellous one, a perfect excuse for everything. The lady for whom the quest is made; it's for the sake of woman as muse that men have made the prairie culturally insane. But muses are static, make nothing. The landscape and its rendering shapes the eye of the viewer. How can we enter fiction.... We can get into it, enter this world, because it belongs to us" ("Spies" 18). These women leave their houses "spying out the lay of the land.... Refusing to be silhouettes, we enter the fiction of the prairies" ("Spies" 19). Men writers appear to want to look and describe; "they are afraid to enter the landscape.... One needs to give up vantage, give up the advantage of scene or vision and enter it. To know prairie, one has to stop looking at prairie and dive" ("Spies" 17).

Acknowledging that prairie man fears the "figure of woman""who contains the space," Kroetsch writes: "We conceive of external space as male, internal space as female. More precisely, the penis: external, expandable, expendable; the vagina: internal, eternal. The maleness verges on mere absence. The femaleness verges on mystery: it is a space that is not a space. External space is the silence that needs to speak, or that needs to be spoken. It is male. The having spoken is the book. It is female. It is closed" ("Fear" 73). So, men writers require that "static" muse to help them fill that female book with language "written as much from fear as from love" ("Fear" 75).

Kroetsch adds, "The male is reluctant to locate and confront the muse. He works by trespass," becoming "the thief of words," which, by digging through the past layerings,[13] builds man's "giant" imaginative "fiction" to place within the pages of "the female ... book" ("Fear" 75). Significantly, the woman as silent book is acted upon by a man and by male language. Yet, also as muse, she is the mystery that entices him to find the language of story.

As a woman writer, van Herk does not want to be the "female book" written upon by a man, so she responds in her own books without fearing or blaming nature or men. Instead, in her writing, she wants to "seduce" her readers with a broad-brushed "erotics of space" ("Fear" 83). She asserts that both writing and reading are acts of "doing," of "lovemaking," and of "anticipat[ing]." "This is obvious," she adds, "if we fixed on replaying the past, we wouldn't actually *do* anything, and in lovemaking, it is the *doing* that counts."[14] It is that powerful loving and writing that connects women writers, texts, and readers in an "uncharted country." While Kroetsch's men work by "trespass" and steal words, van Herk's women are spies who discover the thieves of story and open up the space. She invites readers and women writers to know that when women leave the prairie house to "enter the fiction of the prairies," they must be spies ("Spies" 19). She challenges women writers in these "indifferent prairies" not to be cajoled by male assertions: "If we limit ourselves to what is 'realistic' in our world," it becomes a "neat way for the patriarchal system to keep us in line—and then it's unrealistic to be a writer at all."[15] "Look out" ("Spies" 19).

Gender and sexual differences in prairie fiction occur because a person's "position," attitude, and location "dictate point of view," and women's position "has been neglected" ("Spies" 139). That does not prevent her from understanding man's fears. Women learn by observation, so, while collectively stuck in stasis, they observe men's fears. Their insights about how the human mind works are articulated by observing how other people manage their lives. They "dive" into the human landscape from inside their domestic situations, yielding more awareness of other humans than men achieve outdoors on their horses. For example, Margaret Laurence writes about the landscapes of the prairies, not like the men, but "as an anomaly" ("Spies" 139), "the breakthrough spy" ("Spies" 145).

Significantly, while van Herk's essay "Women Writers and the Prairie: Spies in an Indifferent Landscape" is a commentary on Kroetsch's "The Fear of Women in Prairie Fiction," her novel *The Tent Peg* extends the parodic discourse.[16] There, instead of being separated on the bald prairies, her characters are psychologically closed to each other all summer in tents in an arctic space. Individuals cope with primitive situations through the mountainous landscapes in the north, and "through the eyes of the words of women" ("Spies" 145). While the prairies for women are an "indifferent landscape" because they are prohibited from exploring new regions, are the defining ingredients of women in the northern landscapes so different? If woman resides in an arctic tent, how different is that from a prairie house? Van Herk explains: "Look at the vantage that defined prairie. Name the west. Explorers: David Thompson, Alexander Mackenzie.... McCourt would say, 'men of action who wrote as they lived, with a strict regard for essentials. Missionaries ... scoured deep lines into prairie soul, cornering the poor benighted heathen in the wilderness. Whiskey traders, Mounties, the CPR, settlers.... Writers. Inevitably writers. After realism, history, revolution, rebellion; eulogizing saloons and cemeteries, churches and police barracks. Men. Male vantage, advantage" ("Spies" 140). What happened to those male explorers,[17] miners, and natives who lived in minimal accommodations, bought supplies, wrote journals, and shared experiences in those Canadian landscapes? Historically, they were primarily interested in the adventures for commercial aggrandizement.[18] On the surface, the men who came to both territories lived by male hubristic power over women, First Nations peoples, and Inuit. Kroetsch remarks: "In Edmonton or Winnipeg, you find the men are still sitting around in huge beer parlors, talking about women in that naive way men will talk about women. At one time this division between men and women might have been a very functional distinction. Now it's harmful. The women who want to participate like men are forced into a kind of isolation."[19] Reinforcing these facts, van Herk sharpens parody and satire to a sabre point.

In *The Tent Peg*, readers discover an unfamiliar northern territory, which parodically speaks to Kroetsch's paradigm by emphasizing the male explorer's fear of losing out to the other men when they outnumber women in those unpopulated regions, as well as the female protagonist's desire to "travel," becoming the man on the horse, in order to come to terms with her "dreams of androgyny" (Kroetsch's phrase). Parodied in this novel are mythological bear stories, western gun-slinging target shooting, men's lust, sexual desire for and fear of woman, effrontery, and attempted rape. Under the circumstances of that arctic summer camping foray, water, ice, rocks, animals, and weather are "as changeable and arbitrary as any stereotyped woman."[20] Van Herk asserts: "I wanted a woman character to penetrate that male world, succeed within it and act as an interpreter/interface. The demands on this character are enormous; she needs to be androgynous enough to traverse both worlds successfully and she needs to be powerful enough to serve as a catalyst for the transformation of the men."[21] Practically, then, a woman leaving the prairies and travelling to the north, in contrast to staying cooped up in a house on the prairie, achieves greater self-knowledge, discovers her feminine animal nature perceived in bears, acknowledges a masculine assertiveness in men, and finds there is a difference between solitude and loneliness, each of which "inevitably shape[s]" and changes her.

It all begins with J.L.'s cross-dressing as a male,[22] intended as a way of gaining summer employment as a cook in an arctic geological camp, and even though she is quickly unmasked, her male dress is continued for practical convenience until the very end of the story. Traditionally, a cook is a female job in a house, but want ads assume that for an-all male camp, as for upscale city restaurants, only a male chef need apply. Yet, after she is hired by Mackenzie, the men in this camp immediately recognize her skills. Watching her, Mackenzie remarks, "J.L. is whistling and clearing the table, putting the plates in the dishpan. She works inside this space as if she belongs here, as if it's part of her.... It's inconceivable to me that I could have mistaken her for a boy, she is every inch of her female, marvellously light and easy and quick, carrying the mystery that is only there in women" (*Tent* 145). Though assumed to be "a man," yet "ill at ease" in that attire, J.L.'s identity is strictly female. Taking a male name or dress, like George Sand, George Eliot, or even Moll Flanders, does not presuppose identification with maleness. J.L. makes clear that with a name consisting of initials, potential employers would assume she was male. Mackenzie, the leader, is most moved after first hiring J.L. as a "man," when, in the men's bathroom at the bar, J.L. says, while "staring" at his penis, "Mackenzie, I'm a girl" (*Tent* 20). While her cross-dressing is a pragmatic solution, it also represents an imaginative and independent desire for freedom. J.L.'s behaviour parodies traditional gender expectations and physical distinctions made overt by apparel.[23]

The Tent Peg is replete with parodic contrasts and gender inversions. In addition to the extended prairie parodies of males on their horses (substitute in a helicopter), and females in their houses (substitute in a cook tent), there is air travel (in a bush plane landing on ice and water, or in a helicopter landing perilously on a mountainside), all of which supersede plodding animal travel across the bald prairies. Significantly, these early mythic gender patterns of *horses* vs *houses* still remain with the men in the arctic camp. Van Herk parodies the gender understandings of men in the wilderness by revealing their naïve sexual assertiveness and their fear of their sexuality.

From our first meeting with J.L., we realize she is uncomfortable with men's sexual nature toward women. She comments: "Their inappropriateness never fails to amaze me. They discriminate so little over where and when. To be so much controlled by hormones, excretions. Perhaps if they would learn to start at the beginning it would be easier, they would be able to push me further. But individually, collectively, they assume that I am ready, primed, they behave as if there has been another man immediately before, preparing my anticipation and response" (*Tent* 64). Like the parodic female characters in Sheila Watson's *The Double Hook*, van Herk's J.L. and her alter ego Deborah do not understand and often distrust the men with whom they come in contact.

While referring to Ross's and Cather's novels in "The Fear of Women," Kroetsch suggests that "to attribute the absence of explicit sex—of its language or its actions ... to prudery" is naïve, for that conundrum "is an operative presence in the works of numerous prairie writers." Man's need for "space and place are not quite able to find equation" ("Fear" 81). But van Herk knows that in his prairie novels, Kroetsch equates space and place by including active, assertive male sexuality. Also equating space and place, van Herk shows in *The Tent Peg* how sexual assertiveness by the men in camp against the only woman is a power play made by one man against the other men to see who can sexually take J.L. Is the male game, then, merely a game among the male studs for supremacy of power? Is that why Kroetsch emphasizes the loneliness of men on the prairie?

In van Herk's parody, natural creativity and overt sexuality dominate the scenic crises: the former in the form of a female grizzly who comes to camp with her two cubs, and the latter in the form of Cap and then Jerome. Early on Cap acknowledges: "Shit, a whole summer in camp with a female cook. Hard to believe" (*Tent* 70). But then Cap attempts to take sexual advantage of J.L. by saying, "I'm horny." She responds, "So?" And of course, he responds, "You're responsible.... If you weren't here, I wouldn't be...." She suggests masturbation, saying she's not interested. He then rages. "Cap, if you're goddamn horny," she adds, "go find yourself a grizzly bear" (*Tent* 105). Her powerful emotional response brings her to tears. Instead of being alone, which was her desire that summer, she is "everyone's property"; she belongs "to every one of these men" (*Tent* 106).

This sexual centrepiece between J.L. and Cap is told from both points of view. In his retelling of the story, he is "absolutely pillared in place," for J.L. is standing beside the cook tent, "perfectly relaxed and easy, and facing her, twenty feet away and reared up on her hind legs, is a huge goddamn grizzly bear. J.L.'s face is tilted up and the she-bear's face is tilted down and they're looking at each other like they've met before. And then J.L. sweeps off her hat and bows at the same instant that the bear seems to shrug, and drops to her feet. For a moment more they stand there as if in conversation, then they both turn. J.L. goes back into the cook tent and the bear lumbers away down the valley. From behind the corner of the tent two little cubs scurry to follow her" (*Tent* 108). J.L. assumes that Deborah came to her in the form of the she-bear, telling her not to let men like Cap "drive her away" (*Tent* 111). The men seem only to want to kill her, to "fuck her," to photograph her, and she wonders what the others will want. But Deborah is realistic: "You thought you'd leave all that behind? There isn't a place in the world without it. You can try to escape, but it's better to face it head on" (*Tent* 111). The other side of facing the men's desires head-on is being cradled in their arms, for, earlier, she admitted, "Still I turn to them, I seek them out, I wait for the perfect lover. There is comfort in another body in bed" (*Tent* 64). J.L.'s projection on the grizzly bear with two cubs is assumed to be Deborah's voice helping her to heal herself by listening to the feminine in a mammoth female bear. Her conversation is with nature, not only another female.[24]

A formidable rock slide signifies the complexity of male and female interaction and acts as a natural warning to J.L. to recognize and come to terms with physical sexual differences. In spite of her reluctance to trust the men, and in her desire to understand her body, voice, and feminine nature, she thinks about what makes up a woman: "Lying there [in bed in my tent], I make notes, evaluate, dream, rid myself of their words. Piecing, stitching seams that threaten to come loose, soaking up the emanation of another body. Sponge, a woman is a sponge. We can be infinitely compressed, infinitely engorged, and still spring back to our own shape. And all for them, all at their whim and mercy, the inert weight on the other side of the bed" (*Tent* 64). Then she turns on her side, and "feel[s] the flank of the mountain shift, feel[s] it rumble and groan as if settling the camp in its arms." And she opens her arms, arches her "body in anticipation, waiting. But it is only a greeting; the rumble subsides" (*Tent* 65). The mountain holds the camp as a man holds a woman in bed.

This is the first moving of the mountain, but the larger mountain rock slide that reveals a new find, a core of gold ore, is parodically interpreted as a basic element of value and, simultaneously, the breakdown of relationship between man and woman. Significantly, Mackenzie mourns the fact that his wife walked out on him ten years before. J.L. helps him to understand why, saying, "She left for herself. You were a good man but you couldn't give that to her, it had nothing to do with you. It was herself she was after and the only way she could find that was by leaving" (*Tent* 202). He realizes that he wouldn't have prevented her from finding herself. But J.L. comments: "That's it right there. The very idea that you could allow her or prevent her. That's why she left" (*Tent* 202). The insight dawns: Mackenzie recognizes his hubris: "believing that another life could be at … [his] disposal, that [he] … had any right to try and make it so" and he feels "shame" (*Tent* 203). "I'm not proud of myself," he says. "I did all the wrong things. Hired a private detective, hunted everywhere myself, acted like she was a runaway teenager." But, at the same time, he claimed the moral highroad by "pretending to be faithful, pretending to be noble by being there just in case she came back" (*Tent* 130). But while he could never find her, and realized that leaving was her conscious act, he admitted that "the hardest thing to face" was the "rock slide of her intention" (*Tent* 130). J.L. makes explicit that men think they have the right to determine and control women. Mackenzie's discovery of his own fragile fear of women is reinforced by the rock slide that reveals a large new vein of gold ore. As the land reveals the hidden vein of gold through the earthquake of the mountain, so, metonymically, men and women can see their differences through painful experiences and, perhaps, come to see the other from a different perspective.

While Mackenzie learns how he overstepped his authority in his relationship with his wife, J.L. learns that the men in camp need her more than she needs them. Man desires woman and wants her contained in a house only for himself; woman desires man but wants to travel, be androgynous, isolated, and sometimes chaste. Helping the men to understand their hubris has freed J.L. to see her own, as she listens to the internalized voice of Deborah, her alter ego or "Siamese friend," whose sequences include one memory and one song of the Biblical Ja-el, the wife of the Israeli leader for whom J.L. was named. Ja-el "killed the Canaanite captain, Sisera, by driving a tent peg through his temple, [and] nailing him to the ground as he slept."[25] In this brief reading, this novel has more to do with the nine men's projections on J.L., a signifier for all women, than with the contrast to her Biblical other. In brief, however, what the Israeli woman did to seduce the Canaanite captain and kill him reveals how other women have known how to take power in their hands when the goal of saving their community, lovers, or people is at stake. Killing, to the chief's wife, was an inevitable outcome of the desire to save her husband and the tribe, suggesting that, historically, neither women nor men fear murder or brutality in their effort to save the community. Our narrator is neither a killer nor a wife, nor has she come to camp with an idea of helping; rather, her intention has been her own quest, to be free of men's single-minded sexual assertiveness. While she unwittingly helps them, what she learns fulfills a basic need, to discover and enjoy her own abilities, energies, body, and voice more than she thought possible.

The parody, then, remains in the plot, for her assets become her liabilities. Despite hiding behind her attire, J.L.'s innate attractiveness forces her to face up to taking control of her own situation. That J.L. was sexually wounded before coming to camp is made clear in the beginning. That she isn't sure she can love anyone but her "Siamese friend," Deborah, is left a question. J.L. has learned to live and talk with men about women's needs and desires. In these new insights, J.L. refutes Kroetsch's assumption that "travel, for all its seeking, acts out an evasion" for there are many "face-to-face confrontations" ("Fear" 82). While J.L. has transformed the men's consciousness, as van Herk writes, by driving a "figurative tent peg of self-knowledge through the temples of the men in the Yukon exploration camp of the novel,"[26] she has also been perceived by them more as an equal than as a subservient female camp cook. Like them, she also drives a post into the ground to stake out her own claim for the gold.

Kroetsch remarks in "Fear of Women" that the "male figure, out in this space, out in the open, presumably free, once epic hero, is now the diminished hero. The woman, in the age-old containment of house or town, is, in prairie writing, the more-than-life figure—but one who is strangely sought" ("Fear" 81). Van Herk might say not to bother keeping her in the house; wherever she is, woman is certainly "sought" because she is the projection of the "more-than-life figure." Explaining how woman is sought and how she responds in *The Tent Peg* is van Herk's response to Kroetsch's question, "How do you make love in a new country?" He writes: "This is a new country. Here on the plains we confront the hopeless and necessary hope of originality: constantly we experience the need to begin. And we do—by initiating beginnings. We contrive authentic origins. From the denied Indians. From the false fronts of the little towns. From the diaries and reminiscences and the travel accounts. From our displaced ancestors ("Fear" 82). Picking up on Kroetsch's remarks, van Herk shows how a writer creates "authentic origins." By using "diaries," "reminiscences," and "travel accounts," she shows how women can turn an indifferent landscape into their own scenic space. From beginning as spies searching for the thieves of words, women characters and writers turn away from being an actor in a man's book, and turn their silence into the language of nature, body, and self-nurture in arctic or prairie landscapes.

Applying mythic recollections of women's power, van Herk liberates *The Tent Peg* "into its own potential" by recognizing how male explorer-writers have misunderstood what the wilderness does to both women and men. She has parodied old-fashioned gender absolutes by showing that, like men's, women's desire to travel, to wield a gun, to cook, or to drive a

tent peg or a stake (to save an earlier tribe, or a community, after a mountain earthquake shakes out a new vein of gold) is more than about becoming androgynous; it is what human beings do. Women can live in tents or
houses, cook, and talk with bears, without becoming muses, witches, or
shamans. Van Herk has shown that "position" in the prairies "dictates point
of view by reinforcing the fact that women have 'infiltrated' the landscape
and toppled the 'male vantage'" ("Spies" 149). Certainly, male writers like
Grove, Kroetsch, and Wiebe cover the prairies with "giant fiction," but in
The Tent Peg, western prairie fiction has felt the mountain move, has seen a
new vein of gold appear, providing J.L., a contemporary creative woman,
her own stake in the future.

Endnotes

1. Hilda Kirkwood, "Kiss of the Spider-Lady: An Interview with Aritha van Herk,"
   Canadian Women's Studies/Les Cahiers de la Femme 8, no. 3 (1987): 87.

2. Henry Kreisel, "The Prairie State of Mind," *Proceedings and Transactions of the Royal
   Society of Canada* 6 (1968): 173, 175.

3. Rudy Wiebe, "Canada in the Making," in *Encounters and Explorations: Canadian Writers
   and European Critics,* ed. Franz K. Stanzel and Waldema Zacharasiewicz (Würzburg:
   Konighshausen and Neumann, 1986), p.123. Wiebe's quote may also be found in
   "Passage by Land," in *Writers of the Prairies,* ed. Donald G. Stephen (Vancouver:
   University of British Columbia, 1973), 130-31.

4. George Bowering, "That Fool of a Fear: Notes on *A Jest of God,*" in *A Place to Stand
   On: Essays by and about Margaret Laurence*, ed. George Woodcock (Edmonton: NeWest
   Press, 1983), 210.

5. Jane Tompkins, *West of Everything: The Inner Life of Westerns* (New York: Oxford
   University Press, 1992), 38-39.

6. Ibid., 17-18.

7. Aritha van Herk, "A Gentle Circumcision," in *Trace: Prairie Writers on Writing,* ed. Birk
   Sproxton (Winnipeg, Turnstone Press, 1986), 257.

8. Robert Kroetsch, "The Fear of Women in Prairie Fiction: An Erotics of Space," in
   Crossing Frontiers: Papers in American and Canadian Western Literature, ed. Dick Harrison
   (Edmonton: University of Alberta Press, 1979); rpt. in *Open Letter* V, no.4 (Spring
   1983); rpt. in *The Lovely Treachery of Words: Essays Selected and New* (Toronto: Oxford
   University Press, 1989), 73. Subsequent quotations, from *Treachery,* are referred to as
   "Fear" and given within parentheses in the text.

9. Robert Kroetsch, "Death Is a Happy Ending: A Dialogue in Thirteen Parts," in *Figures
   in a Ground: Canadian Essays on Modern Literature Collected in Honour of Sheila Watson,*
   ed. Diane Bessai and David Jackel (Saskatoon: Western Producer Prairie Books, 1978),
   215.

10. Thompkins, *West of Everything*, 45.

11. In "The Fear of Women in Prairie Fiction," Kroetsch refers to Willa Cather's novel *My Antonia* and Sinclair Ross's novel *As For Me and My House*.

12. Aritha van Herk, "Women Writers and the Prairie: Spies in an Indifferent Landscape" *Kunapipi* 6, no. 2 (1984): 15-24; rpt. in *Canadiana: Studies in Canadian Literature,* ed. Jorn Carlsen and Knud Larsen (Aarhus, 1984); originally a lecture given at the 1st Canadian Studies Conference, University of Aarhus, Aarhus, Denmark, May 3, 1984; collected in *A Frozen Tongue* (Sydney, Australia: Dangeroo Press, 1992), 139-51. Subsequent quotations, from the first publication, are referred to as "Spies" and given within parentheses in the text.

13. To read or write the land, Kroetsch suggests, requires unearthing the past "archaeological deposits" to understand and grasp the palimpsests of the people and animals who lived before. Following Foucault, he suggests that "Archaeology allows for discontinuity. It allows for layering. It allows for imaginative speculation." See "The Moment of the Discovery of America Continues" in *The Lovely Treachery of Words* (Toronto: Oxford University Press, 1989), 7.

14. Aritha van Herk, "A Literary Affair," in *Driving Home: A Dialogue between Writers and Readers*, ed. Barbara Belyea and Estelle Dansereau (Waterloo: Wilfred Laurier University Press, 1984), 71-74; originally a lecture given at Driving Home, a workshop conference sponsored by the Calgary Institute for the Humanities, August 1982; collected in *A Frozen Tongue* (Sydney, Australia: Dangeroo Press, 1992), 86-89.

15. Aritha van Herk, "Of Viscera and Vital Questions," in *Language in Her Eye: Writing and Genre,* ed. Libby Scheier et al. (Toronto: Coach House Press, 1990), 274.

16. The form of *The Tent Peg* (Toronto: McClelland and Stewart, 1981; rpt. New York: Seaview Press, 1982), according to van Herk, is "taken directly from [William Faulkner's] *As I Lay Dying*, a funeral odyssey through which each character in that novel achieves self-knowledge as well." As in Faulkner's novel, each chapter is told from the point of view of one of the characters. In an interview with Hilda Kirkwood, van Herk reiterates Faulkner's influence on her writing. For references to van Herk's use of the grizzly, see Rosella Mamoli Zorzi, "Faulkner and a Contemporary Feminist Novel: From Faulkner's *The Bear* to Aritha van Herk's *The Tent Peg,*" in *Faulkner, His Contemporaries and His Posterity,* ed. Waldemar Zacharasiewicz (Tubingen: A. Francke Verlag, 1993), 309-16. Subsequent quotations, from the New York edition, are referred to as *Tent* and given within parentheses in the text.

17. I.S. Maclaren suggests, in "Alexander Mackenzie and the Landscapes of Commerce," *Studies in Canadian Literature* 7, no. 2 (1982): 141-50, that Sir Alexander Mackenzie's (1764-1820) journals and trips were motivated by "commercial" and not "aesthetic" interests. His "sensibilities were too commercial, possessing neither the careful and sensitive discrimination of David Thompson, nor the artistic temperament of George Back, Robert Hood, Sherard Osborn or even John Franklin" (143). One reviewer concluded that "Mackenzie's account of the North and West reinforced the myth of the regions as, largely, a wasteland" (142). As an employee of the Hudson's Bay Company at the time of his travels, and "effectively under [the] control of the North West Company," Mackenzie deplored the lack of trees, suggesting a lack of beaver or other animals whose fur was commercially important.

18. For background see Alexander Mackenzie, *The Journals and Letters of Sir Alexander Mackenzie,* ed. W. Kaye Lamb (Cambridge: Cambridge University Press for the Hakluyt Society, 1970); T.D. MacLulich, "The Explorer as Hero: Mackenzie and Fraser," *Canadian Literature* 75 (Winter 1977); Eric W. Morse, *Fur Trade Canoe Routes of Canada / Then and Now* (Ottawa: Queen's Printer, 1968); Doug Owram, *Promise of Eden: The Canadian Expansionist Movement and the Idea of the West 1856-1900* (Toronto: University of Toronto Press, 1980), chapter 1; E.E. Rich, *The Fur Trade and the Northwest, to 1857* (Toronto: McClelland and Stewart, 1967).

19. Alan Twigg, "Male: Robert Kroetsch," in *For Openers: Conversations with 24 Canadian Writers* (Madeira Park, BC: Harbour Publishing, 1981), 107-16.

20. Aritha van Herk, "*Judith* and *The Tent Peg:* A Retrospective," in *A Frozen Tongue* (Sydney, Australia: Dangeroo Press, 1992), 280.

21. Ibid., 281.

22. In Ross's *As For Me and My House,* as well as in van Herk's *The Tent Peg,* and Kroetsch's *The Puppeteer: A Novel* (Toronto: Random House, Vintage Books, 1993), cross-dressing follows the prominent literary tradition that questions socially constructed gender patterns and sexual orientations.

23. In *Coyote Country: Fictions of the Canadian West* (Durham: Duke University Press, 1994), 114-15, Arnold E. Davidson writes, "If the cross-dressing comes out, so to speak, in the fiction yet is still retained, then it becomes an ongoing crisis for everyone and especially for characters—and readers—who previously had no doubts about which sex was which, with what each one was endowed, just who belonged where, and to what end all of this division worked. The confusions of those mostly male certainties are all dramatized in *The Tent Peg.*"

24. Personal comment to J'nan Morse Sellery from Aritha van Herk.

25. Dorothy Jones, "Restoring the Temples: The Fiction of Aritha van Herk," *Kunapipi* 6, no. 1 (1994): 422.

26. Van Herk, "*Judith* and *The Tent Peg,*" 281.

The Female Body as Garrison in Three Prairie Biotexts

Claire Omhovère

THE STONE DIARIES by Carol Shields, *Mothertalk: Life Stories of Mary Kiyoshi Kiyooka* as written by Roy Kiyooka, and "The Poetics of Rita Kleinhart" by Robert Kroetsch resist the neat categorization of literature into clearcut genres and subcategories. Rather than biography, autobiography, or (auto)biographical fiction, "biotext"[1] is the term I will be using here to round up works that exceed generic barriers and include heterogeneous documents—photographs, poems, letters, shopping lists—in order to explore a central question: how does a life translate into narrative? Research on (auto)biography has exposed to what extent fiction informs the reconstructions of memory.[2] In its opening warning, Roland Barthes's autobiography alerts the reader to the unavoidable fictionalization of the self: "All this should be read as if it were said by a character in a novel."[3] With the dismantling of the Cartesian ego, post-structuralists took an even more drastic stance when they argued that no subject ever coincides with him/herself. The self is irremediably lost in the play of *differance*, which defers indefinitely the completion of a concluded subject through the writing process.[4]

The biotexts I selected go further in questioning prior conceptions about the autobiographical subject by foregrounding the problematic question of agency. Carol Shields's novel shuttles between incompatible stances as Daisy Goodwill simultaneously occupies the contradictory positions of active narrator and passive object within the same narrative. The resulting dislocation finds a striking formulation in sentences that challenge the rules of grammatical coherence: "the long days of isolation, of silence, the torment of boredom—all these pressed on me, on young Daisy Goodwill, and emptied her out."[5] In the life stories of Mary Kiyooka, the singular "I" results from a collaboration between various voices. Mary's story in Japanese was initially recorded on tapes by her son, Roy Kiyooka.[6] Once the tapes were translated into English by Matsuki Masutani, Roy Kiyooka transcribed them and interspersed his mother's stories with some of his own poems. After Kiyooka's death in 1994, the arrangement of the text into book form was completed by the editor, Daphne Marlatt. Robert Kroetsch concludes his autobiography, *A Likely Story: The Writing Life,* with the first instalment of a piece entitled "The Poetics of Rita Kleinhart."[7] The introspection of the writing self becomes externalized as the autobiographical subject splits into two personae: Rita, the Alberta poet who disappeared in the Museum of Modern Art in Frankfurt while gazing at James Turell's *Twilight Arch,* and Raymond, her lover, reader, and maybe rival in poetry. Whether on the authorial or on the narrative level, these biotexts undermine the traditional construction of autobiography in a singular voice by foregrounding the plurality of voices converging to recreate a life in writing. Such texts therefore open onto the notion of collective biography.

The shift from the individual to the collective might be traced as far back as the implications of Northrop Frye's theory of the garrison mentality. That paradigm, grounded in the Canadian colonial past, has survived as a defence the human mind sets up "to preserve its integrity or even its sanity [against] the vast unconsciousness of nature."[8] The protection of small, tightly knit communities has implied, as a counterpart, that the individual should abide by group-accepted norms: "The real terror comes when the individual feels himself becoming an individual, pulling away from the group."[9] This double bind would explain why, according to Frye, the Canadian climate and Canadian culture have combined to become inhospitable to literary genius, the term referring here to this superlative form of subjectivity whereby individuality reaches universality.[10]

Frye's position, however, is informed by a prescriptive assumption ranking individual achievement above collective practices. Just as classic autobiography supposed the model of a separate and unique selfhood,[11] the garrison paradigm makes it difficult to value the collective, no matter how crucial it may be in the individuation process of women and minorities.[12] In that respect, Susan Friedman demonstrates that women developed a dual consciousness that enabled them to negotiate with the demands of the group: "the self as culturally defined and the self as different from cultural prescription."[13] My hypothesis will be that in these three prairie biotexts, the female body is constructed as a version of garrison where the collective, the individual, and exterior space articulate.

Monumental Bodies

In *The Stone Diaries*, the female body is envisioned by men as a rampart to resist the chaotic expansion of prairie space. The novel does not conform to the cliché presenting the area as a region one leaves "to get away from Northrop Frye winters."[14] Instead, summer is the most dangerous season, when days are spent outside in the hazy horizontality of fields crouching under the sizzling heat: "The Quarry Road takes [Cuyler] across flat, low-lying fields, marshy in spots, infertile, scrubby, the horizon suffocatingly low, pressing down on the roofs of rough barns and houses" (*Diaries* 36). In winter, when people safely remain indoors, space does not exert the same portentous threat (*Mothertalk* 97). At the turn of the century, in sunny Manitoba, there is no eye-soothing landscape in the old sense of a com-posed nature,[15] and Winnipeg's "struggling civic flower beds" (*Diaries* 274) echo Daisy's father's longing for consolidation and structure. Similarly, her husband, Barker, finds solace against chaos in the nomenclature of botanical charts: "The discovery at the age of twelve or thirteen that the whole of the natural world had been classified, that someone other than himself had guessed at the need for this ordering, struck him like a bolt of happiness" (*Diaries* 142). When Barker leaves Manitoba and moves to Ontario, his Sunday strolls take him past urban gardens and manicured lawns where nature, confined as it is within man-made limits, does not question the bond between word and world (*Diaries* 163).

Whereas Rita Kleinhart has an "aversion to intentional space" ("Rita" I, 200), her preference for randomness showing in the disposition of her ranch "at once rambling and severely unprotected" ("Rita" I, 190), Raymond is another male character in search of frames. He counteracts Rita's child-hood fantasy of having a cherry tree grow out of her belly with his own memory of an old woodcut. The possibility that the inside and the outside might interact within the body and threaten its integrity is negated by the vignette in which the cherry tree is securely "cramped into a small, rectan-gular space" ("Rita" I, 179). Then, Raymond digresses towards a senten-tious description of the Alberta township grid, finding here again the reassurance that space can be metered out into a succession of identical units ("Rita" I, 180).

Raymond's partiality for structure looms large in his reading of Rita's cryptic verse: "The old forms were good enough for me, on occasion I now take one of her poems and give it the look it should have by finding in her disorder a quatrain or two" ("Rita" I, 208). Analogy is the rhetorical ploy Raymond uses to make sense of the traces Rita left behind after her disappearance. For him, comparison is reason enough. However, as Raymond contemplates Rita's welter of verse, anxiety arises:

> Poetry is excrement. It is marginally useful as fertilizer. In using it as fertilizer we run the risk of transmitting a variety of venereal diseases.
> Rita Kleinhart saw in me the klutz who might bumble her obscurity into the annals—and why not anals?—of that morbidity we call literature.
> What torpor is it that enables the poet to drowse a few scribbles onto the beauty of a white page?
> Is not the elegance of almost any naked ass to be preferred to the puffy regurgitation of accumulated consonants?
> *Kick a dong of lick pence,*
> *A belly full of blear.*
> It is high time we got down to the text. ("Rita" I, 209)

The verse illustrates Raymond's theory on the affinity between poetic discharge and excremental production. Although the two lines make up a grammatical sentence complete with imperative, object, and apposition, its meaning does not coalesce. Semantic dispersal is nevertheless counteracted by consonance and metric cohesion: two trochees are followed by a pivotal spondee initiating the iambic reversal in the second line: /- /- // -/ -/ -/. Poised as it is on the brink of signification, the poem as pleasure (s)tool recalls Kristeva's analysis of the "semiotic" as the resurgence in adult discourse of a dimension of language preceding the child's access to the symbolic order. The semiotic, Kristeva explains, is composed of non-signifying units, sound-patterns, and rhythms, which gradually disappear from the child's discourse as it begins to perceive itself as distinct from its mother's body.[16] Raymond and Rita both recall how in infancy words are composites that bind the haphazardness of breath, sound, and gesture into a rhythmed articulation. In the couplet that concludes the first instalment, Raymond echoes Lewis Carroll by writing "*Tickle tickle little tum. / How I wonder where you bum*" ("Rita" I, 216). And this finds a parallel in Rita's own memory:

> Somewhere in my childhood I read a poem that said
>
> pussycatpussycatwherehaveyoubeen?
> I'vebeentoLondontoseetheQueen.

Pussycatpussycatwhatdidyouthere?
Ifrightenedalittlemouseunderachair.

and after that I was a poet. ("Rita" II, 31)

The stringing together of words compacts each line into a mouthful of
rhythm, exposing the insignificance of the signified as opposed to the overwhelming matter of the signifier. Rita's free play with sound substance
creates unease in Raymond, for it recalls an age when the body is umbili-
cated to the maternal tongue and does not yet exist as a proper, individuated
territory.[17] Poetic discharge therefore both fascinates and repels Raymond:
"What small perversions of the body make us sing? Tickled in the groin,
we giggle poems. Fuck it" ("Rita" I, 208). Poetry conjures up the skin-
deep experience of a vulnerable body whose orifices cannot resist the intrusion of the exterior: "Her restless words begin, like the hot lick of snow,
their incisions" ("Rita" I, 184).[18]

Raymond's injunction, "It's high time we got down to the text," checks
the autonomous spurting out of signifiers to ensure the constriction of
meaning. Shaping meaning out of Rita's verbal dejections, in other words,
shifting from the *anal* to the *annals*, is a tactic to tap verbal leakage and
convert the corpus into a monument. Bataille provocatively showed in "La
notion de dépense" that there is no safe passage into art. As Rita disappeared precisely *into art* ("Rita" I, 204), she can well tease Raymond about
being a constipated writer: "You should drink your apple juice, it will
relieve your anxiety about your bowel movements" ("Rita" I, 213), followed by: "You are the prisoner of space, not I, Raymond. And please, if
nothing else, I beg you, drink your apple juice" ("Rita" I, 214).

Raymond's amorous reconstruction of Rita's textual body parallels the
relationship between Daisy's parents in *The Stone Diaries*. Mercy's massive
body does not leak: it is a fluid-tight container out of which perspiration,
menstrual blood, words even, hardly ever ooze (*Diaries* 5-6, 60). Her body
is consistently described as a stronghold complete with floor ("the floor of
her chest" [*Diaries* 4]), vault (*Diaries* 7), and walls ("her abdominal walls"
[*Diaries* 6]; "the folded interior walls of her body" [*Diaries* 7]). She seems to
have inherited this heaviness along with the name of the place she was
given at the Stonewall Orphans' Home: "Mercy Stone weighs forty stone"
(*Diaries* 30).

Contrary to Mercy's fortress, male bodies are described as leather pouches
holding fluids, their private parts "a sack of loose blue flesh between [their]
legs" (*Diaries* 22). Their fragility is most strikingly shown in the accident

that befalls Daisy's first husband in the French city of Corps, an emblematic name, since it fittingly translates as "body": "and then [she] hears a bang, a crashing sound like a melon splitting, a wet injurious noise followed by the screaming of children" (*Diaries* 119-20). As in "The Poetics of Rita Kleinhart," the emission of words or fluids threatens the male subject with a radical form of dissolution. Only a body as formidable as Mercy's can therefore safely receive and contain Cuyler's ardour: "There in the sheeted width of their feather bed, his roughened male skin discovering the abundant soft flesh of his wife's body, enclosing it, entering it—that was the moment when the stone in his throat became dislodged....Words gathered in his mouth then, words he hadn't known were part of his being. They leapt from his lips: his gratitude, his ardor, his most private longings" (*Diaries* 84).

After Mercy's death in childbirth, the stonecutter erects a limestone tower to commemorate his beloved. The building of the tower coincides with Cuyler's discovery that he is a gifted orator. The passionate words he poured into his wife's willing ear are followed by cataracts of speeches addressed to the tourists who come to admire the structure, then, later, to larger audiences as the obscure Manitoba worker rises in status to the position of associate partner in a large American stonecutting company (*Diaries* 85). As a metaphor, however, the tower fails to replace Mercy: the seeping out of words opened an unstoppable breach in Cuyler. He loses his carving gift and gradually shrinks into a blathering garden dwarf (*Diaries* 115). Cuyler's end somehow echoes Red Rorty's in Howard O'Hagan's paradigmatic novel *Tay John*: "the word has choked him."[19]

To preserve a contained fullness, the male characters react as if they had internalized Northrop Frye's pronouncement by constructing the female body as a place their discourse can securely invest. The female body is all the more safe as it is rhetorically fixed, formulated. Feminist criticism has convincingly argued that female autobiography is characterized by its double stance, women presenting themselves both as the product of the discourse of others and as individuals.[20] The subsequent questions therefore arise: Can women use their own bodies as a version of garrison to protect their individuality? What happens when women presume to leave the garrison of discourse erected around them?

Minimal Bodies / Invisible Selves

In these biotexts, the reader comes to the disturbing realization that the female body hardly exists outside the discourse that embodies it.[21] Contrary to expectations, the photographs included in *The Stone Diaries* and in

Mothertalk do not satisfy the reader's curiosity. As Simone Vauthier points out, the pictures in *The Stone Diaries* "derealize" more than they confirm the narrative account.[22] Mercy's picture belies the bloated, barrel-like figure the reader had come to expect. As for her daughter Daisy, although she stands at the very centre of narrative speculation, there is no picture of her. In Kiyooka's book, the effect is slightly different, as the set of photographs showing Mary does not bear a caption. As a result, her body cannot be identified as distinct from the surrounding constellation of family and friends (*Mothertalk* 80-93). It is only after reading the subsequent chapter that the reader can match body and description (*Mothertalk* 94-104). Even as we shuttle back and forth between pictures and commentary, Mary Kiyooka remains part of a continuum between her children—the first two pictures—and her father, whose photo in traditional dress caps the series. Rita's blurred snapshots of her neighbours' back doors translate into the flow of her poems ("Rita" I, 174-75). Similarly, the posed pictures in *The Stone Dairies* and *Mothertalk* release the body back into the movement of narrative, confirming Barthes's intuition that the perception of our body exceeds visual representation.[23]

The paradoxical failure of these photographs to *represent* may be approached if we bear in mind that women do not readily perceive their bodies as circumscribable entities insofar as the boundaries between the inside and the outside that define the universal (male) subject do not apply to them. In Sidonie Smith's words: "There is no isolable core of selfhood there for woman for in the act of heterosexual intercourse, the female body is penetrated by the body of the other and in the experience of pregnancy, that other that is part of the subject takes up greater and greater space until it is suddenly expelled. Inside is outside; outside inside. The cultural notion of autonomous individuality is totally confused."[24]

The example of Mary Kiyooka is here particularly telling. She belonged to a generation of Japanese women whose existence depended solely on their position within the group. A woman was born a daughter to a man, to be given as a wife to another. There was no way out of marriage for Meiji women who, on their wedding day, received a nuptial sword with the words: "If you have to leave his household use the sword" (*Mothertalk* 69). Mary Kiyooka's use of the singular "I" therefore inevitably borders onto the collective "we." As her narrative proceeds, it aggregates the stories of countless picture brides for whom sailing to Canadian shores towards an unknown bridegroom was the sole option to keep body and soul together. The reader senses the satisfaction of the folktale teller weaving the cohesion of social fabric into her story when she concludes after recounting these women's lives: "They had several kids and lived long useful lives" (*Mothertalk* 52).

Her own body achieves singularity as a vector for symbolic exchange between the living and the dead:[25] she successfully transmits her father's writing gift to one of her sons and reciprocates the gift by erecting a stone to commemorate the grandfather. The question of the monumental stone therefore frames *Mothertalk*. The book opens with Mary's restless worrying about the stone ghost of her father: "The big stone has been inscribed and is lying half asleep ... I would like to see that big stone hold its blunt head up to the sun" (*Mothertalk* 19, see also 163). It reaches its close as Mary gets confirmation that her father's disciples have gathered enough money to erect the stone on consecrated ground (*Mothertalk* 170). The stratification of authors that elaborated *Mothertalk* performs a ritual whose function is identical to the inscribed stone's: "to tell others who we Oes were" (*Mothertalk* 165). This sentence is echoed in the book's final words: "When I pass away there won't be a soul left to tell how the heart-of-Tosa sang in our home behind an English facade" (*Mothertalk* 172). And yet, the book proffers its eloquent answer as Mary's circulated stories are enshrined into book form, the fabric of stories a fitting monument to the spinner of yarns who died in 1996 in Edmonton at the age of 100.

Born in 1905, Daisy Goodwill almost belongs to Mary Kiyooka's generation. In spite of the culture gap between the real woman and Shields's character, Daisy is said to have a "talent for self-obliteration" (*Diaries* 124) that is somehow reminiscent of Mary's. Carol Shields has constructed a novel in which Daisy's personal account is bracketed in and is undercut by others' discourses. Probing the novel's aporetic narrative stance, Simone Vauthier concludes that *The Stone Diaries* obliges readers to avoid "the regressive entanglement of self-referentiality."[26] I would like to confront the text's demand for a "new, non-mimetic reading"[27] with the emphasis it lays upon mimicry and the implicit suggestion that the eye never sees the subject as it is, but as it intends to be seen.

It is vital for living organisms on a prairie landscape to develop a system of concealment to avoid exposure and to negotiate existence. Unlike the prostitutes Barker used to visit in Montreal, his wife Daisy does not threaten his sense of self-possession, provided she remains a flower, as charmingly innocuous as the species listed in his botanical charts. To be approached, she needs to undergo transformations that disguise her corporeality: "The house is orderly, the children asleep, and she herself is bathed, powdered, diaphragmed, and softly nightgowned" (*Diaries* 186). When sexual intercourse follows, it is described with a scientific detachment that recalls how the small prairie orchid called lady's slipper lures an insect inside its pouched lip to ensure pollination (*Diaries* 191). Daisy's body is referred to in terms that displace her femininity towards the vegetal: "her own buttocks—like soft fruit spreading out beneath her on the firm mattress" (*Diaries* 192, see also 160).

"Mimicry," Jacques Lacan writes, "reveals something in so far as it is distinct from what might be called an itself that is behind. The effect of mimicry is camouflage.... It is not a question of harmonizing with the background, but against a mottled background, of becoming mottled."[28] Here the translator opted for the word *mottled* to render the French *bigarré*. Another possible translation would have been "motley." What Daisy Goodwill discovered in Clarentine Flett's Winnipeg garden is a motley world where wildflowers have mouths, teeth, and tiny tongues (*Diaries* 338). By turning into a flower, Daisy responds to the prairie environment in a way that opens onto the collective experience of the carnival, when identity becomes unstable and subject to multiple definitions.[29] As Lacan emphasizes, it would be pointless to look for a unified subject behind the motley background with which Daisy merges. When the moment of her death approaches, she dissolves into the daisy of the popular song: "Daisy Daisy / Give me your answer true / Day's eye, Day's eye / The face in the mirror is you" (*Diaries* 344). The mirror reflection conjures up the image of an eye or "I" that blends with the passing of days, the love of men, the birth of children, the seasons she spends tending the garden. As her learned daughter puts it: "that garden of hers, it functioned like a kind of trope in her daily life" (*Diaries* 236). The shape-shifter does not exist behind her garden; she is the garden. The metaphorical displacement of woman into flower provides her with a culturally coded, in other words, acceptable, alias. Later, and this time through synecdochic reduction, it also initiates her entry into writing as "Mrs. Green Thumb," the successful writer of a weekly column on gardening.

In Prairie society, where gender construction has traditionally been strict, men with few words[30] might also find it convenient to borrow from women their ploys to negotiate social prescriptions. After Clarentine has left him, Magnus Flett finds in her sewing basket the penny novelettes his wife read on the sly. Among them he discovers Currer Bell's *Jane Eyre*. In a desperate attempt to grasp why his wife escaped the attic of their marriage, Magnus inverts Charlotte Brontë's devious mimicking of a male voice. He learns the whole novel by heart, as if the expression of grief and longing could only be allowed by incorporating a woman's diction: "If this talky foolishness was her greatest need, he would be prepared to meet her, a pump primed with words full of softness and acknowledgement: O beautiful eyes, O treasured countenance, O fairest of skin. Or phrases that spoke of the overflowing heart, the rising of desire in the breast, the sudden clarities of one body saluting another or even the simple declaration. I love you, he whispered, into her waiting ear" (*Diaries* 100-01).

Once again, words have the instability of fluids that rise and overflow. And yet, Magnus preserves his bodily integrity as he memorizes the whole unadulterated text. His case of ventriloquism therefore prevents leakage and the impending danger of losing hold of oneself, a risk the Rita/Raymond duo does not avoid.

In "On the Art of Building in Ten Hornbooks," Dawne McCance eloquently debunks attempts to dress Rita and Raymond in the trappings of classic Doppelgängerism.[31] They are neither "the two halves of a whole, the once-perfect being of Plato's *Symposium*," McCance writes, nor a reconfiguration of "the Greek couple Hestia and Hermes, two sides of the theoretical binary private/public, interior/exterior, passivity/activity."[32] Challenging the law's "single voice," which would confine the autobiographer to house arrest ("Rita" II, 28),[33] Rita and Raymond open the possibility of a "contamination" between voices, thus radically upsetting fixed binaries.[34]

Starting from McCance's reading, I would suggest that contamination occurs when the repressed body of traditional male autobiography gets dislocated and relocated into a female body whose leakages "sap the power of self-unification."[35] "*Retreating from his own back door / the invisible man stepped on his invisible dog / and, having been bitten, bled red blood*" ("Rita" I, 181). By trading places with Rita, Raymond's disembodied self achieves the paradoxical visibility of the writerly trace. As he crosses the threshold of both her house and her poems, he enters writing—"I read them and am compelled by their knotted intentions into words of my own" ("Rita" I, 192). Through his repeated crossing of the female text, Raymond comes to exist beside himself, as part of a flux where body and prairie drift into momentary convergence:

> "Sometimes," Rita said, "I want to go all the way up to the tree line."

> We were hiking together, into the bare, south-facing coulee hills to the west of the ranch. I helped Rita take off her hiking boots and her socks. I kissed the blisters on the bottom of her toes. As I knew on my lips the changing taste of her sweat I knew I had strayed from her toes to her ankles, then from her ankles to the backs of her knees, then from the

sweaty backs of her knees to her inner thighs. She said, at the edge of my hearing, "All I can see is empty sky."

Lying on my belt, facing east, all I could see was the bush of her body.

"Bush" I whispered. ("Rita" I, 211-12)

Rita seeks erasure through space; her gaze takes her always further north or west, thus adumbrating the promise in Hornbook #13: "Somewhere out there / the fence is down" ("Rita" II, 29). Conversely, in Raymond's charted, east-oriented vision, the female body intersects with space on the literal level. The textual blur that results from the sudden shift in vision is an example of how "The Poetics of Rita Kleinhart" shuttles between perceptions, decentring the self towards a periphery where it comes into contact with the outside: a lover's skin, but also "the deceptive randomness of wind and rain and sky ... the violence and the blinding inevitability of prairie sun" ("Rita" I, 200).

Maybe the word "friction," rather than "contamination," would here better evoke the abrasion that occurs between Rita's verbal leakage and Raymond's yearning for form. Rita teases the archivist: "If urine came forth as song, you'd still manage to remain silent" ("Rita" I, 204). And yet, the scatological imagery[36] that runs throughout "The Poetics of Rita Kleinhart" points obliquely toward the possibility of shaping the amorphous. Raymond arranges Rita's drafts and notes into colours "Blue-One," "Yellow-Three," "Blue-Two," which do not register as a code but sound like a chord of colours in a non-figurative painting, dissipating even further the non-linear arrangement of the hornbooks' sequence.

Raymond compulsively quotes fragments that involve minimal shaping: in Exhibit A, an argumentative scaffold holds together a riot of signifiers;[37] in Hornbook #81, the prescribed alphabetical order of lines and initials is contradicted by the unpredictable configuration of words within each line: "antiquarian apes arrange ancestors / bees brush berries' bosoms / crimped clowns cuddle catastrophes" ("Rita" I, 212). A similar tension is evident in lines where excessive repetition does not quite allow the exhaustion of the signified, as incremental variations let a halo of signification persist:[38] *"crushed shale in my lane, / rain falling on fallen rain on / crushed red shale, fire, flood."* ("Rita" I, 190).[39]

The lovers bicker: "'Embrace,' I suggested.'Not surround.' 'Surround she said'" ("Rita" I, 205). Rita's insistence recalls[40] her "conviction that she might so write her poems that she would leave each object or place or person that fell under her attention undisturbed" ("Rita" I, 179). Far from freezing the substance of Rita's art, Raymond propagates her words as he delineates the contours of her poems. In fact, the textual loopholes that bind Rita and Raymond are reminiscent of a line by René Char that, according to Maurice Blanchot, encapsulates the poet's "torn unity":[41] "Le poète est la genèse d'un être qui projette et d'un être qui retient."[42] In Char's vibrant formulation, the poet is born again and again out of himself in the spasm of his utterance, between release and retention. As a result, poetry coincides neither with a surrender to shapelessness nor with a consolidation into form. Rather, it occurs when the trajectory of the line takes it beyond these two poles. In "The Poetics of Rita Kleinhart," poetry defines itself against the impossible horizon of an ecstasy under strictures. As such, it borders on the enigmatic, ineffable experience of a jouissance *in the feminine*;[43] as such it is also akin to the erasure that prairie space promises.

Bodies in Translation

In *The Stone Diaries, Mothertalk,* and "The Poetics of Rita Kleinhart," the Prairies do not register as a place of origin. They appear instead as a place of arrivals and departures, a transient home for the homeless as in Mary Kiyooka's immigrant story: "O I'll never forget that trip through the Rockies and that slow trip across the limitless prairies. Papa and I had never seen anything like it. We Issei came from one small prefecture or another we knew the boundaries of. I was dismayed by the distances between people, places and things in Canada" (*Mothertalk* 69).

After the initial shock, the boundlessness of the new place is welcomed, as it will contribute to preserving intact the etched memory of lost Nippon: "There's a landscape-of-the-heart you won't locate in any geography book" (*Mothertalk* 160). In its abundance, Mary's tongue-tide or tongue-tied chatter[44] somehow silences the possibility that the female body might serve other purposes than being a vector for the family line, and this at any expense. For readers, it is difficult to resist the suggestion that there might be a concealed story in the prostitution anecdotes that recur obsessively in the narrative:[45] "There were Issei women who made a living by sleeping around. Most of them had husbands who knew what was going on but simply put up with it. After all it didn't matter where the money came from when the going was tough" (*Mothertalk* 72, see also 103-04). No matter what it might have cost them, women of Mary's calibre never deserted the garrison.[46] Their resilience and their dignity command respect from the group.

The overwhelming presence of the group also comes to the fore in *The Stone Diaries*. It finds an expression in the metaphor of the fossil, as the layers of voices surrounding Daisy's elusive presence encase the wilting flower and retain its fragile imprint (*Diaries* 292, 301). The mausoleum Daisy's father erected against death and the horizontality of space disappears as visitors take away its exquisitely carved stones, one by one (*Diaries* 267). The mother's huge body consequently survives oblivion once its scattered fragments are shared collectively.[47] The Prairies' sense of the collective therefore gives rise to challenging literary practices, something Northrop Frye could not necessarily have foreseen in an age of individualism. Whereas in traditional male autobiographies, "the man is forever adding himself to himself,"[48] the biotexts that get elaborated around the absence of Daisy and Rita work by way of subtraction. Against the male positioning of an eternal feminine, the female body insists that it exists otherwise, in other guises. Rita's, and Daisy's surrender of authorship in their respective stories is not perceived as a loss but as an entry into writing, as the traces their disappearing bodies leave behind offer us the tantalizing possibility of a reconstruction.

Endnotes

1. Sandra Carolan-Brozy uses the term "biotext" in relation to texts that do not conform to traditional autobiographical patterns. See Sandra Carolan-Brozy, "'You Just Don't Concern Me Now' vs. 'Why We Must Talk': Lee Maracle's Biotexts," *Anglophonia, Canada: Fractures mais non ruptures*, 1 (1997): 55-66.

2. Georges Gusdorf, "Conditions and Limits of Autobiography," in *Autobiography: Essays Theoretical and Critical,* ed. James Olney (Princeton, NJ: Princeton University Press, 1980), 43.

3. "Tout ceci doit être considéré comme dit par un personnage de roman." Roland Barthes, *Roland Barthes par Roland Barthes, Oeuvres complètes*, vol. III: 1974-80 (Paris: Seuil, 1994), 80. The translation is mine.

4. "The concept of the unified self completely deconstructed, autobiography becomes, in Paul de Man's formulation, impossible, disfiguring that which it figures forth. An autobiographer, such as Derrida or Barthes, can only displace and dislocate the signature of the 'I' of the text, can only enact the impossibility of making the self present, so to speak, to oneself." Shirley Neuman, "Autobiography: From Different Poetics to a Poetics of Differences," in *Essays on Life Writing: From Genre to Critical Practice*, ed. Marlene Kadar (Toronto, Buffalo, London: University of Toronto Press, 1992), 215.

5. Carol Shields, *The Stone Diaries* (London: Fourth Estate, Ltd., 1994), 75. Subsequent quotations from this edition are referred to as *Diaries* and given within parentheses in the text.

6. Roy Kiyooka, *Mothertalk: Life Stories of Mary Kiyoshi Kiyooka*, ed. Daphne Marlatt (Edmonton: NeWest Press, 1997). Subsequent quotations from this book are referred to as *Mothertalk* and are given within parentheses in the text.

7. Robert Kroetsch, "The Poetics of Rita Kleinhart," in *A Likely Story: The Writing Life* (Red Deer, AB: Red Deer Press, 1995). The second instalment was published in *Prairie Fire* 17, no. 2 (Summer 1996): 28–31. Subsequent quotations are referred to as "Rita" I and "Rita" II for each instalment, respectively, and are given within parentheses in the text.

8. Northrop Frye, *The Bush Garden: Essays on the Canadian Imagination* (Concord, ON: Anansi, 1995), 227.

9. Ibid., 228.

10. Ibid., 218.

11. Susan Stanford Friedman, "Women's Autobiographical Selves, Theory and Practice," in *The Private Self: Theory and Practice of Women's Autobiographical Writings,* ed. Shari Benstock (Chapel Hill: University of North Carolina Press, 1988), 34.

12. Ibid., 35.

13. Ibid., 39.

14. George Bowering, "The Stump," in *The Rain Barrel* (Vancouver: TalonBooks, 1994), 199.

15. See W.H. New's chapter "The Artifice of Landscape" in *Land Sliding: Imagining Space, Presence, and Power in Canadian Writing* (Toronto, Buffalo, London: University of Toronto Press, 1997).

16. Julia Kristeva, *Polylogue* (Paris: Seuil, 1977), 14.

17. Julia Kristeva uses the conclusions of anthropologist Mary Douglas on the rites that transform profane dirtiness into sacred taintedness. She demonstrates that the notion of abjection points to a logic of exclusion whereby each social group defines itself as proper. What is true for the group also holds for the individual as the child's access to the symbolic order coincides with the age of sphyncteral training. *Pouvoirs de l'horreur, essai sur l'abjection* (Paris: Seuil, 1980), 80.

18. See, for instance, the dwindling flow in the following lines: "Once upon a time, long ago. / Long a time. Once upon a go. / Long upon ago a once a time. / A time ago upon. A long. A once. / I was trying to tell you a story, Rita. I had troubled getting stopped" ("Rita" I, 196). In its ambiguity—"I had trouble(d) getting stopped"—the last statement testifies to Raymond's anxiety.

19. Howard O'Hagan, *Tay John* (Toronto: McClelland and Stewart [1939], 1974), 28.

20. Neuman, "Autobiography," 218.

21. See Sidonie Smith's reading of Judith Butler: "the masculine 'I' is the noncorporeal soul. The body rendered as Other—the body repressed or denied and, then, projected—reemerges from this 'I' as the view of others as essentially body. Hence, women become the Other; they come to embody corporeality itself. This redundancy becomes their essence." *Subjectivity, Identity and the Body: Women's Autobiographical Practices in the Twentieth Century* (Bloomington and Indianapolis: Indiana University Press, 1993), 11.

22. Simone Vauthier, "Ruptures in Carol Shields's *The Stone Diaries," Anglophonia. Canada: Fractures mais non ruptures* 1 (1997): 188.

23. Roland Barthes, *The Pleasure of the Text*, trans. Richard Miller (New York: Hill and Wang, [1973] 1975), 232.

24. Smith, *Subjectivity*, 12.

25. I am referring here to Baudrillard's analysis of the symbolic exchange in feudal societies in *L'Echange symbolique et la mort* (Paris: Gallimard, 1976).

26. Vauthier, "Ruptures," 191.

27. Ibid., 187.

28. Jacques Lacan, *The Four Fundamental Concepts of Psychoanalysis*, trans. Alan Sheridan, (London: The Hogarth Press and the Institute of Psycho-analysis, 1977), 99.

29. See Robert Kroetsch's essay: "Carnival and Violence: A Meditation," in *The Lovely Treachery of Words: Essays Selected and New* (Toronto, New York, Oxford: Oxford University Press, 1989), 95-107.

30. Cf O'Hagan, *Tay John*, 91: "Those with few words must know how to use them."

31. Dawne McCance, "On the Art of Building in Ten Hornbooks," *The New Quarterly* 18, no. 1 (Spring 1998): 161-73. Jean Baudrillard connects the *Doppelgänger* with Freud's notion of the uncanny. In the double that comes back to haunts the self, Baudrillard sees a resistance to the imposition of the Law of the Father. *L'Echange symbolique et la mort*, 218.

32. McCance, "Art of Building," 166.

33. Dawne McCance shows that "house," "archive," and "autobiography" are etymologically as well as historically connected. The moment when architects thought of creating a central place in the house, a closet, where the master of the house would devote himself to writing, coincided with the emergence of autobiography as a distinct literary genre. McCance, "Art of Building."

34. McCance, "Art of Building," 167.

35. Smith, *Subjectivity*, 20.

36. The back door, the irresistible ass of LiPo's beloved, and Rita's perfect behind insist that "at the bottom, we might say, is an ass, rather than a reflection of the autobiographer's face." (Kroetsch, "Rita" I, 164).

37. For a fascinating analysis of Kroetsch's poem as hubbub, see Pamela Banting, *Body, Inc.: A Theory of Translation Poetics* (Winnipeg: Turnstone Press, 1995), 115 *et passim*.

38. Barthes, *The Pleasure of the Text,* 41: "[R]epetition itself creates bliss. There are many ethnographic examples: obsessive rhythms, incantatory music, litanies … to repeat excessively is to enter into loss, into the zero of the signified."

39. See also: "*You are what remains after night's fall. / You are what remains after nights fail*" (Kroetsch, "Rita" I, 213).

40. The embracing and/or surrounding debate is just as difficult to settle as the question of how to eat a peach: "She had a way of splitting a peach with a knife, then removing the stone. I prefer to eat the stone free of the sweet smelling flesh" (Kroetsch, "Rita" I, 204).

41. Maurice Blanchot, *L'Espace littéraire* (Paris: Gallimard, 1955), 305.

42. "The poet is the genesis of a being that projects and of a being that holds back." The translation is mine. Blanchot analyzes Char's line at length in *L'Espace littéraire*, 300-04.

43. Feminine *jouissance*, Lacan argues, occurs beyond the Phallus; as such it remains unspeakable. See also *Le Séminaire,* vol. XX, *Encore* (Paris: Seuil, 1975): 68-69: "Il n'y a de femme qu'exclue par la nature des choses qui est la nature des mots.... Il n'en reste pas moins que si elle est exclue par la nature des choses, c'est justement de ceci que, d'être pas toute, elle a, par rapport à ce que désigne de jouissance la fonction phallique, une jouissance supplémentaire. ... Il y a une jouissance ... jouissance du corps, qui est ... *au-delà du phallus."*

44. The pun is Roy Kiyooka's: "a tongue-tide language" (*Mothertalk* 77) and "I've been left with a tied tongue" (*Mothertalk* 181).

45. I am here referring to discussions among the participants of Robert Kroetsch's seminar on female autobiography. We all admitted, however reluctantly, that the possibility of this unofficial story had indeed come to our minds.

46. By way of contrast, quite a number of her anecdotes recount how both the family and the individual break down as soon as one of its members becomes estranged (*Mothertalk* 32, 139, 169).

47. McCance, "Art of Building," 163: "Collective biography resists the myth of community as wholeness, the narrative of a (male) unitary being that preexists writing and is made manifest through it. What it suggests is spacing: rather than sameness, the particularity of place, the play of the juncture, where differences touch, tumble into each other, without ever fusing into one. Collective biography opens onto the infinite singularity of the common world."

48. Gusdorf, "Conditions and Limits," 45.

Life Sentence, passwords, and local pride: prairie in the poetic journals of Eli Mandel and Dennis Cooley

Karen Clavelle

EARLY AUG/98

It occurs to me, as I begin to write this essay, that I might consider writing a journal on the journals: Dennis Cooley's *passwords*[1] and Eli Mandel's *Life Sentence.*[2]

But, aren't essays journals, in a manner of speaking?

Why not? What's happening, for example, in Mandel's *long liner's*[3] notes, in essays in Kroetsch's *Lovely Treachery of Words,*[4] in Cooley's *The Vernacular Muse?*[5]

> treachery
> anarchy
> breaking the line, breaking the form
> metaphorically breaking the sod
> breaking ground
> breaking wind!

:defining the prairies

How do you define the prairies? Markus Müller[6] asks, and my answer surprises me. "Not with words," I say. "You absorb them and they you." It's a case of immersion; the medium. I don't want to argue that the above essays *are* journals, only to suggest that as peculiar kinds of essays they demand a larger reading than the form would ordinarily allow. Similarly, *passwords* and *Life Sentence* demand readings beyond what might be afforded *journal,* the genre to which, deceptively, they lay some claim. These texts do appear in part to be quotidian accounts of a number of journeys, Cooley's and Mandel's, respectively, hence their manifestation as journals. The subject at hand is double-edged: there is definition and then there is the question of *how* things are defined, an oblique working toward prairie, I would say.

Here, the Great Plains, curiously doubled with the plain in Spain, Cooley and Mandel there together and not there at all. "Wherever you are, you are here," Molly Rhutabaga says, quoting her father, in what looks suspiciously like a journal in Méira Cook's *The Blood Girls*.[7] More prairie poetry, the question of genre. What's Cooley writing? and Mandel? I want to argue long poem, but here, in the landscape, I have not space; space, place not interchangeable; they're binaries, one dis-placing the other. Place takes space. Occupies it, fills it up.

Aug 13

Separated by place, separated by time: Mandel in 1978, Cooley in 1990, put together by occupation, journal, by place, by our reading, in 1998. Mandel, born in Estevan, Saskatchewan, 1922. Cooley, born in Estevan, Saskatchewan, 1944. They are doubles by fate and no less by design. Dennis Cooley, twenty-two years younger than Mandel, with, as he likes to point out, two sets of double letters in his name. Mandel, who loved doublings, would have loved looking at these two texts together.

Cooley doubles for Mandel, does not re-place or stand in for him, but creates a reference to Mandel through the text, coolly doubling with his own. Mandel, in Spain, recalls in memory, memory of riot scenes he's known at home: "Estevan 1932, Regina when the South Saskatchewan Regiment went on the rampage against the Germans in Regina in early WWII and my Uncle Ike, the Colonel of the Regiment bringing the men into order riding their truck down 11th Avenue and ordering them to their places through a bullhorn" (*Sentence* 128).

What evokes the South Saskatchewan Regiment for Cooley, I would say, is Mandel's text; its inclusion in *passwords* inspired by Cooley's conscious desire for poly-textuality, polymorphosity, perhaps, for repetition, for patterns, for doubling in his journal, his desire to evoke Mandel, moreover, his desire as writer (aware, too, of the construct of writer) for palimpsest.

"Dennis," Cooley writes, "here's where the South Saskatchewan Regiment attacked at Pourville, near Dieppe on July 19th, 1942 [the date is crossed out, deliberately written under erasure, a parallel to the people figuratively crossed out, literally under erasure, a whole regiment] Aug 19th, 1942. "The beach is not as expansive as it looks here" (*passwords* 213). As it looks "here"? Where is "here"? The real beach? Which is the real beach?

Cooley may be looking at the construct of a beach but he is not looking at *the* beach; he is nowhere near Dieppe. Is he looking at a map, at a photo, at an article in a magazine? Cooley, clearly aware of hermeneutics, foregrounds the role of the writer as interpreter, as mediator (or, in a sense, casting the writer as a boundary) between what he sees and what he records.

Aug 14

Meeting, my first, with Birk Sproxton,[8] here, in St. John's College, who says the Japanese word *utaniki* … mentions Roy Miki's writing on bp (nicol). The idea suits perfectly the journals I am reading: poetic journals, a more satisfying name by far. A blurring of borders. Writing about borders is popular right now; the word *border* shows up everywhere. Mandel introducing the segment of *Life Sentence* on Spain in the following words: "We have come to a border France/Spain. The border between past and present, there and here, this place that time" (*Sentence* 126). These are the words that immediately precede the section of *Life Sentence* entitled "Barcelona." In two small sentences Eli Mandel grasps the whole universe and chronos besides.

In music, this kind of transition is called a bridge; it may contain elements of musical concern common to each of the sections being joined. In *passwords*, Cooley bridges place in a way uncannily similar to what Mandel does above: "Metaphor—a bringing across, from one site to another. / Metaphor, a Greek taxi. / We travail, we cross over. / The traffic of words & bodies" (*passwords* 201). These are words that precede Cooley's *spain: gijon*, following the heading "July 2." But Cooley's transition has yet to be made. "Lindy, we are going to Portugal," he writes (*passwords* 202). In point of fact, Cooley is *not*, at that point, headed for Portugal. He is going to Spain, and he will get there in writing, making many, many crossovers. His friends in Winnipeg and Germany, by virtue of being named in this passage, make their own contributions to Cooley's juxtapositions of place. Lindy is in Winnipeg; Zirker is planning a Canadian conference for Trier. Cooley-from-the-prairie in the train in France, headed for Spain, "They say it has hailed in Winnipeg," Cooley writes, "& the world is rank with green" (*passwords* 202). Crossing out of Germany, crossing through France to Spain in early July, Cooley is in a *world* of rank green. Two worlds: the world *outwith* and the world within. "But there's the local beer, he says [he being Zirker], that pun. A source of pride for those raised here: Dorothee Gressnich, Markus Müller, Dorothee tells me it's the best beer in the world" (*passwords* 202). Cooley's reference is doubled, taking in not only Zirker's reference to *Bittburger* Beer, pondering, I'm told, the words *Bitt Bitte*, one of the few puns available in the German language, but also William Carlos Williams's opening words in his long poem, *Paterson,*[9] "a local pride." References to prairie, in Cooley as in Mandel, demonstrate the poets' own local pride.

> *July 3*
> *5:30 p.m.*
>
>   Through Luxembourg on our way to Paris. Last night in the flat I woke everyone laughing in my sleep. Love this countryside again the way it is. 'Messy' less filled. Spaces where animals can be and there they are. Cows–Holsteins–loll around pastures, being cows, & there are other ones lying, flour sacks or sandstone. (*passwords* 202)

This is Cooley in transit.

> *July 4/90*
> *8:00 a.m.*
> *Irun, Spain*

I look ahead: although Cooley will arrive in Irun, Spain, on July 4th, it will be July 7th when he actually mentions Gijon again. His transition, then, *in writing*, will take an entire week to travel what, in point of fact, will take a few days, and during that time, Cooley, gravitating back to Winnipeg, to the prairies, will figuratively cross and re-cross the Atlantic ocean a dozen or more times.

Reading about hermeneutics in *place/culture/representation.*[10] The reader understands a text by situating it within two interpenetrating fields of reference, the extra-textual, the reader's experiences in the world, and the inter-textual, the context of other texts. The world in the text is continually compared to the world outside the text. This is what they do, Cooley and Mandel. Interpenetrating fields of reference, the plains in Spain, the readers' writers' experience in the world: their's, foregrounding writing, foregrounding place, foregrounding the *home* place, the world outside the new text, the landscape of the new place.

Aug 20

Reading Edward S. Casey's *The Fate of Place* and Plato's *Receptacle* comes in to the discussion.

> *Hupodoché'*, one of its [*Receptacle's*] names in Greek (besides dechomenon, literally, "the recipient"), gives a crucial clue [to what it is]. The Receptacle is what lies *under* (hupo) that which appears in the physical world. It is an underlying "region of regions," to borrow a concept from Husserl (who, however, applied it to consciousness, not the material world). Not being that "out of which" (*ex hou*) things are made . . . it is the "in which" (en hoi) on which things (qualities, powers, notions: ultimately perceptible things) come to appearance, exchange position and gain their place.[11]

I am reading "receptacle" in part as vessel, which seems more positive, separating what is outwith from that which is within, functioning, in part, as a border. (I've chosen the word *outwith* because although the words that comprise it are simply in reverse of common order, I don't want to evoke the element of absence. I want, instead, to explore/promote the idea of border with relation to a vessel of containment, without its being *ex*-clusive.) As a poem or journal is to a book, so is a poem or a journal to a poet/ writer, the book and the person being the receptacle or recipient/holder of the words. Within this view, the body of words held can be read as a "region of regions," lying under that which appears in the physical world; in this case, the body or the text. This reading, then, renders the "region of regions" portable as receptacles are portable. It is a small step from a vessel of containment to a vessel of inscription, and, clearly, prairie poets and their poems are both: containing on the one hand and simultaneously inscribed and inscribing on the other.

Moreover, Cooley and Mandel, inscribed and inscribing *prairie,* are imprinted, taking with them wherever they go their "region of regions" under their skin and transposing (another musical concept) the "region of regions" to words within, in this case, the skin of a poetic journal.

Aug 30

Defining the Prairies: the whole impulse behind this discussion. Thought I'd try to focus on how Cooley's and Mandel's journals define the prairies but perhaps it is true that the prairies, instead, define them. I don't think the question of "how" is any smaller in either case. Inscribed; inscribing. Cooley names his anthology of prairie writing *Inscriptions*. The understanding of prairie resides in the inscriptions; in the case of the poets, in the *fixed* variables comprising the "region of regions" they carry within themselves. Fixed variable: an oxymoron that perfectly describes the prairie as efficiently as it describes the sea in another oxymoron: constant motion.

Thinking of place as a receptacle: prairie. A receptacle always has something in it; even when we see and observe that it is empty, it is full of air. So it is with the prairie, as Cooley remarks in the long poem *Fielding*: "not empty this space is not empty."[12] So it is with the poets away from home in a place devoid of the western Canadian prairie. We look through the poets' eyes and see not the absence of prairie in the European place but instead the vessel, the "region of regions" in an other place: Spain. The word "vessel": vassal, a *holder* of land. Cooley and Mandel, vassals, too.

Aug 31

How do you get there from here? How do you get here from there? One of the things that traditional poetry has done through the years is to disembody the voice behind the poem. The task of actually getting a body into a literary work is formidable; in a very real sense, I suppose, impossible: literally, it cannot be done. A journal, on the other hand, is at best arguably disembodied. At best, the only manifestation of writer will be words purported to represent the self, something we usually take as perhaps the main attribute of a journal. Although Cooley retains the reflexiveness of a journal in certain places, both as poet and narrator, in the Spanish section he privileges place. (Note the subtle separation of the poet Cooley from his narrator "cooley," a distinction made clear by the use of the upper and lower case letter "c.") Moreover, he privileges *prairie* place, "the home place," to include a "Kroetsch-ism," so to speak, as opposed to Spanish place. As I have already shown, even as he enters Spain, Cooley brings to the journal people from home and what has become, in the journal at least, people from home away from home (Germany).

> Dreamt a BlueJays[13] game much of the night, he writes, they played beautifully. [This is still a dream.] ... Sun bright 8 hours from Gijon, he writes. A Winnipegger looking forward to these parts. Gardens beside the railway here, too, gardens throughout Europe only here the soil looks like soil. [When does soil not look like soil; don't know if the reference is to home or Europe.] 10:30 country easy on the prairie eye, open country soil looks poor. [Another "region of regions." The point of reference becomes clear. And a reference to the landscape of the mind:] How numbingly incomprehensible the notion of puritanism was to the students in Germany when we earlier discussed it.

> 1:15 Nearing Lyon where we change trains. Land looks remarkably like home—miles and miles of wheat and canola, few houses. "The landscape

takes my imagination, as at home," Eli Mandel found, over a decade ago, passing through Spain. (*passwords* 204-05)

It is interesting to notice here, however briefly, the parallel journey of the two writers, both physically and imaginatively. And

Cooley, up to placing and *re*-placing

placed and re-placed, no, re:place

no replacements for this one

no replace meant couldn't re place him if I tried

continues to read the home (place) in Spain:

Tractors, cultivators, combines. Yes, combines! now and then in the fields. [As the train moves along the landscape, the following lines.] Beside us the land has convulsed, some hills with perfect vertical striations caves cut into hill faces.... Houses all alone, no trees—the outskirts of town are like Estevan's too. Many abandoned buildings that would have been very handsome once. (*passwords* 205, 206)

Cooley's concern with placement is by no means incidental; he titles his works accordingly (think of *RePlacing*).[14]

July 6

The concrete sculpture high on the headland. Out into the ocean, winds, its huge & simple beauty. You take pictures and think of Mike Olito. Mike should see this. He will be amazed when he sees Pat and Diane[15] walking into it, backs to us, small bodies at the bottom of one pillar. The dozen bodies he can see bunched within the sculpture, the sea thousands of miles behind. (*passwords* 207)

Another element of the Cooley journal, the looking forward in time, anticipation that really doubles back on itself. (Cooley's is not an "ordinary" journal.) While in one reading the narrator looks forward in time, in another Cooley actually looks backwards at the time of writing, which is in the future of the journal's present. Always the binaries here and there mean time, mean place. How do you get there from here? But to return to prairie, Mike Olito, although not marked as such in the journal, is from home: one of the *fixed variables*?

early Sept.

Sat. July 7, finally *Gijon* (*passwords* 209). Three paragraphs without a single comma or period. A single capital letter "s" used three times in the last seven lines. Breathless writing, words falling like seeds of grain, slipping through your fingers, spilling onto the page, out of one receptacle to another. Cooley unpunctuates. *cooley unpunctuated*. cool-ly unpunctuated. But what is a punctuation mark on the prairie? A grain elevator, a receptacle, inscribed and inscribing. A fixed variable, the receptacle fixed, the contents always being replaced. Gijon is, in this instant, Cooley's prairie, with nothing to break the landscape of the page.

> at 1000 on a Saturday morning in Spain in the summer you are a prairie boy so buoyed you stand flat-footed in the side walk amazed you cannot enter the wet tide of flesh flatter yourself you will get flatter and in a prairie way a little relieved and learn later in Spanish "sin" means "without" to be without to be without sin let he who is without be she who is. (*passwords* 208)

> *spain: gijon to madrid*

> HHHEE-HOH they pronounce it. [This is how this section begins.] a donkey, calling, sort of, what up until now you have read in a french way as ghee-yoh. Throaty sounds, rasps & sometimes clicks. Phlegm. Are they phlegmatic the people of Gijon? Do they go for the throat? Sweet-tempered people I saw. (*passwords* 209)

Punning. Cooley moves on to joy and says so. And not only in puns. Everything in this place (but there are really two places, the physical place occupied for the duration of the journal, and the place caught in the vessel that is Cooley), everything in this place comes to him charged with energy, exquisite and intense. *"A joy,"* he says, *"an absolute joy, this trip"* (*passwords* 209). Cooley, as writer, of course (opposed to Cooley, the narrator), addresses joy primarily through words that he harvests, gathers in to the "region of regions," gathers in under his skin, gathers in to himself. The fixed variable constantly re-placing himself, like Mandel, out of place—*from* place, i.e., *out* of *the* place from which he comes. Cooley's sense of "out of place" is quite different from Mandel's. Cooley's sweet-natured and somewhat bewildered narrator celebrates the world in which he finds himself, while Mandel's narrator reveals his anxieties and disillusionment. One evokes a certain affection and perhaps even a degree of protectiveness on the part of the reader; the other, empathy over the narrator's profound disappointments. Cooley's losses are not in *passwords*, but Mandel's, in *Life Sentence*, cannot be missed.

Sept 8

Still in *Gijon to Madrid*:

> Land dry and scabby here, a bit like Estevan. Light industry—gravel and concrete. Field of corn barely up, patchy and stunted. All over Europe, here too, cereal crops are squashed into the ground in big patches. Lodging, my Dad would have said, it's lodging. (*passwords* 211)

A *bit* like Estevan? Like enough that the landscape evokes that place; powerful enough, too, that it evokes Cooley's father. The word "lodging" chosen to evoke a sense of permanence of place, while, ironically, the narrator being "out of place" (i.e. not home).

Sept 10

Over the past few weeks, preparing to write this paper, reading Andrew Stubbs's *Dennis Cooley and his Works*, Cooley's *RePlacing* and *Inscriptions*,[16] essays in post-colonial literature, on place, culture, representation, looking for signs of engagement with place. I have found receptacles, "regions of regions." But in the introduction to *Inscriptions* Cooley names what I have been doing. His words express concern that the writing in that anthology shows itself to be engaged with *prairie* place. I have, I discover, been seeking *Engagement*, and I have found it . . . in Spain of all places.

Sept 11

Gijon to Madrid, reduced to *Leon to Madrid,* where the snow ptarmigan makes its way into Cooley's text, and brings with it, somehow, "nivation," the word from Jon Whyte's *Homage, Henry Kelsey*.[17] Cooley writes, "'Nivation,' he said, resting or sleeping or growing under, snow, the Canadian winter, equivalent to. Under the snow, breathing. Unknown, without name" (*passwords* 213). Palimpsest, too: one layered above a white page, the other, beneath it. "Bewildered Canadians, under snow, a huge winter they sleep under" (*passwords* 278). Under the white page, the Canadian sleeps. *On* the page, too, palimpsest/nivation, year after year, fixed variables, like the contents of the receptacle; like the grain elevator, season after season.

The journey filling the writer, the writing, filling the pages. Cooley re-placing Mandel in Spain, not taking the place of, and yet, perhaps a little of that, too, but re-placing; Cooley, aware of placing (re: place, about place) and deliberately and intentionally placing again words connected to Mandel so that there is a doubling of placement of prairie in Spain, in Cooley's text. If I were to take Mandel's poem "On the Murder of Salvador Allende" (*Sentence* 19) and abridge to it Cooley's piece dated *July 7/90*, one text would simply move into the other. Both juxtapose a chilling lyricism with the graphic, Mandel and Cooley both writing with uncharacteristic vio-lence, smooth words that recoil and linger in the emotions the way the acrid smell of gunpowder lingers in the mouth. Mandel:

> . . . the silent explosion of guns
> it changes nothing: it goes on:
> today in Omonia Square   guns in the mouth of speech
> yesterday in Mozambique
>   the same taste
> of death and torture
>   admirals calculating
> losses and reserves (*Sentence* 21)

Cooley, Mandel clearly firing both his imagination and emotions, bringing Mandel, prairie writer ("region of regions") to Madrid:

> *July 7/90*
> nearing Madrid where
> was it they shot Lorca & why
>
> not he used all the wrong words
> though not so the story
>
> in America goes he was not
> active as a Republican he was
> a good man but they shot him
>
>   for good measure
>   perhaps just
> for the pleasure
>   maybe it was a mistake
> maybe he was just getting
>   out of line

one night he is sitting at home, say . . .
his mother there & they are drinking
a glass of wine it's been hot
it often is they have some wine
when coolness comes, into the stones
        & out of them
the lizards crawl out it is too
dark it is too late for lizards yet
lizards squirm out anyway
into the chocolate night

wear their leather pouches
a slackness hangs from them
the dry men from Franco crawl
out of the rocks on the rocks
they can smell blood
      & they want some
      thing to break

    open a bottle
    rip open some skin
    Lorca for his sins will do

death a prodigality in him
spills his life over (*passwords* 215)

The texts do not appear to have a lot to do with prairie, but clearly, something in the experience of being in Spain and the mutual experience of these two prairie writers evoked the strong emotions evident in these poems. In Cooley's text, what we have is a collision of prairie with other place, achieved by the sandwiching of this historical event, of 1936, between specific references to home.

July 9 12:00 noon. [A new heading.] "Leaving Madrid. An hour late & it is hot, hot and foul, air so thick pollution floats in it. Over 40 during the day and nights down to only 26 or so" (*passwords* 216). This sounds like my most recent experience with the south Saskatchewan prairie when I could *see* the heat in the air. "Dry," writes Cooley, "terribly dry. A scabbiness" (*passwords* 216). Just prior to this, he has written, "Land dry and scabby here, a bit like Estevan" (*passwords* 210). Engagement. I was working off engagement. Cooley is engaged. Engaging. Gauging. Working in a series of *enchaînments*, landscape within him and outwith en-chained, joined link by logical link. For Mandel it is a double *enchaînment* indicated even in the title of the journal *Life Sentence*, the linkage of place with place the same as Cooley's, but doubled yet again by virtue of being imported into the Cooley text.

Sept. 20

I'm still crossing Spain with Cooley. Here and yet there. There and yet not there at all. Can't get to the end, can't even get to Barcelona. Have to leave Cooley behind but continue the journey, the journal, a "region of regions" in writing; it's as long as the prairie, or, in Cooley's words (to give him the last word) *it's a long long way to go.*

Endnotes

1. Dennis Cooley, *passwords: Transmigrations between Canada and Europe* (Kiel, Germany: I&F Verlag, 1996). Subsequent references are referred to in the text as *passwords*.

2. Eli Mandel, *Life Sentence* (Victoria, BC: Press Porcépic, 1991). Subsequent references are referred to in the text as *Sentence*.

3. Mandel discusses the cross-genre possibilities of the long poem in the article entitled "The long Poem Journal and Origins," in *The Family Romance* (Winnipeg: Turnstone Press, 1986). Concerned with poetics and clearly written in response to the "long liner's conference," the "essay" comprises a series of journal entries, musings, poems, quotations, and "found" materials. Mandel's original title of the essay, "The Proceedings of the Long Liner's Conference on the Canadian Long Poem, York University, Toronto, May 29-June 1, 1984: Documentary Autobiography Alternatives Poetics Locality Origins Origins Origins Journal," provides an apt, if not succinct, description of what he is up to.

4. Robert Kroetsch, *The Lovely Treachery of Words* (Toronto, Oxford University Press, 1989).

5. Dennis Cooley, *The Vernacular Muse* (Winnipeg: Turnstone Press, 1987).

6. Markus Müller, a Graduate Student Canadian Literature specialist from the University of Trier, Germany, was a contributor in the Defining the Prairies Conference.

7. Méira Cook, *The Blood Girls* (Edmonton: NeWest Press, 1998).

8. Birk Sproxton, a prairie writer from Red Deer College and a contributor to the conference, referred me to Miki's work on bp nicol and the long poem as well as to a collection of essays edited by Miki, *Tracing the Paths Reading and Writing* The Martyrology (Vancouver: Talonbooks, 1988).

9. William Carlos Williams, *Paterson* (Toronto: George J. McLeod Ltd., 1958).

10. James Duncan and David Ley, eds. *place/culture/representation* (London and New York: Routledge, 1993), 9.

11. Edward S. Casey, *The Fate of Place: A Philosophical History* (Berkeley and Los Angeles: University of California Press, 1997), 36.

12. Dennis Cooley, "Fielding," in *a/long prairie lines*, ed. Daniel Lenoski (Winnipeg: Turnstone Press, 1989), 245.

13. The (Toronto) Blue Jays are a professional baseball team; the narrator is clearly a baseball fan.

14. Dennis Cooley, *RePlacing* (Winnipeg: Turnstone Press, 1980).

15. Cooley refers to friends and family in this passage.

16. Dennis Cooley, *Inscriptions* (Downsview: ECW, 1992).

17. John Whyte, *Homage, Henry Kelsey*, in *a/long praire lines,* ed. Daniel Lenoski (Winnipeg: Turnstone Press, 1989), 213. Originally published by Turnstone Press in 1981.

Don't Give Me No More of Your Lip; or, the Prairie Horizon as Allowed Mouth

Robert Kroetsch

A GRADUATE STUDENT who grew up in Pamela Banting country near Birch River, Manitoba, came to interview me in Victoria. She was doing her graduate work in Kingston, Ontario, and had been advised by her advisor that she'd find me silent, reluctant to communicate, and hard to get started talking. After the interview that same advisor began the debriefing by saying, "Kind of a strange bird, isn't he?" The graduate student replied, "There's nothing strange about him. He's just prairie."

My mind has been boggled for some months now by that simple sentence. I heard the story from the advisor, a belligerent, colonizing Easterner, so I have no idea of what the student's tone might have been. Already, a problem in the complex dialects of place.

He's just prairie.

Does that mean that I'm silent, or does it mean that I talk? Granted, I do spend a few months now and then without speaking. But I spoke to the student for almost an hour. Did her cryptic naming act imply a kind of erotic transcendentalism? Or was she being abrupt rather than cryptic, and did her too brief summary imply that I might be one brick short of a load?

Whatever the case, the student was obviously suggesting that prairie is people. Prairie is actual, identifiable, and describable (though that modifier raises new questions) people.

I began to cast a cool and objective eye at some of my friends. I considered, for instance, the faculty and staff of St. John's College, their many students, their many associates. I had, before the occasion of the interview, late one night, when awakened from sleep in Trier, Germany, and just to placate Dennis Cooley so that I might get back to sleep, agreed to say a few words at a meeting in St. John's College on a subject he announced as prairie. "What do you mean?" I asked him. "Ah, you know," he said. And hung up.

Back in my narrow bed in Wolfgang Klooss's subterranean guest room, contrived especially for claustrophobic visiting prairie people, I had a dream of David Arnason. I saw and perhaps remembered Arnason trying to get wet in Lake Winnipeg. I saw him, large and luminous, wading towards a far and vague prairie horizon, ever trying to find deep water. In my dream he spoke as he waded. Just as he moved beyond earshot, he began to tell me what Cooley would have said if Cooley had answered my question. What do you mean?

Prairie, then, is as much performance as it is either place or answer.

Or to put it another way, it is possible that to become "just prairie" is to recognize and even celebrate the predicament whereby one can either gain utterance by enacting the impossibility of arrival (and the speculations of Gerry Friesen loom large here), or one can be rendered silent (and here looms the spectre of the unnameable) by the merest cognitive acknowledgment of a real prairie horizon.

I thought of Robert Enright, speaking without surcease to the round horizon. I thought of Meeka Walsh, the writer, the prairie editor, seeking out the reassurance and consolation of the acute and quite often naked image, carefully framing it onto a rectangular page. What, then, is the mathematics of prairie? The curved straight line? I thought of Nicole Markotic, her novel *Yellow Pages*, her Alexander Graham Bell reversing the physic of prairie, imagining the immediate as silence, the distant as sound. I dial, and I cannot hear the phone where it rings. The inventor of the telephone named Bell. This is a Dennis Cooley joke. On the prairies, one is always presently deaf. I thought of Charlene Diehl-Jones, that quintessential St. John's prairie person, inside her stone house in Ontario, speaking and speaking against a forest that blurs all possibility of horizon. Always, an heuristic vision. (And I can't remember what heuristic means. I've looked it up four times.) Always, one brick short of a load.

I turned (and the verb, to turn, here, is basic) to the writings of that somewhat silent theorist and writer, Mark Libin. Libin offers that a prairie text might be "propelled by means of circumlocution." Already the horizon at once recedes and looms, all around us.

For Libin prairie is motion.

Now we're getting somewhere.

He says, and he is speaking either of himself or of me, it isn't clear: "The Alberta that Kroetsch performs for us—the Alberta I perform in tandem and tangent, an alibi for my extrapolations—is always already a replica, a catafalque, a diptych in which map and legend are folded into each other seamlessly, full of inconvenient seams...."[1]

Libin is just prairie.

The folds of which Libin speaks become, in the work of that fast-talking prairie poet, Dennis Cooley, puns. Cooley believes that the prairies are, both figuratively and literally, a sequence of puns—a consequence of punning. Consider the abundant prairies that are not there. What patch of earth is more a cultivated garden than the prairies? And yet the prairies tease us with origins, with traces and hints of what was or might still be wild.

If we consider the machinations and fate of Bloody Jack, we realize that we are at once and always escaping and ever able to escape. Surely the book *Bloody Jack* is one of the finest autobiographies written on the prairies— and yet it might be said to contain hardly a word of truth. Cooley, by subverting the details of his own life, constructs the catafalque, the diptych, the replica that enables him to fast-talk his alibis right past us. We are seduced by our own criminal longings for a just world.

If we read in the issue of *Prairie Fire* devoted to the writings of Dennis Cooley, we quickly discover that we do not in fact have a reliable or complete text of the poem, *Bloody Jack*. The shape-shifter says, in reply to an honest but interrupted question from Rob Budde:"When Arnason assembled the pieces shortly before publication, he grabbed most of the narrative things and stuck them in. On the sly, I took out some of those things and re-inserted some love poems."[2]

Re-inserted a love poem. Again, the mind boggles. And is this, too, to be "just prairie"?

The idea of flirtation is essential to any definition of pun, and to any definition of prairie. To flirt is to tease with possibility. Surely that is a prairie condition. We live with possibility and yet that possibility is at once and always invited and frustrated by the gaps in the narrative. That gap might be anything from a ten-minute hailstorm to a ten-year drought. Cooley proposes a love poem as remedy. He names it *Bloody Jack*.

Here on the prairies we are always trying to name or generalize about an incomplete or fractured text. Facing the riddle of self, and community and horizon; we carefully mumble our answers.

Dawne McCance, more than any writer I have read, sees the prairie as construct. Prairie, for her, is architectural and archival. I use the adjectival forms, because McCance applies the terms, architectural, archival, to a non-existent noun.

Now we're getting somewhere.

Dawne McCance is the woman in the prairie city, reading that city, living that city. She is fascinated by the cartouche. A cartouche is, for instance, the ornamental frame at the bottom of a map that contains the map's name. Again, it is an oval or oblong figure (as on ancient Egyptian monuments) enclosing a sovereign's name. The cartouche, then, is both architectural and archival.

The cartouche is the frame, the container, the architectural device that presents the name, and keeps us from it. It is one of the paradoxes of the archive that we place in that public space—our personal lives.

Dawne McCance has written brilliantly on the obscure works of that prairie poet, Rita Kleinhart. I quote McCance, who begins by quoting Rita:

> In Hornbook #48, ... "Rita stands at her back door, guessing where she might put a new birdhouse" (p. 187). The ways in which her house defies modernity's spatial logic will be given, I want to suggest, by the back door. Rather than issuing her poetry from a detached centric point available only to the male holder of vision, Rita writes on back doors. For her, autobiography does not deliver a deposit of self-referential content to be hermeneutically unsealed, but inscribes the process itself, the play of the frame, an insistent crossing of inside and out. I read the back door in "The Poetics of Rita Kleinhart" as figure of what architect Peter Eisenman calls "a text of between: writing that dislocates authorial and natural value, and that does not symbolize use, shelter or vertical structure."[3]

She's just prairie.

Aha, you say to yourself—so much for prairie as motion. But let me quote again from McCance—and this time from her review, in *Prairie Fire*, of a book by Robert Enright called *Peregrinations: Conversations with Contemporary Artists*. "For Lyotard, the word [peregrinations] suggests something about what he calls the 'event' of writing—or for that matter, of thinking, speaking and art-making. Far from proceeding along a fixed linear course from beginning through middle to end, the event ... is more of roaming across overlapping boundaries, more of a wandering among clouds. What fascinates me about peregrinations, the word and the event, is not just the responsive, seeking *movement*, but also the *shapes* it creates."

The vindication of Libin and Cooley—the prairies as event and as shape—the prairies as boundaries, as crossings, as border crossings.

And again, where Dawne McCance would build, Birk Sproxton burrows.

Where she acknowledges light and air, the birdhouse impulse, he acknowledges the underpinning of the Precambrian Shield; that is, even as we stand or sit here, only a few yards beneath our feet. For Sproxton, in his tellingly named book *Headframe:,* prairie is a clutch of addled eggs, contained in a basket of rock. And again, where Sproxton betrays his concealment by laughter, Doug Reimer speaks soberly a prairie dialogue of forgetfulness and ecstatic memory. As the country & western song has it: "remember to forget me." I am silence itself, and . . . now let me tell you. . . .

Consider the predicament made eloquent by Gerry Friesen. Consider two of the titles he offers to us, his avid and grateful readers. For our larger consolations, *The Canadian Prairies: A History.* And for this collection, "Why the Prairies Don't Exist."

Maybe he's just prairie.

If McCance's cartouche contains everything I have been trying to say, Friesen's history anticipates it. My belatedness, always, or at least sometimes, appalls me. When am I ever, in this new country, going to be young?

Friesen's *A History* is the epic of unassuming people in an assuming landscape. He locates that epic predicament, not originally but, rather, continuously, in the natural world that preceded both white and native arrivals.

With reference to the buffalo herds that reached to the round horizon, he quotes from an early traveller—and with that traveller Friesen looks not up, but down: "Every drop of water on our way was foul and yellow with their wallowings and excretions."[5]

One recognizes immediately that Friesen finds our epic and the communality of that epic not in what rises but, rather, in what falls. And falling is sometimes a violence.

Friesen goes on to say:

> The sound of the bisons' roaring could be heard for miles and the path upon which the animals travelled resembled a war zone. . . . Bison dung was sufficient to fuel camp-fires for generations, and bison bones sustained a small fertilizer industry into the modern pioneer era. Bison trails criss-crossed the plains like highways. Where the herds encountered bluffs, the trees would become rubbing posts, and the barks of stronger specimens would be torn off to a height of six feet; the small brush would simply be beaten to death by the cyclonic force of the bisons' passage. The buffalo landscape had a character all its own.[6]

The buffalo landscape performs itself. This is a landscape not as something fixed and static, but as motion, as gesture, as event, as turmoil. Consider Mark Libin on his imaginary horse, really riding out of Calgary, and always and never returning. Consider David Arnason, yearning across the dreamed lake toward the real horizon—or is it the other way round?

Consider Bloody Jack as if he might be Cooley himself, in his jail cell, forever fashioning his bed sheets not into a bed but, rather, into a rope.

Here is our buffalo landscape, we enter into elaborate mimicry.

I remember from my childhood a bird we called the slough-pumper— a strange bird. The American Bittern, I learned to call it, once I went to school and looked at pictures in books. In the slough across the road from our farm, the slough-pumper was a bird that made a sound like that of an old-fashioned, long-handled, back-busting water pump. As simple as that. Except that one ornithologist renders the sound as pump-er-lunk, pump-er-lunk, pump-er-lunk, while another renders it as oong-ka'-choonk, oong-ka'-choonk, oong-ka'-choonk. Once again, the difficulties of transmission, the awkward shape of archival longing.

I was a few years into my childhood before I actually saw the actual bird. I saw it quite by accident.

The woman who lived in the old homestead house near the slough across the road from our farm had been widowed by a battle somewhere in France during the First World War. Mrs. Beddoes, that was the only name I ever knew her by. She had one child, a son who was considered to be "not quite all there." Leroy's prized—and I could even say only—possession was a saddle horse. He rode that horse for hours, for days, along or beside the dirt roads, even in farmers' carefully tended fields of wheat, and he never, as my mother put it, "helped out" at home, so she now and then sent me across the road to do chores—such as pumping water with a pump that I can still hear—for Mrs. Beddoes. It was Mrs. Beddoes who one spring day asked me to go to the foot of her very messy garden and look for an abandoned rhubarb patch.

That's when I chanced to notice the slough-pumper. You see, the slough-pumper is so well disguised that it's almost impossible to recognize, standing as it sometimes does, in a rather unbirdlike way, rigidly still, its beak pointed upward in what seems a slightly demented manner, its striped body all the while perfectly matching the reeds and grasses at the edge of a slough.

What if the slough-pumper, in trying to look like its surroundings, actually looked like its surroundings? Or—what if the slough-pumper, in trying to look like its surroundings, didn't succeed in looking like its surroundings? Hmmm.

Endnotes

1. Mark Libin, "Home and Inscription In and Around Robert Kroetsch," *The New Quarterly* XVIII, no.1 (Spring 1998): 222.

2. Dennis Cooley, "Cooley Dreams His Way into the World: A Conversation," Interview with Todd Bruce and Robert Budde, *Prairie Fire* 19, no. 1 (Spring 1998): 50.

3. Dawne McCance, "On the Art of Building in Ten Hornbooks," *The New Quarterly* XVIII, no. 1 (Spring 1998): 162.

4. Dawne McCance, *Prairie Fire* 19, no. 2 (Summer 1998): 152.

5. J.G. Nelson, "Animal, Fire and Landscape in Northwestern Plains of North America in Pre and Early European Days," *Prairie Perspectives* 2 (1973), cited in Gerald Friesen, *The Canadian Prairies, A History* (Toronto: University of Toronto Press, 1987), 8.

6. Friesen, *The Canadian Prairies*, 8.

Selected Bibliography

Adam, Ian. "Iconicity, Space and the Place of Sharon Butala's 'The Prize.'" *Studies in Canadian Literature* 23, no.1 (1998): 178-89.

Allen, Richard, ed. *A Region of the Mind, Interpreting the Canadian Plains.* Canadian Plains Studies No. 1. Regina: Canadian Plains Studies Centre, 1973.

Ayers, Edward L., Patricia Nelson Limerick, Stephen Nissenbaum, and Peter S. Onuf. *All Over the Map.* Baltimore: Johns Hopkins University Press, 1996.

Bahktin, M.M. *The Dialogic Imagination.* Austin: University of Texas Press, 1981.

Bannatyne-Cuget, Jo. *A Prairie Alphabet.* Illustrated by Yvette Moore. Montreal: Tundra, 1992.

Banting, Pamela. *Body Inc.: A Theory of Translation Poetics.* Winnipeg: Turnstone Press, 1995.

Bark, D. "History of American Droughts." In *North American Droughts, AAAS Selected Symposium 15,* edited by N.J. Rosenberg. Boulder: Westview Press, 1978.

Barkley, T.M., ed. *Flora of the Great Plains.* Lawrence: University Press of Kansas, 1986.

Barron, Hal S. *Mixed Harvest.* Chapel Hill: University of North Carolina Press, 1997.

Barthes, Roland. *The Pleasure of the Text.* Translated by Richard Miller. 1973. Reprinted, New York: Hill and Wang, 1975.

_____. *Roland Barthes par Roland Barthes, Oeuvres complètes.* Vol. III: 1974-80. Paris: Seuil, 1994.

Baudrillard, Jean. *L'Echange symbolique et la mort.* Paris: Gallimard, 1976.

Becker, Susanne. "Ironic Transformations: The Feminine Gothic in Aritha van Herk's *No Fixed Address.*" In *Double Talking: Essays on Verbal and Visual Ironies in Contemporary Canadian Art and Literature,* edited by Linda Hutcheon. Toronto: ECW Press, 1992.

Bell, Edward. *Social Classes and Social Credit in Alberta.* Montreal and Kingston: McGill-Queen's University Press, 1993.

Belyea, Barbara, and Estelle Dansereau, eds. *Driving Home: A Dialogue between Writers and Readers.* Waterloo: Wilfrid Laurier University Press, 1984.

Bercuson, David Jay, ed. *Western Perspectives 1.* Toronto: Holt, Rinehart and Winston of Canada Ltd., 1974.

_____, and Philip Buckner, eds. *Eastern and Western Perspectives.* Toronto: University of Toronto Press, 1981.

Bergland, Betty. "Postmodernism and the Autobiographical Subject: Reconstructing the 'Other'." In *Autobiography and Postmodernism*, edited by Kathleen Ashley, et al. Amherst: University of Massachusetts Press, 1994.

Berman, Marshall. *All that Is Solid Melts into Air: The Experience of Modernity*. New York: Simon and Schuster, 1982.

Best, Edward E. "Memoirs of a School Inspector, 1888-1932." Winnipeg: Public Archives of Manitoba, MG 9 A-95-1.

Blanchot, Maurice. *L'Espace littéraire*. Paris: Gallimard, 1955.

Bliss, Michael. "Privatizing the Mind: The Sundering of Canadian History." *Journal of Canadian Studies* 26 (Winter 1991-92).

_____. "'Pure Books on Avoided Subjects': Pre-Freudian Sexual Ideas in Canada. *Historical Papers* (1970).

Bouchard, Dave. *If you're not from the prairie....* Illustrated by Henry Ripplinger. Vancouver: Raincoast, 1994.

_____. *Prairie Born*. Illustrated by Peter Shostak. Victoria, BC, and Custer, WA: Orca, 1997.

Bowering, George. "That Fool of a Fear: Notes on *A Jest of God*." In *A Place to Stand On: Essays by and about Margaret Laurence*, edited by George Woodcock. Edmonton: NeWest Press, 1983.

_____. "The Stump." In *The Rain Barrel*. Vancouver: Talonbooks, 1994.

Brandt, Di. "Questions I Asked Dennis Cooley about the Vernacular Muse." *Prairie Fire* 9, no. 3 (Autumn 1988): 94-96.

Braudel, F. *The Identity of France (L'Identité de la France)*. Trans. edition, New York: HarperCollins, 1986.

Breen, David H. *The Canadian Prairie West and the Ranching Frontier, 1874-1924*. Toronto: University of Toronto Press, 1983.

Brodie, Janine. *The Political Economy of Canadian Regionalism*. Toronto: Harcourt, Brace, Jovanovitch, 1990.

Brown, Annora. *Sketches from Life*. Edmonton: Hurtig Publishers, 1981.

Brown, Lauren. *Grasslands*. New York: Alfred A. Knopf, 1985.

Brückner, E. *Klimaschwankung seit 1700, nebst Bemerkungen über die Klimaschwanjungen der Diluvialzeit*. Vienna: Hölzel, 1890.

Buckner, Philip. "'Limited Identities' Revisited: Regionalism and Nationalism in Canadian History." *Acadiensis* XXX (Autumn 2000): 4-15.

Butala, Sharon. *The Perfection of the Morning: An Apprenticeship in Nature*. Toronto: HarperCollins, 1994.

_____. "The Reality of the Flesh." In *Writing Saskatchewan: 20 Critical Essays,* edited by Kenneth G. Probert. Regina: Canadian Plains Research Centre/University of Regina, 1989.

Butler, Robert. "The Life Review: An Interpretation of Reminiscence in the Aged." *Psychiatry* 26 (1963): 65-76.

Calder, Alison. "'The nearest approach to a desert': Implications of Environmental Determinism in the Criticism of Prairie Writing." *Prairie Forum* 23 (1998): 171-82.

Careless, J.M.S. "'Limited Identities' in Canada." *Canadian Historical Review* L, no. 1 (March 1969): 1–10.

_____. "'Limited Identities':Ten Years Later." *Manitoba History* 1, no. 1 (1980).

Carolan-Brozy, Sandra. "'You Just Don't Concern Me Now' vs 'Why We Must Talk': Lee Maracle's Biotexts." *Anglophonia. Canada: Fractures mais non ruptures* 1 (1997): 55–66.

Casey, Edward S. *The Fate of Place: A Philosophical History.* Berkeley and Los Angeles: University of California Press, 1997.

Cavanaugh, Catherine, and Jeremy Mouat, eds. *Making Western Canada.* Toronto: Garamond Press, 1996.

Collini, Stefan. *Public Moralists: Political Thought and Intellectual Life in Britain, 1850-1930.* Oxford/New York: Clarendon Press/Oxford University Press, 1991.

_____. "The Idea of 'Character' in Victorian Political Thought." *Transactions of the Royal Historical Society* 35, Fifth Series, 1985.

Conn, H.W. *Elementary Physiology and Hygiene.* Toronto: Copp, Clark, 1903.

Connerton, Paul. *How Societies Remember.* New York: University of Cambridge Press, 1989.

Connor, Ralph. *The Foreigner: A Tale of Saskatchewan.* Toronto: Westminster Co., 1909.

Conrad, Margaret. "Recording Angels: The Private Chronicles of Women from the Maritime Provinces of Canada, 1750-1950." In *The Neglected Majority: Essays in Canadian Women's History,* edited by Alison Prentice and Susan Mann Trofimenkoff. Toronto: McClelland and Stewart, 1985.

Cook, Méira. *The Blood Girls.* Edmonton: NeWest Press, 1998.

Cook, Ramsay. "The Burden of Regionalism." *Acadiensis* VII, no. 1 (Autumn 1974).

_____. "Canadian Centennial Celebrations." *International Journal* XXII (Autumn 1967): 659–63.

_____. "The Golden Age of Canadian Historical Writing." *Historical Reflections* V, no. 1 (Summer 1977).

_____. "Regionalism Unmasked." *Acadiensis* XIII, no. 1 (Autumn 1983).

Cooley, Dennis. *Bloody Jack: A Book.* Winnipeg: Turnstone Press, 1984.

_____. *Eli Mandel.* Monograph. Toronto: ECW Press, n.d.

_____. *passwords: Transmigrations between Canada and Europe.* Kiel, Germany: I&F Verlag, 1996.

_____. *The Vernacular Muse: The Eye and Ear in Contemporary Literature.* Winnipeg: Turnstone Press, 1987.

_____, ed. *Inscriptions: A Prairie Poetry Anthology.* Winnipeg: Turnstone Press, 1992.

_____, ed. *RePlacing.* Downsview: ECW Press, 1980.

Creighton, Tom. "How Flin Flon Got its Name." *Northern Lights* 1, no. 5 (July 1942): 32.

Dainotto, Roberto Maria. "'All the Regions Do Smilingly Revolt': The Literature of Place and Region." *Critical Inquiry* 22 (1996): 486–505.

Davey, Frank. "Toward the Ends of Regionalism." In *A Sense of Place: Re-Evaluating Regionalism in Canadian and American Writing,* edited by Christian Riegel and Herb Wyile. Vol. 9. *Textual Studies in Canada* (Spring 1997).

Davidson, Arnold. *Coyote Country: Fictions of the Canadian West*. Durham: Duke University Press, 1994.

Dickinson, Peter. "'Orality in Literacy': Listening to Indigenous Writing." *Canadian Journal of Native Studies* 14, no. 2 (1994): 319-40.

Dorscht, Susan Rudy. *Women, Reading, Kroetsch: Telling the Difference*. Waterloo: Wilfrid Laurier University Press, 1991.

Driedger, Leo. *Mennonite Identity in Conflict*. Lewiston, NY: E. Mellen Press, 1988.

Duke, John. "How Far North Is North?" *The Canadian* (October 1929): 6-7; 36-37.

Duncan, James, and David Ley, eds. *place / culture / representation*. London and New York: Routledge, 1993.

Durkin, Douglas. *The Heart of Cherry McBain*. Toronto: The Musson Book Company, 1919.

_____. *The Lobstick Trail: A Romance of Northern Canada*. Toronto: The Musson Book Company, 1921.

_____. *The Magpie*. Toronto: The Musson Book Company, 1921.

Dyck, Harvey L, ed. and trans. *A Mennonite in Russia: the Diaries of Jacob D. Epp, 1851-1880*. Toronto: University of Toronto Press, 1991.

Easthope, Anthony, and Kate McGowan. *A Critical and Cultural Theory Reader*. Toronto: University of Toronto Press, 1992.

Eddy, J.A. "Climate and the Role of the Sun." In *Climate and History, Studies in Interdisciplinary History*. Princeton: Princeton University Press, 1981.

Enright, Robert. *Peregrinations: Conversations with Contemporary Artists*. Winnipeg: Bain and Cox, 1997.

Epp. Frank H. *Mennonites in Canada, 1786-1920: The History of a Separate People*. Toronto: University of Toronto Press, 1974.

Epp, Ingrid I., and Harvey L. Dyck. *The Peter J. Braun Russian Mennonite Archive, 1803-1920: A Research Guide*. Toronto: University of Toronto Press, 1996.

Eyles, John. *Senses of Place*. Warrington, UK: Silverbook Press, 1985.

Falconer, Sir Robert. *Idealism in National Character: Essays and Addresses*. London: Hodder and Stoughton, 1920.

Fentress, James, and Chris Wichkham. *Social Memory*. Oxford, UK: Blackwell, 1992.

Finkel, Alvin. *The Social Credit Phenomenon in Alberta*. Toronto: University of Toronto Press, 1989.

_____. "Paradise Postponed: A Re-examination of the Green Book Proposals of 1945." *Journal of the Canadian Historical Association*. New Series 4 (1993): 120-42.

Fothergill, Robert. *Private Chronicles: A Study of English Diaries*. London/New York: Oxford University Press, 1974.

Foucault, Michel. *Power/Knowledge: Selected Interviews and Other Writings, 1972-1977*. New York: Pantheon, 1980.

Fowke, Vernon C. "The National Policy—Old and New." *Canadian Journal of Economics and Political Science* 18, no. 3 (August 1952): 271-86.

Francis, R. Douglas. "In Search of a Prairie Myth: A Survey of the Intellectual and Cultural Historiography of Prairie Canada." *Journal of Canadian Studies* 24, no. 3 (Fall 1989).

_____, and H. Ganzevoort, eds. *The Dirty Thirties in Prairie Canada.* Vancouver: Tantalus Research Limited, 1980.

Friedman, Susan Stanford. "Women's Autobiographical Selves, Theory and Practice." In *The Private Self: Theory and Practice of Women's Autobiographical Writings*, edited by Shari Benstock. Chapel Hill: University of North Carolina Press, 1988.

Friedmann, Robert. *Mennonite Piety through the Centuries: Its Genius and Its Literature.* Goshen: The Mennonite Historical Society, 1949.

Friesen, Gerald. *The Canadian Prairies: A History.* Toronto: University of Toronto Press, 1987.

_____. *The West: Regional Debate, National Ambitions, Global Age.* Toronto: Viking/ Penguin, 1999.

_____. *River Road: Essays on Manitoba and Prairie History.* Winnipeg: University of Manitoba Press, 1996.

Fritts, H.C. *Reconstructing Large-Scale Climatic Patterns from Tree-Ring Data.* Tucson: University of Arizona Press, 1991.

_____, and X.M. Shao. "Mapping Climate Using Tree-Rings from Western North America." In *Climate Since A.D. 1500,* edited by R.S. Bradley and P.D. Jones. Rev. ed., London: Routledge, 1995.

Frye, Northrop. *The Bush Garden: Essays on the Canadian Imagination.* 1991. Reprint, Concord: Anansi, 1995.

Gagan, David. P., ed. *Prairie Perspectives.* Toronto: Holt, Rinehart and Winston of Canada, Ltd., 1969.

Geertz, Clifford. *After the Fact: Two Countries, Four Decades, One Anthropologist.* Cambridge: Harvard University Press, 1995.

Gerber, David. "You See I Speak Wery well English." *Journal of American Ethnic History* 12 (1993): 56–65.

Gibbins, Roger, and Sonia Arrison. *Western Visions: Perspectives on the West in Canada.* Peterborough: Broadview, 1995.

Gingell, Susan. "When X Equals Zero: The Politics of Voice in First Peoples Poetry by Women." *English Studies in Canada* 24, no. 4 (December 1998): 447–66.

Gjerde, Jon. *The Minds of the West: Ethnocultural Evolution in the Rural Middle West, 1830-1917.* Chapel Hill: The University of North Carolina Press, 1977.

Goody, Jack. *The Interface between the Written and the Oral.* New York: Cambridge University Press, 1987.

Graff, Harvey J. Introduction to *Literacy and Social Development in the West: A Reader.* New York: Cambridge University Press, 1981.

Granatstein, J.L. *Who Killed Canadian History?* Toronto: HarperCollins Publishers, 1998.

Grove, J.M. *The Little Ice Age.* London: Methuen, 1988.

Gruending, Dennis, ed. *The Middle of Nowhere.* Saskatoon: Fifth House, 1996.

Gusdorf, Georges. "Conditions and Limits of Autobiography." In *Autobiography: Essays Theoretical and Critical,* edited by James Olney. 1956. Reprint, Princeton: Princeton University Press, 1980.

Halbwachs, Maurice. *The Collective Memory.* 1950. Reprint, New York: Harper & Row, 1980.

Hall, Jacqueline Dowd. "'You Must Remember This': Autobiography as Social Critique." *Journal of American History* 85 (September 1998): 439–65.

Hareven, Tamara. "The History of the Family and the Process of Social Change." *American Historical Review* 96 (1991).

Harris, Cole. "The Emotional Structure of Canadian Regionalism." Lecture delivered at McGill University. In *The Walter L. Gordon Lecture Series 1980-81*. Vol. 5. *The Challenges of Canada's Regional Diversity*. Toronto: Canada Studies Foundation, 1981.

Harrison, Dick, ed. *Crossing Frontiers: Papers in American and Canadian Western Literature*. Edmonton: University of Alberta Press, 1979.

Hedman, Valerie, Loretta Yauck, and Joyce Henderson. *Flin Flon*. Flin Flon: Flin Flon Historical Society, 1974.

Hesketh, Bob. *Major Douglas and Alberta Social Credit*. Toronto: University of Toronto Press, 1997.

_____. " The Company A, Company B Charges: The Manning Government, the Treasury Branches and Highways Contracts." MA thesis, University of Alberta, 1989.

Hewitt, Irene, "What's Yours Is Mine. Creighton vs Collins. Who Really Found Flin Flon?" *The Winnipeg Tribune Magazine* (May 24, 1980): 8–10.

Highway, Tomson. *Kiss of the Fur Queen*. Toronto: Doubleday Canada, 1998.

Hirsch, E.D., Jr. *Cultural Legacy: What Every American Needs to Know*. New York: Random House, 1988.

Horowitz, Helen Lefkowitz, ed. *Landscape in Sight*. New Haven: Yale University Press, 1997.

Houghton, J.T., G.J. Jenkins, and J.J. Ephraums, eds. *Climate Change, The IPCC Scientific Assessment*. New York: Cambridge University Press, 1990.

Houghton, J.T., B.A. Callander, and S.K. Varney, eds. *Climate Change 1992, The Supplementary Report to The IPCC Scientific Assessment*. New York: Cambridge University Press, 1992.

Hutcheon, Linda. *The Canadian Postmodern: A Study of Contemporary Canadian Fiction*. Toronto: Oxford University Press, 1988.

Innes, Matthew. "Memory, Orality and Literacy in an Early Medieval Society." *Past and Present* 77 (1998): 3–36.

Ivins, William M., Jr. *Prints and Visual Communication*. 1953. Reprint, Cambridge: MIT Press, 1969.

Johnson, K.L. *Rangeland through Time: A Photographic Study of Vegetation Change in Wyoming 1870-1986*. Wyoming Agricultural Exp. Station. Misc. Pub. 50. Laramie, WY, 1987.

Jones, Dorothy. "Restoring the Temples: The Fiction of Aritha van Herk." *Kunapipi* 6. no. 1 (1994): 416–31.

Jordan. David M. *New World Regionalism: Literature in the Americas*. Toronto: University of Toronto Press, 1994.

Jordan, Terry G. *North American Cattle-Ranching Frontiers*. Albuquerque: University of New Mexico Press, 1993.

Jussim, Estelle. *The Eternal Moment*. New York: Aperture Foundation, 1989.

_____, and Elizabeth Lindquist-Cock. *Landscape as Photograph*. New Haven: Yale University Press, 1985.

Kammen, Michael. *Mystic Chords of Memory*. New York: Alfred A. Knopf, 1991.

Karasick, Adeena. *Genrecide*. Vancouver: Talonbooks, 1996.

Keahey, Deborah. *Making it Home: Place in Canadian Prairie Literature*. Winnipeg: University of Manitoba Press, 1998.

Kelly, Ursula. *Marketing Place: Cultural Politics, Regionalism, and Reading*. Halifax: Fernwood, 1993.

Kirkwood, Hilda. "Kiss of the Spider-Lady: An Interview with Aritha van Herk." *Canadian Women's Studies / Les Cahiers de la Femme* 8, no. 3 (1987).

Kiyooka, Roy. *Mothertalk: Life Stories of Mary Kiyoshi Kiyooka*. Edited by Daphne Marlatt. Edmonton: NeWest Press, 1997.

Klett, M., E. Manchester, J. Verburg, G. Bushaw, R. Dingus, and P. Berger. *Second View, The Rephotographic Survey Project*. Albuquerque: University of New Mexico Press, 1984.

Klassen, Henry C. *The Canadian West: Social Change and Economic Development*. Calgary: Comprint Publishing Company, 1977.

Klooss, Wolfgang. "Multiculturalism, Regionalism and the Search for a Poetics of Disparity in Contemporary Canadian Writing." In *Anglistentag 1991 Düsseldorf*, edited by Wilhelm G. Busse. Tübingen: Niemeyer, 1992.

Kreisel, Henry. "The Prairie State of Mind." *Proceedings and Transactions of the Royal Society of Canada* 6 (1968).

_____. "The Prairie: A State of Mind." In *Trace: Prairie Writers on Writing*, edited by Birk Sproxton. Winnipeg: Turnstone Press, 1986.

Kristeva, Julia. *Polylogue*. Paris: Seuil, 1977.

_____. *Pouvoirs de l'horreur, essai sur l'abjection*. Paris: Seuil, 1980.

Kroetsch, Robert. *Completed Field Notes. The Long Poems of Robert Kroetsch*. Toronto: McClelland and Stewart, 1989.

_____. *A Likely Story: The Writing Life*. Red Deer: Red Deer Press, 1995.

_____. *The Lovely Treachery of Words: Essays Selected and New*. Toronto: Oxford University Press, 1989.

_____. *The Puppeteer: A Novel*. Toronto: Random House, Vintage Books, 1993.

_____. *Seed Catalogue*. 1986. Reprint, Winnipeg: Turnstone Press, 1977.

_____. "Death Is a Happy Ending: A Dialogue in Thirteen Parts." In *Figures in a Ground: Canadian Essays on Modern Literature Collected in Honour of Sheila Watson*, edited by Diane Bessai and David Jackel. Saskatoon: Western Producer Prairie Books, 1978.

_____. "from 'The Poetics of Rita Kleinhart.'" *Prairie Fire* 17, no. 2 (Summer 1996): 28-31.

Lacan, Jacques. *The Four Fundamental Concepts of Psychoanalysis*. Translated by Alan Sheridan. London: The Hogarth Press and the Institute of Psycho-analysis, 1977.

_____. *Le Séminaire*. Vol. XX. *Encore*. Paris: Seuil, 1975.

LaDurie, E. L. Roy. *Times of Feast, Times of Famine, A History of Climate Since the Year 1000.* Translated from the French *Histoire de Climat Depuis l'an Mil.* New York: Farrar, Strauss, and Girous, 1971.

Lamb, H.H. *Climate, History and the Modern World.* London: Methuen, 1982.

_____. *Climate, Present, Past and Future.* Vol. 1. *Fundamentals and Climate Now.* London: Methuen, 1972.

Lang, S.E. "Better Organisation of Educational Agencies." *Western School Journal* I, no. 5 (May 1906).

Lawson, M.P., and C.W. Stockton. "Desert Myth and Climatic Reality." *Annals of the Association of American Geographers* 7, no.1 (1981): 521-35.

Lenoski, Daniel, ed. *a/long prairie lines.* Winnipeg: Turnstone Press, 1980.

Libin, Mark. "Home and Inscription In and Around Robert Kroetsch." *The New Quarterly* XVIII, no. 1 (Spring 1998): 216-29.

Limerick, Patricia Nelson. *The Legacy of Conquest: The Unbroken Past of the American West.* New York: W.W. Norton, 1987.

_____, Clyde A. Milner, II, and Charles E. Rankin, eds. *Trails.* Lawrence: University Press of Kansas, 1991.

Loewen, Royden. *Family, Church and Market: A Mennonite Community in the Old and New Worlds, 1850-1930.* Urbana and Chicago: University of Illinois Press, 1993.

_____. "Ethnic Farmers and the Outside World: Mennonites in Manitoba and Nebraska." *Journal of the Canadian Historical Association* 1 (1990): 195-214.

Maclaren, I.S. "Alexander Mackenzie and the Landscapes of Commerce." *Studies in Canadian Literature* 7, no. 2 (1982): 141-50.

Mandel, Eli. *The Family Romance.* Winnipeg: Turnstone Press, 1986.

_____. *Life Sentence.* Victoria: Press Porcépic, 1981.

_____. "Images of Prairie Man." In *A Region of the Mind: Interpreting the Western Canadian Plains,* edited by Richard Allen. Regina: Canadian Plains Research Centre/University of Regina, 1973.

_____. "Romance and Idealism in Western Canadian Fiction." In *Prairie Perspectives 2: Selected Papers of the Western Canadian Studies Conference, 1970, 1971,* edited by Anthony W. Rasporich and Henry C. Klassen. Toronto: Holt, Rinehart and Winston, Canada, 1973.

_____. "Writing West: On the Road to Wood Mountain," In *Essays on Saskatchewan Writing,* edited by E.F. Dyck. 1977. Reprint, Regina: Saskatchewan Writers Guild, 1986.

Mangan, J.A., and James Walvin. *Manliness and Morality: Middle-Class Masculinity in Britain and America, 1800-1940.* Manchester: Manchester University Press, 1987.

McCance, Dawne. "On the Art of Building in Ten Hornbooks." *The New Quarterly* XVIII, no. 1 (Spring 1998): 161-73.

McLeod, R.C., ed. *Swords and Ploughshares: War and Agriculture in Western Canada.* Edmonton: The University of Alberta Press, 1993.

Medick, Hans. "'Missionaries in a Rowboat'? Ethnological Ways of Knowing as a Challenge to Social History." *Comparative Studies in Society and History* 29 (1987): 76-98.

Miller, Jim Wayne. "Anytime the Ground Is Uneven: The Outlook for Regional Studies and What to Look Out For." In *Geography and Literature: A Meeting of the Disciplines,* edited by William Mallory and Paul Simpson-Housley. Syracuse: Syracuse University Press, 1987.

Miller, William L., Annis May Timpson, and Michael Lessnoff. *Political Culture in Contemporary Britain: People and Politicians, Principles and Practice.* Oxford: Clarendon Press, 1997.

Milne, Courtney. *Prairie Dreams.* Grandora, SK: Earth Vision, 1989.

Milner, Clyde A., II. "The View from Wisdom: Four Layers of History." In *Under an Open Sky,* edited by William Cronon et al. New York: W.W. Norton, 1992.

Morton, W.L. *Manitoba: A History.* Toronto: University of Toronto Press, 1967.

_____. "Clio in Canada: The Interpretation of Canadian History." In *Context of Canada's Past: Selected Essays of W.L. Morton,* edited by A.B. McKillop. Toronto: Macmillan, 1980.

Mouat, Jeremy, and Catherine Cavanaugh, eds. *Making Western Canada: Essays on European Colonization and Settlement.* Toronto: Garamond Press, 1996.

Mullen, Patrick B. *Listening to Old Voices.* Urbana: University of Illinois Press, 1992.

Myerhoff, Barbara. *Number Our Days.* New York: E.P. Dutton, 1978.

_____. *Remembered Lives.* Ann Arbor: University of Michigan Press, 1992.

Neth, Mary. *Preserving the Family Farm.* Baltimore: Johns Hopkins University Press, 1995.

Neuman, Shirley. "Autobiography: From Different Poetics to a Poetics of Differences." In *Essays on Life Writing: From Genre to Critical Practice,* edited by Marlene Kadar. Toronto, Buffalo, London: University of Toronto Press, 1992.

New, W.H. *Land Sliding: Imagining Space, Presence, and Power in Canadian Writing.* Toronto, Buffalo, London: University of Toronto Press, 1997.

Newcombe, Chas. K. "The High Schools and Their Relation to the Community." *Western School Journal* I , no. 4 (April 1906).

Newman, Russell W., Marion R. Just, and Ann N. Crigler. *Common Knowledge: News and the Construction of Political Meaning.* Chicago: University of Chicago Press, 1992.

Nischik, Reingard M. "Narrative Technique in Aritha van Herk's Novels." In *Gaining Ground: European Critics on Canadian Literature,* edited by Robert Kroetsch and Reingard M. Nischik. Edmonton: NeWest Press, 1985.

Norris, Kathleen. "Can You Tell the Truth in a Small Town?" In *Dakota: A Spiritual Geography.* Boston and New York: Houghton Mifflin, 1993.

Nyce, James M., ed. *The Gordon C. Eby Diaries: Chronicle of a Mennonite Farmer, 1911-1913.* Toronto: Wilfrid Laurier University Press, 1982.

O'Hagan, Howard. *Tay John.* 1939. Reprint, Toronto: McClelland and Stewart, 1974.

Olinder, Britta. *A Sense of Place. Essays in Post-Colonial Literature. The Proceedings of the Gothenburg University Congress of Commonwealth Language and Literature, 1982.* Göteborg: Gothenburg University, 1984.

Ong, Walter. *Orality and Language: The Technologizing of the Word.* New York: Methuen, 1982.

Owram, Doug. "Narrow Circles: The Historiography of Recent Canadian Historiography." *National History* 1, no. 1 (Winter 1997).

Palliser, J.M. *The Publications of the Champlain Society—The Papers of the Palliser Expedition 1857-1860*. Edited by I.M. Spry. Toronto: Champlain Society, 1968.

Palmer, Howard, ed. *The Settlement of the West*. Calgary: Comprint Publishing Company, 1977.

_____, and Donald Smith, eds. *The New Provinces: Alberta and Saskatchewan 1905-1980*. Vancouver: Tantalus Research Limited, 1980.

Parry, M.L. "Climate Change and the Agricultural Frontier: A Research Strategy." In *Climate and History, Studies in Past Climates and Their Impact on Man*, edited by T.M.L. Wigley, M.J. Ingram, and G. Farmer. New York: Cambridge University Press.

Petrone, Penny. *Native Literature in Canada: From the Oral Tradition to the Present*. Toronto: Oxford University Press, 1990.

Pielou, E.C. *After the Ice Age: The Return of Life to Glaciated North America*. Chicago: University of Chicago Press, 1991.

Pollock, Sheldon. "The Cosmopolitan Vernacular." *The Journal of Asian Studies* 57, no. 1 (February 1998).

Preston-Muddock, J.E. *The Sunless City*. London: F.V. White & C. Ltd., 1905.

Quinn, W.H., and V.T. Neal. "The Historical Record of El Niño Events." In *Climate Since A.D. 1500*, edited by R.S. Bradley and P.D. Jones. Rev. ed., London: Routledge, 1995.

Raaen, Aagot. *Grass of the Earth*. 1950. Reprint, St. Paul: Minnesota Historical Society Press, 1994.

_____. *Measure of My Days*. Fargo: North Dakota Institute for Regional Studies, 1953.

Rabinow, Paul. "Representations Are Social Facts: Modernity and Post-Modernity in Anthropology." In *Writing Culture*, edited by James Clifford and George E. Marcus. Berkeley: University of California Press, 1986.

Rasporich, A.W., ed. *The Making of the Modern West: Western Canada since 1945*. Calgary: The University of Calgary Press, 1984.

_____, ed. *Western Canada: Past and Present*. Calgary: McClelland and Stewart West Ltd., 1975.

_____, and H.C. Klassen, eds. *Prairie Perspectives 2*. Toronto: Holt, Rinehart and Winston of Canada Ltd., 1973.

Ricou, Laurence. *Vertical Man / Horizontal World: Man and Landscape in Canadian Prairie Fiction*. Vancouver: University of British Columbia Press, 1973.

Riegel, Christian, and Herb Wyile, eds. *A Sense of Place: Re-Evaluating Regionalism in Canadian and American Writing*. Textual Studies in Canada. Edmonton: University of Alberta Press, 1998.

Riley, D., and L. Spolton. *World Weather and Climate*. New York: Cambridge University Press, 1974.

Robbins, Bruce. "Comparative Cosmopolitanism." *Social Text* 10, no. 2-3 (1992): 169-86.

Rodoway, Paul. *Sensuous Geographies*. London: Routledge, 1994.

Roorda, Randall. *Dramas of Solitude: Narratives of Retreat in American Nature Writing*. Albany: State University of New York Press, 1998.

Roper, Michael, and John Tosh. "Introduction: Historians and the Politics of Masculinity." In *Manful Assertions: Masculinities in Britain since 1800*, edited by Michael Roper and John Tosh. London: Routledge, 1991.

Roth, Michael S. *The Ironist's Cage*. New York: Columbia University Press, 1995.

Schama, Simon. *Landscape and Memory*. New York: Alfred A. Knopf, 1995.

Scott, Joan W. "The Evidence of Experience." *Critical Inquiry* 17 (Summer 1991): 773-97.

Scott, W.J. Gordon. "Democracy in the Classroom." *Western School Journal* XV, no. 6 (June 1920).

Seeley, L. "Character as an End of Education." *Western School Journal* 8 (October 1906).

Shao-Wu, Wang, and Zhao Zong-Ci. "Droughts and Floods in China, 1470-1979." In *Climate and History, Studies in Past Climates and Their Impact on Man*, edited by T.M.L. Wigley, M.J. Ingram, and G. Farmer. New York: Cambridge University Press, 1989.

Shields, Carol. *The Stone Diaries*. 1993. Reprint, London: Fourth Estate Ltd. 1994.

Shields, Rob. *Places on the Margin: Alternative Geographies of Modernity*. London and New York: Routledge, 1991.

Shover, John L. *First Majority—Last Minority*. De Kalb: Northern University of Illinois Press, 1976.

Simons, Judy. *Diaries and Journals of Literary Women: From Fanny Burney to Virginia Woolf*. Iowa City: University of Iowa Press, 1990.

Simpson-Housley, Paul, and Glen Northcliffe, eds. *A Few Acres of Snow*. Toronto and Oxford: Dundurn Press, 1992.

Smith, D.A. "A Country of Stupendous Mountains: Opening the Colorado San Juans, 1870-1910." In *The Mountainous West, Explorations in Historical Geography*, edited by W. Wyckoff and L.M. Dilsaver. Lincoln: University of Nebraska Press, 1995.

Smith, Sidonie. *Subjectivity, Identity and the Body: Women's Autobiographical Practices in the Twentieth Century*. Bloomington and Indianapolis: Indiana University Press, 1993.

Sollors, Werner. Introduction to *The Invention of Ethnicity*. New York: Oxford University Press, 1989.

Sproxton, Birk. *Headframe:*. Winnipeg: Turnstone Press, 1985.

_____, ed. *Trace: Prairie Writers on Writing*. Winnipeg: Turnstone Press, 1986.

Stabler, J.C., and M.R. Olfert. *Restructuring Rural Saskatchewan, The Challenge of the 1990s*. Regina: Canadian Plains Research Centre/University of Regina, 1992.

Stevens, I.I. *Narrative and Final Report of Explorations for a Route for a Pacific Railroad near the Forty-Seventh and Forty-Ninth Parallels of North Latitude from St. Paul to Puget Sound*. Washington, DC: War Department, 1855.

Stubbs, Andrew. *Myth, Origins, Magic: A Study of Form in Eli Mandel's Writing*. Winnipeg: Turnstone Press, 1993.

_____. *Dennis Cooley*. Monograph. Toronto: ECW Press, n.d.

Thompson, John Herd. *Forging the Prairie West*. Don Mills: Oxford University Press, 1998.

tjsnow. *I do not know this story*. Calgary: House Press, 1998.

Tompkins, Jane. *West of Everything: The Inner Life of Westerns*. New York: Oxford University Press, 1992.

Tosh, John. "What Should Historians Do with Masculinity? Reflections on Nineteenth-century Britain." *History Workshop Journal* 38 (1994).

Trofimenkoff, Susan, ed. *The Twenties in Western Canada.* Ottawa: National Museum of Man, 1972.

Tuan, Yi-Fu. *Space and Place.* Minneapolis: University of Minnesota Press, 1977.

_____. *Topophilia.* New Jersey: Prentice-Hall, 1974.

Twigg, Alan. "Male: Robert Kroetsch." In *For Openers: Conversations with 24 Canadian Writers.* Madeira Park: Harbour Publishing, 1981.

Urry, James. *None but Saints: The Transformation of Mennonite Life in Russia, 1789-1889.* Winnipeg: Hyperion, 1989.

Valverde, Mariana. *The Age of Light, Soap, and Water: Moral Reform in English Canada, 1885-1925.* Toronto: McClelland and Stewart, 1991.

Van Herk, Aritha. *A Frozen Tongue.* Sydney: Dangeroo Press, 1992.

_____. *The Tent Peg.* 1981. Reprint, New York: Seaview Books, 1982.

_____. "Of Viscera and Vital Questions." In *Language in Her Eye: Writing and Genre,* edited by Libby Scheier et al. Toronto: Coach House Press, 1990.

_____. "Women Writers and the Prairie: Spies in an Indifferent Landscape." *Kunapipi* 6, no.2 (1984): 15-24.

Vaughan, R.M. "Lobster Is King: Infantilizing Maritime Culture." *Semiotexte(e)* 6, no. 2 (1994): 169-72.

Vauthier, Simone. "Ruptures in Carol Shields's *The Stone Diaries.*" *Anglophonia. Canada: Fractures mais non ruptures* 1 (1997): 177-92.

Voisey, Paul. *Vulcan.* Toronto: University of Toronto Press, 1988.

Walker, David. "Continence for a Nation: Seminal Loss and National Vigour." *Labour History* 48 (1985).

_____. "Energy and Fatigue." *Australian Cultural History,* no. 13 (1994).

Webb, Walter P. *The Great Plains.* Lincoln: University of Nebraska Press, 1931.

West, Elliott. *Growing Up with the Country.* Albuquerque: University of New Mexico Press, 1989.

White, Richard. *It's Your Misfortune and None of My Own: A History of the American West.* Norman: University of Oklahoma Press, 1991.

Whyte, Jon. *Homage, Henry Kelsey.* Winnipeg: Turnstone Press, 1981.

Wiebe, Rudy. "Canada in the Making." In *Encounters and Explorations: Canadian Writers and European Critics,* edited by Franz K. Stanzel and Waldemar Zacharasiewicz. Würzburg: Konighshausen and Newmann, 1986.

_____. "Passage by Land." In *Writers of the Prairies,* edited by Donald G. Stephen. Vancouver: University of British Columbia Press, 1973.

Wilson, Adrian. "Foundations of an Integrated Historigraphy." In *Rethinking Social History: English Society 1570-1920 and Its Interpretation.* Manchester: Manchester University Press, 1993.

Williams, William Carlos. *Paterson.* Toronto: George G. McLeod, Ltd., 1958.

Wright, H.E. Jr., J.E. Kutzbach, T. Webb III, W.F. Ruddiman, F.A. Street-Perrott, and P.J. Bartlein, eds. *Global Climates Since the Last Glacial Maximum*. Minneapolis: University of Minnesota Press, 1993.

Wyile, Herb. "Regionalism, Postcolonialism, and (Canadian) Writing: A Comparative Approach for Postnational Times." *ECW* 63 (Spring 1998): 139-61.

Young, William R, "'A Highly Intelligent and Unselfish Approach': Public Information and the Canadian West, 1939-45." *Canadian Historical Review* 62, no. 4 (December 1981): 502.

Robert Kroetsch is a Killam scholar and Professor Emeritus at the University of Manitoba. He has published nine novels, including *The Studhorse Man* (winner of the Governor General's Award for Fiction), *Alibi*, *The Puppeteer*, and, most recently, *The man from the Creeks: A Novel*. His many collections of poetry include *Seed Catalogue* and *Completed Field Notes: The Long Poems of Robert Kroetsch*. His literary essays have been collected in *The Lovely Treachery of Words*. He lectures extensively around the world.

Royden Loewen is Chair of Mennonite Studies at the University of Winnipeg. He is the editor of *The Journal of Mennonite Studies*, and the author of *From the Inside Out: The Rural World of Mennonite Diarists, 1863-1929* (University of Manitoba Press), and of *Family, Church, and Market: A Mennonite Community in the Old and New Worlds, 1850-1930* (University of Illinois Press).

Clarie Omhovère is Assistant Professor of English at University Nancy 2 (France). She has published articles on the novels of Robert Kroetsch, Aritha van Herk, and Thomas Wharton. She is currently interested in investigating the connections between geography and Canadian culture.

Molly P. Rozum received her MA in folklore and is a doctoral candidate in US history at the University of North Carolina at Chapel Hill. Her dissertation is entitled "Grasslands Grown: A Twentieth Century Sense of Place on North America's Northern Prairies and Plains." She is the author of "The Regional West," an overview article of recent scholarship on the history of the American West, included in the volume *A Companion to 19th Century America* (Blackwell Publishers, 2001).

J'nan Morse Sellery is the Louisa and Robert Miller Professor of Humanities at Harvey Muddy College and Claremont University in California, teaching literature, media, and women's studies. Her publications include articles and books on gender, poetry, and film. Currently, she is writing a book on Aritha van Herk and Robert Kroetsch, developed from her Fulbright Senior Fellowship in 1998-99 at the Calgary Institute for the Humanities.

Birk Sproxton was born in Flin Flon, Manitoba, and has taught at the universities of Regina, Manitoba, and Winnipeg; currently he teaches at Red Deer College. His books include a novel, *The Red-Headed Woman with the Black Black Heart*; a long poem, *Headframe:*; and a book of short fiction, *The Hockey Fan Came Riding*. He is the editor of *Trace: Prairie Writers on Writing*, and, more recently, *Great Stories from the Prairies*. He loves rocks.

Robert Wardhaugh is Assistant Professor of History at the University of Winnipeg. He was an organizer of the Defining the Prairies Canadian Studies Conference at the University of Manitoba in 1998. He is the author of several reviews, articles and essays on Canadian history, published in books and journals. His most recent book is *Mackenzie King and the Prairie West* (University of Toronto Press, 2000).

Jason Wiens is a doctoral candidate at the University of Calgary, where he is completing his dissertation on the Kootenay School of Writing in Vancouver. His published works include articles on Dionne Brand and George Bowering.

Contributors

Alison Calder is Assistant Professor at the Department of English, University of Manitoba, where she teaches literature and creative writing. She has published several articles on regionalism and prairie writing, as well as essays about Guy Vanderhaeghe and Sky Lee. She is currently working on a project on regional iconography that focusses on the ultimate prairie icon: the gopher.

Dr. Gerald T. Davidson was a member of the Space Sciences Laboratory at Lockheed Palo Alto Research Laboratories in California for 29 years. He received his PhD in theoretical physics from the University of Wisconsin. His experience embraces a wide range of topics in computational physics, astrophysics, space physics, and the Earth's environment. Now retired, he continues research on climate variations and their impacts.

Alvin Finkel is Professor of History at Athabasca University. He has published extensively on the history of the Canadian welfare state and the political history of the Canadian West. His books include *Business and Social Reform in the Thirties; The Social Credit Phenomenon in Alberta; History of the Canadian Peoples*, Volumes 1 and 2 (co-authored with Margaret Conrad); *Our Lives: Canada after 1945*; and *The Chamberlain-Hitler Collusion* (co-authored with Clement Leibovitz).

Gerald Friesen is Professor of History at the University of Manitoba. He is the author of *The Canadian Prairies: A History* (1984) and *of Citizens and Nation: An Essay on History, Communication, and Canada* (2000). He published *River Road: Essays on Manitoba and Prairie History* at the University of Manitoba Press in 1996.

R. Rory Henry received his PhD from the Australian National University for a thesis examining higher education and middle-class identity and citizenship in Canada and Australia. Since returning to Canada, he has been working on a project that examines the development of middle-class culture and concepts of citizenship in western Canada.